A TRAILS BOOKS GUIDE

HORSING AROUND
IN WISCONSIN

THE STATE'S BEST STABLES, BARNS, AND TRAILS FOR LESSONS AND TRAINING

ANNE M. CONNOR

TRAILS BOOKS

Black Earth, Wisconsin

Library of Congress Control Number: 2004104309
ISBN: 1-931599-38-6

Editor: Stan Stoga
Photos: Anne M. Connor, except where noted
Maps and Illustrations: Pamela Harden
Book Design: Emily Culp
Cover Photo: Anne M. Connor

Printed in the United States of America by Sheridan Books, Inc.

09 08 07 06 05 04   6 5 4 3 2 1

TRAILS BOOKS
A division of Trails Media Group, Inc.
P.O. Box 317 • Black Earth, WI 53515
(800) 236-8088 • e-mail: books@wistrails.com
www.trailsbooks.com

For Cal, Zoe, and Kate.
May you always have time to ride!

Contents

Preface

Every book is written for a reason. My reason for writing this book is simple.

As a horse owner and lover, I live in the country. My husband and I often invite friends to our farm, and invariably, head up to the barn for a ride. If these friends have kids, they gravitate to our children's pony, a 10-hand Shetland named Half a Lump of Sugar. Dutiful beyond reason, Sugar carries (some would say drags) these kids around without complaint, bringing them smiles and laughter. At the end of these visits, their parents always ask where in Wisconsin they can take their kids to ride, or how old their son or daughter needs to be to take lessons.

Being a writer, I figured there must be a book that answered these questions, so I started hunting around. What I found were a few outdated Web sites, a few books on trail riding, and not much else. I approached Trails Media Group about writing one myself, and what you hold in your hands is my attempt at answering these questions. Whether you ride English or western, participate in roping or jumping, or simply want to start riding, there's something in this book for you.

In addition to listing riding facilities, show grounds, and trails, I've included a few sections that can help the horseperson, new and old, on buying horses, finding trainers, and choosing proper apparel.

Background

I grew up as a barn rat in southern Wisconsin. My family played golf, and I did everything I could to stay off the range and in the barn. We didn't own horses; we owned clubs and I didn't get ponies for Christmas; I got golf balls. So I took every opportunity I could to clean stalls, offer to groom horses, and ride at friends' farms. Sensing that I was serious about this, my parents signed me up for lessons at Hoofbeat Ridge in Mazomanie. Never one to jump out of bed for school, I couldn't wait to get to the bus that would take me to Hoofbeat every Saturday. Once there, I did whatever needed doing. While the other kids played blind man's bluff in the horse pasture, I was pestering owners John and Betty Bennett to let me clean tack so I could earn an extra ride that day. I balked at doing homework, but had my horse science down to, well, a science.

I was 21 before I got my own horse, but prior to that I rode just about every discipline. I trail rode, I jumped, and I dabbled in polo (see, that golf game came in handy after all). As an adult I rode and showed hunter/jumpers, evented a bit, and in my late thirties, took up dressage. I introduced my husband to riding at the age of 35, and a dozen years later, he events at the preliminary level.

If you're like me and thousands of other Wisconsinites, you know that horses can provide a respite from the stresses of daily life. When I walk into a barn, my blood pressure drops, and to hear my friends talk, I know I'm not alone in this.

My hope is that with this book, you can find a place to take your own horse or ride somebody else's, take up a new discipline, or just find some quality horse time for yourself. It's time, if not money, well spent. So saddle up and enjoy. There's a whole world of horses waiting out there for you!

Acknowledgments

No book involving this much information can be written by itself. I'd like to thank the following people for their assistance, guidance, and knowledge of the horse industry in Wisconsin. In alphabetical order they include Dick Black of the Dane County Parks Department; Ken Carpenter of the Glacial Drumlin Horse Trails Association; Marsha Cooper of the Wisconsin State Horse Council; Raven Flores; Doris Green; Terri Keene of the Tomah Saddle Club; Lisa Otto of the Glacial Drumlin Horse Trails Association; Wayne Schutte of the Wisconsin Department of Natural Resources; Malcolm Stack of Ridge Run Farm; and Caryn Vesperman of the Wisconsin Dressage and Combined Training Association.

Sincere thanks to Karla Ching, Trinity Evans, Lucie Frohlichova, Pili Maturana, Stephanie McCluskey, and Joan Stack for their dedication and assistance. I wouldn't have had the opportunity to ride and write without your help!

I'd also like to acknowledge members of the Wisconsin State Horse Council, Wisconsin Horses, the Tomah Saddle Club, and the Southern Kettle Moraine Horse Trails Association, who voiced their opinions on the trails.

Lastly, thanks to my husband and riding companion Tim Connor, plus our four-legged friends, Pizzazz, London Taxi, and Sugar, who take me and my family on riding adventures in this state and beyond.

Introduction

Riding horses is fun, not unlike child's play. It makes us feel young at heart and carefree. It's important to remember, however, that riding and owning horses is serious business.

Horses are domesticated animals and, as such, deserve our care and respect. They're large, weighing 1,200 pounds on average, so one might find owning a horse more responsibility than, say, owning a dog. Still, nothing can match the nicker you hear when you walk in the barn or the freedom you feel cantering through a field on a fresh spring day. Here are a few guidelines to help you on your way. Ride safe, and as always, have fun!

What to Wear

In the old days, some of us were used to watching movie cowboys jump on horses with no saddle, a rope for a bridle, and not much else. Their riding "apparel" consisted of jeans, a button-down shirt, boots, and sharp spurs. These days, things are a bit more refined. Most horses wear saddle pads, saddles, and leather bridles. Riders, too, have realized that proper riding attire not only looks good but also stops the chafing that often comes from riding in jeans.

Riding still takes place in all kinds of attire, but the three things I recommend come without regard to discipline. They are:

A hard hat, preferably one with a chin strap. Helmets should be approved by the American Society for Testing and Materials and the Safety Equipment Institute. Approved helmets will have an ASTM-SEI sticker prominently featured on the inside. The American Medical Equestrian Association estimates that ASTM/SEI-approved helmets have decreased riding-related head injuries by 50 percent.

Long pants. Take a ride in a saddle wearing shorts, and you'll understand what I mean!

Boots with a heel. Flat-soled shoes can easily slip through stirrups, causing a rider's foot to become stuck. Quality trainers of all disciplines recommend boots or paddock shoes with a minimum 1/2-inch heel.

What to Look for in an Instructor

Contrary to some riders' experiences, riding instructors who adhere to the football coach style of training are not (usually) the most effective. Trainers, especially for beginners, should be patient yet firm, and should have a good understanding of training and riding techniques. The following is a list of questions to ask yourself when choosing a trainer:

What kind of riding do I want to do? Those who want to learn dressage should not go to someone who specializes in barrel racing, or vice versa.

What kind of personality suits me? I like trainers who are calm, knowledgeable, and focused. Others like more animated, rah-rah types. While one rider may be unfazed by an instructor who yells as a matter of course, others are traumatized. Watch a potential trainer teaching other students to see if his or her style matches your personality.

How much money are you willing to spend to learn how to ride correctly? Consider whether you want to take private or group lessons, and what you're willing to spend for training. If you have your own horse, you'll find that some boarding facilities will keep your horse only if you enter into a training program.

Do you want to show a horse? Some barns and trainers are geared toward the show market; others are not. Choose the one that's right for you.

Remember, it's always okay to go watch a trainer teach before you sign up for lessons. If he or she doesn't want you there, you probably don't want to take lessons from the person. Trainers should be able to answer any questions you have about their lesson policies and provide you with a copy of the facility's liability waiver. Make sure you do all this before you mount your first horse!

Ready for a Horse of Your Own?

There comes a time in many riders' lives when they want a horse of their own. Horse ownership is a joyous, heartwarming experience. It's also expensive, and a huge responsibility. How can you tell when you're ready for a horse of your own?

You should be both a competent rider and a competent horse person. Horse ownership isn't just about riding; it's about caring for the animal and being able to make good decisions on its behalf.

It goes without saying that horses are expensive and time consuming. Some joke that you're not ready for your first horse until you can flush a $100 bill down the toilet without crying. That said, there are ways to make ownership more cost-effective.

If you're not sure you're ready for the commitment of ownership, try leasing, or half leasing a horse at a local, reliable stable. Make sure you know the horse well and like the trainer. Some leases require contracts; others do not. Ask about different options.

If you're set on ownership, ask yourself the following questions. If you're confident that you're making a good decision, jump in, and enjoy the years of companionship that ensue!

Do you think of horses as investments? Financially speaking, horses are usually bad investments. They need to eat every day, and you rarely get what you paid for them once you're ready to sell. Often, the joy you receive from their companionship is the only payback you get—but that's an enormous gift.

Can you afford to care for a horse? Horses require regular trimming and shoeing, worming, vaccinations and veterinary care, not to mention what you'll spend on training and board. Horses require a fairly steady flow of disposable income. If you have that and are willing to commit it to your horse, you're on the right track.

Do you have a place to keep a horse? Boarding options include keeping your horse on your own land, or boarding in a pasture or in a stall at another facility. Pasture board costs the least, stabling the most. What will you want for your horse?

Do you have the time and experience to own your own horse? Horse ownership is time consuming, especially if you keep your horse at home. Ask yourself if you're ready for this animal to become an integral part of your life.

Do you understand that the purchase price is often the cheapest part of horse ownership? Again, look at the long-term costs.

Do you have the proper tack and grooming supplies for a horse? Visit a local tack shop to check for used equipment, which is often much cheaper than buying new.

Do you have a big heart? Horses have a way of climbing in and making themselves at home. Once you fall in love with horses, it's hard to fall out!

Trail Etiquette

All riders should be ambassadors for courteous and safe riding, so it's important to have good etiquette when we're out on the trails. Check out these great etiquette tips from the Maryland Horse Council. Then go and enjoy the trails!

1. Make sure your horse has the temperament and training for riding on congested public trails. Busy multi-use trails are not the proper place for schooling green horses.

2. Advise other trail users of your horse's temperament, e.g. a horse with a tendency to kick should always wear a red ribbon in the tail or a stallion should wear a yellow ribbon. Assume that not everyone will know what these ribbons mean, so be prepared to explain or take the necessary precautions to avoid trouble.

3. Obey posted speed/gait limits, and use common sense in crowded areas (cantering or galloping on crowded trails endangers everyone).

4. Move to the right to allow faster trail users to pass.

5. Announce your intention to pass other trail users, and reduce speed in order to pass safely. Pass on the left only.

6. Remove your horse from the trail if you begin experiencing behavior problems.

7. Stay on equestrian-approved trails.

8. As a courtesy to others in your group, use appropriate hand signals for turning, slowing, etc., and give verbal warnings for dangers on the trail (e.g. holes, low branches).

9. On multi-use trails, remember that other trail users may not be familiar with horses or their reactions to new experiences. Your horse may be another trail user's introduction to horses; what you do is a reflection of the local horse community. Cheerfully answer questions about your horse. You are an ambassador for the entire equestrian community.

10. If you trailer to a location, do not clean out your trailer in the parking area.

11. On multiple-use trails, step off the trail (if possible) if your horse needs to relieve itself, or kick the droppings off the trail.

Notes & Errata

It should be noted that in the trail section of this book, there are several places where I've referred riders to the yellow pages when looking for rental horses to ride on public lands. Barns regularly change their policies on whether they allow their horses to leave their property, and for this reason it is best to call facilities directly.

Key for the boarding rates given in the "Stables and Barns" sections of the book.

$. $100–199/month
$$. $200–299/month
$$$. . . . $300–399/month
$$$$. . . $400 and above

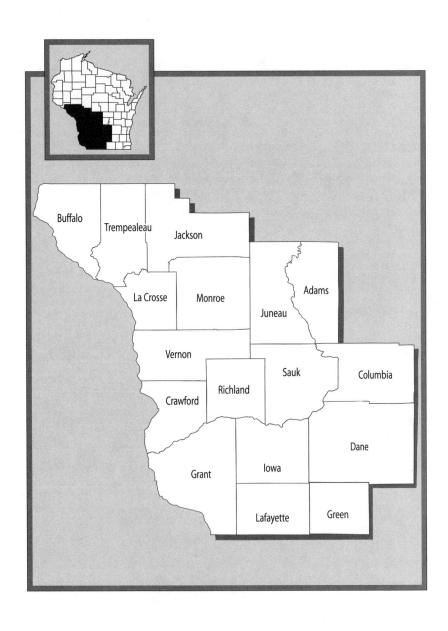

Southwest
Wisconsin

Stables and Barns

Breakaway Farm
Oregon

Horse lovers looking for a place to learn and have fun in the southwestern part of the state will love Breakaway Farm in Oregon. This hunter/jumper barn is a hit with adults and children alike, and with good reason. It is easily accessible from County Road M, and the owners host and travel to shows. Most important, however, is that people enjoy themselves at Breakaway.

As at any show facility, the students at Breakaway work hard to perfect that imperfect seat. But the owners strive to ensure that the facility is friendly, the competition is important but not overwhelming, and the overriding goal is to have fun. While the setup at Breakaway is older (there is one new barn), the horses are well cared for, and the indoor and outdoor arenas provide an impressive array of jumps. There are several instructors, all of whom are qualified to teach children and adults.

The folks at Breakaway host fun shows twice a year, introducing their students to the show world without the high stress of rated shows. Fall shows are complete with costume classes as well as the more traditional lead line, walk/trot, and jumping classes.

Getting started at an early age, at Breakaway Farm. Photo courtesy of Caryl Farkas.

Location: 5353 County Road M, Oregon, WI 53575.

Phone: (608) 835-2486.

Year founded: 1996.

Owner(s): Ginny and Dave Dvorak.

Hours: Flexible. Call for appointment.

Specialization(s): Hunter/jumper, equitation, hunter under saddle.

Facilities: Barn, 60 x 180-foot indoor arena with viewing area, outdoor arena, turnout paddocks, pasture, outdoor wash rack, tack room. All riding arenas have jumps.

Number of stalls: 28 in two barns.

Board: $$$. Includes daily stall cleaning, feedings, and turnout. Breakaway keeps all farrier and vaccination schedules, freeing owners of these responsibilities.

Lessons: Private, semiprivate, group, adult. Minimum age is 6.

School horses: 3 horses and 2 ponies.

Requirements: Boots or paddock shoes, approved riding helmet.

Shows/clinics: Two on-site schooling shows per year. Trainers and students travel to several shows per year.

Transportation: Available to shows and clinics.

Capitol View Stables
Oregon

Capitol View, formerly Thunder Hooves Equestrian Center, is one of the largest riding facilities in southwestern Wisconsin. Located in Oregon, Capitol View boasts 92 stalls and runs everything from training programs to day camps and birthday parties. For those interested in lessons, the barn employs several trainers. Lessons are offered in hunt seat, saddle seat, trail, western pleasure, and jumping.

The facility hosts several camps, the most popular being a weeklong day camp, which is offered in the summer and over school vacations. These offer "getting to know the horse" sessions plus riding lessons, sometimes two a day. Capitol View also hosts an overnight summer camp, which runs from 6 p.m. on Friday through 6 p.m. on Sunday. Kids bring their tents and own supplies, and they receive multiple riding lessons. If your child likes roughing it, this is the camp he or she will enjoy.

Of Capitol View's amenities, the best is its 100 x 220-foot indoor arena, which can be rented for clinics and shows. (4-H clinics are particularly popular, as was one with an equine chiropractor.) "You should see our electric bill," jokes one of the trainers, speaking of the arena's lights provided for night riding. "It's amazing."

Capitol View is host to several shows per year, including "come as you are" shows the first Sunday of each month. No grooming, no dressing up—riders can just show up ready to ride.

There are scheduled vet and farrier visits, although boarders are welcome to use their own, as long as they make the appointments. The guidelines at Capitol View are flexible and allow everyone to be responsible, work hard, and have fun.

Location: Capitol View Stables, 4452 County Road B, Oregon, WI 53575

Phone: (608) 835-8000.

E-mail: wildrose@jvlnet.com

Web site: http://www.capitolviewstables.com

Year founded: 2003.

Owner(s): Dave Bruce.

Hours: 7:00 a.m.–10:00 p.m. daily, including holidays.

Specialization(s): Hunt seat, saddle seat, trail, and western pleasure, jumping.

Facilities: Barn, 100 x 220-foot indoor arena, 150 x 300-foot outdoor arena, 143 acres of trails, individual tack lockers, heated bathroom, heated lounge, hot water wash stall, outdoor wash stall.

Number of stalls: 92, some open for shows and clinics.

Board: $$–$$$. Includes turnout in mare or gelding pasture (private turnout available for extra fee), matted stalls, two feedings per day. Stalls cleaned daily.

Lessons: Private, semiprivate, and group. Six packs are available at a discount.

School horses: 5.

Requirements: Helmets are required for those under 18.

Shows/clinics: Hosts several shows per year. See Web site for schedule.

Transportation: Sometimes available to shows.

Other: Horses for sale, lease, and half lease.

Carriage Ridge Stables
Waunakee

When Tom Bunbury envisioned Carriage Ridge Stables, he was thinking in grand terms. The stables, which are part of the larger Carriage Ridge community off County Road M in Waunakee, are indeed impressive. With 29 stalls, the facility boasts indoor and outdoor riding areas, heated indoor, luxurious 12 x 12-foot stalls with automatic waterers, and a sparkling-clean lounge.

To top it off, the environment at Carriage Ridge is friendly, professional, and accessible. While some boarders are residents of the Carriage Ridge community, residency is not required, and stalls do occasionally become available. There are more phases of the residential development planned, so while the day may come when the barn is only open to residents, it is well off in the future.

One of the prime features of Carriage Ridge is the bridle trail that runs through the property. The five miles of trails that weave in between houses, fields, and developments are fenced on both sides and very safe—sturdy, with no exposed nails.

Reminiscent of equestrian neighborhoods like Pebble Beach in California, Carriage Ridge strikes a perfect balance between people and horses.

Carriage Ridge has a handful of quality school horses that are used by both residents and the general public. The level of instruction is superb and flexible enough to meet the needs of a wide range of learners. The fees tend to be high, but the value of what customers get for their money is top notch.

Location: 5500 Surrey Lane, Waunakee, WI 53597.

Phone: (608) 850-5012.

E-mail: tbunbury@carriageridgestables.com

Web site: http://www.carriageridgestables.com

Year founded: 2000.

Hours: 8:00 a.m.–9:00 p.m. daily

Owner(s): Tom Bunbury

Specialization(s): Hunter/jumper, western pleasure, English pleasure, dressage, gaited/saddle seat.

Facilities: Barn, heated indoor arena, outdoor arena, clubhouse, indoor wash rack, outdoor wash rack, tack room, turnout paddocks, pasture, lights for night riding.

Number of stalls: 29.

Board: $$$$. Includes daily turnout, blanketing, two feedings per day, daily stall cleaning. Vets and farriers visit every other week.

Lessons: Private, semiprivate, group. Minimum age is 6.

School horses: 4.

Requirements: Boots/paddock shoes, long pants, and helmets required.

Shows/clinics: Fun shows for boarders, small clinics.

Other: Horses for half-lease.

Children's Ranch
Prairie du Chien

Children's Ranch is unique: While the facility offers trails, and plenty of them (descriptions can be found in the Trails section later in this chapter), it is also a show facility that offers board, trails, and lessons, all for free.

Years ago, Children's Ranch copresidents Jim White and Dwight Boom had a vision. They wanted to develop an equestrian facility that catered to at-risk children, families, and groups that promoted horsemanship. They also had volunteers who helped them raise the money to buy 470 acres, adjoining LaRiviere Park in Prairie du Chien. And thus, the Children's Ranch was born.

Children's Ranch is a nonprofit organization that runs a horse-adoption program in addition to its many other programs. White opened his facility to the general public, and regularly hosts events such as trail rides and campouts, as well as drill team, team penning, and cattle round-up competitions. The Upper Midwest Buckskin Horse Association regularly holds shows on Children's Ranch property, again, all for free. The place is teeming with volunteers (more are always needed), and boarders are asked to donate eight hours of ranch time per month in exchange for keeping their horse(s) on the property.

Children's Ranch has a popular program for at-risk youth called "The Steps to a Cowboy," in which kids take lessons to move their way up from Pilgrim to Cowboy. The pride in these riders' faces is reward enough for all those who volunteer.

Between Children's Ranch and LaRiviere Park, trail riders can enjoy more than 100 miles of trails, which are in the bluff country along the Mississippi River. They are suitable for beginners and advanced riders alike. The facility is a rugged kind of place, where hard work is needed and appreciated.

Location: 405-1/2 South Beaumont Road, Prairie du Chien, WI 53821.

Phone: (608) 326-4682.

E-mail: youthranch@yahoo.com

Web site: http://www.childrensranch.org

Year founded: 1996.

Owner(s): Jim White and Dwight Boom.

Hours: 8:00 a.m.–8:00 p.m.

Specialization(s): Western pleasure, rodeo, English pleasure, eventing.

Facilities: Barn, 135 x 340-foot outdoor arena, pasture, viewing area, outdoor wash rack, tack room, lights for night riding, more than 100 miles of trails.

Number of stalls: 72.

Board: Free. Requires eight hours of work per month.

Lessons: Private, semiprivate, group.

School horses: 12.

Requirements: Helmet, boots with heels.

Shows/clinics: Many shows and events are held on Children's Ranch property, including Upper Midwest Buckskin Horse Association show and team penning.

Transportation: None.

Other: See Web site for information on horse-adoption program. Children's Ranch is a 501(c)3 organization, and all donations are tax-deductible to the extent of the law.

Doby Stables
Dodgeville

Doby Stables has been serving trail riders in southwestern Wisconsin for more than 30 years. This facility, located just off Highway 23 near Dodgeville, is both easy to find and easy to navigate. The owners, Dave and Sandy Johnson, have been leading trail rides so long they have it down to a science.

One of the great things about Doby Stables is its location. Located across the highway from Governor Dodge State Park, which includes one of the most-used equestrian trail systems in the state, the facility uses a highway underpass to access the park and its more than 20 miles of trails. Doby offers one- and two-hour guided trail rides through the park (call ahead for reservations), or a 45-minute ride on the stable's property. Located in the Driftless Area, Doby features scenery that is beautiful year-round.

Location: 4334 State Highway 23, Dodgeville, WI 53533.

Phone: (608) 935-5205.

Year founded: 1970.

Owner(s): Dave and Sandy Johnson.

Hours: Open 9:00 a.m.–4:00 p.m. in the spring, summer, and fall. The state park is open from May 1 to November 15. Note: Doby is in the Chronic Wasting Disease eradication zone, so trail dates in Governor Dodge change from year to year. Call ahead for reservations.

Specialization(s): Guided trail rides through Governor Dodge State Park and on 180 acres of Doby Stables' property.

Facilities: Doby Stables sits on 190 acres of rolling hills and valleys blanketed with woods and open fields. They have a gift shop with souvenirs and a mineral museum with an on-site rock shop.

Number of stalls: n/a

Board: n/a

Lessons: n/a

Trail horses: 25.

Requirements: Recommends boot with a heel and safety helmet.

Shows/clinics: n/a.

Transportation: n/a

Other: Horses occasionally for sale.

Endless Valley Stables
Spring Green

Endless Valley is unique in that it successfully integrates many kinds of riding, including hunt seat, equitation, and jumpers in the English disciplines, and lunge line, halter, pleasure, and trail classes for those who ride western. The owners host several clinics a year, including those for barrel racing, gaited horses, and dressage, as well as one called Zen and the Horse.

There is also a listing for Endless Valley in the Trails section of this chapter, because the more than 30 miles of trails are every bit as good as the facility. Those who like to vacation with their horses (Endless Valley does not currently lease horses for trail rides) should call for reservations. While the scenery is outstanding year-round, it is especially beautiful in the fall.

Endless Valley, which has a three-bedroom guesthouse that sleeps eight, is a labor of love built by the on-site owners. The stable area is meticulous, and the 10 x 12-foot stalls are first-rate. This is a barn that compares to Carriage Ridge in its layout and construction. The board is reasonable (both pasture and indoor board are available), and a vet and farrier visit regularly, freeing owners from the responsibilities of calling for appointments.

The bucolic setting of Endless Valley Stables near Spring Green.

Location: 5975 County Road T, Spring Green, WI 53588.

Phone: (608) 753-2887.

E-mail: lsmurphy@execpc.com

Web site: http://www.endlessvalleystables.com

Year founded: 2003.

Owner(s): Lori and Steve Murphy. Owners live on-site.

Hours: 7:00 a.m.–10:00 p.m. daily.

Specialization(s): Hunt seat, hunter/jumper, western pleasure, natural horsemanship, lunge line, trail classes, and trails.

Facilities: Barn, newly constructed 60 x 120-foot indoor arena, heated viewing lounge, two bathrooms (one with shower), indoor and outdoor hot/cold wash racks, large tack room, and washer/dryer. There is space for one tack trunk per boarder. Primitive camping or three-bedroom lodge is available for overnight guests.

Number of stalls: 30.

Board: $–$$. Includes daily turnout, blanketing, and unblanketing. Regular vet and farrier visits.

Lessons: Private, semiprivate, group. Minimum age is 4.

School horses: 10, English and western.

Requirements: Boots or paddock shoes with a heel, helmet for those taking lessons.

Shows/clinics: Clinics hosted on-site year-round. Travel to shows.

Transportation: Available to some clinics and shows.

Other: Horses occasionally for sale and lease.

Grandview Equestrian Center
McFarland

Horse lovers looking for a facility that treats their horses as well as its own should check out Grandview Equestrian Center in McFarland. Grandview offers all the amenities of a top barn, from an indoor arena to hot/cold water wash stalls, but its real strength lies in how it treats its customers (those customers, of course, being horses).

Relatively new to the market, Grandview has been in business since 1999 and offers quality instruction in eventing and dressage. Some boarders ride western, but they must bring their own trainers to the barn for a small fee. To supplement its dressage and eventing lessons (most lessons are private, but trainers will consider requests for group or semiprivate lessons), Grandview hosts clinics on a regular basis. They also host Pony Club rallies, but those, says owner Sharon Scallon, "pretty much run themselves."

Grandview has a jump field and plenty of room for trailer and carriage parking. The indoor arena is 60 x 120 feet and gets hopping in the winter. There are lights for night riding, and there is plenty of room for outdoor riding as well.

Location: 2348 Dyerson Road, McFarland, WI 53558.

Phone: (608) 838-6992.

Year founded: 1999.

Owner(s): Sharon and Gerald Scallon.

Hours: 7:30 a.m.–10:00 p.m.

Specialization(s): Dressage, eventing. Boarders can bring trainers in for western lessons.

Facilities: Barn, indoor arena with lounge and heated bathroom, indoor hot/cold water wash rack, tack room, outdoor arena, turnout paddocks, pasture, trails, and jump field. Trailer parking available on-site, carriages welcome.

Number of stalls: 20.

Board: $$$. Includes hay three times a day, grain twice a day, hand-led turnout to paddocks (pasture available in summer months), daily stall cleaning, and personalized care.

Lessons: Mostly private, although some trainers may teach group lessons.

School horses: None.

Requirements: Riders must either wear a helmet or sign a helmet waiver.

Shows/clinics: Facility hosts pony club rallies on a regular basis. Also hosts dressage and eventing clinics.

Transportation: Boarders provide own transportation to shows.

Green Meadows
Belleville

With access to more than 600 acres of land, Dave Judd has built himself a piece of horse heaven. Judd, a former dairy farmer, says he is used to getting up early and getting things done, and that shows at Green Meadows, a 55-stall barn in Belleville.

Dealing mainly with the English disciplines (Judd hires trainers based on demand), boarders at Green Meadows range from dressage enthusiasts to hunter/jumper riders and eventers. Boarders have access to an extensive trail network, so Judd attracts a fair share of trail riders as well. The facility is extensive, with two indoor arenas, an outdoor arena, several jump fields, and the trails.

"If I was going to get into the horse business," which he did in 1997, "I'm going to make it look good, not like a makeshift dairy farm," Judd says. Others agree. The footing is excellent and the horses well cared for. Green Meadows is a real horseperson's place.

The terrain at Green Meadows is rolling, and the farm is nestled snugly into a valley. It is a great place for horses and riders with or without show aspirations.

Location: 6312 County Road A, Belleville, WI 53508.

Phone: (608) 424-3801.

Year founded: 1997.

Owner(s): Dave Judd.

Hours: No set hours.

Specialization(s): Hunter/jumper, eventing, jumpers, dressage, trail riding.

Facilities: Barn, outdoor arena, two indoor arenas, small lounge, tack room, jump fields, trails on approximately 600 acres.

Number of stalls: 55.

Board: $$$. Includes turnout, two feedings per day, daily stall cleaning.

Lessons: Private, semiprivate, group, adult.

School horses: 3.

Requirements: Helmets and boots with a heel recommended.

Shows/clinics: Hosts clinics on a regular basis.

Transportation: Boarders have own trailers and help each other arrange transportation to shows.

Other: Horses occasionally for sale and lease.

A view of the impressive layout at Green Meadows.

Hickory Knoll Farm
Fitchburg

Located just south of Madison, Hickory Knoll provides a top-notch, professional place to ride. Hickory Knoll is a multi-service, English-based barn that caters to dressage riders, carriage drivers, jumpers, and polo players on a year-round basis.

Hickory Knoll is also host to Madison Polo Club games and practices (see description later in this section). The facility hosts polo lessons for beginners and more advanced players on a regular basis. Competitors play on a regulation-sized field in the summer and a roomy indoor surface in the winter. Lessons for first-year players are surprisingly inexpensive and include the use of a school horse.

Polo players are not the only ones who use Hickory Knoll. The facility caters to dressage riders and employs up to six professional instructors and clinicians at a time. The owners also host 4-H clinics.

In addition to mounted riding, Hickory Knoll offers driving instruction and clinics, including a Dairyland Driving Club beginners' clinic in May, when 10 safe schooling turnouts are available. The facility caters to beginning and advanced riders alike.

Location: 5438 County Road M, Fitchburg, WI 53575.

Phone: (608) 835-7473.

E-mail: frei@chorus.net

Web site: http://www.hickoryknoll.net

Year founded: 1998.

Owner(s): John and Betsy Freiburger.

Hours: 9:00 a.m.–9:30 p.m. daily.

Specialization(s): Dressage, driving, polo, hunter/jumper, eventing, Pony Club.

Facilities: Heated barn and arena, standard 60-meter dressage arena, lights for night riding, clubhouse, indoor wash rack, outdoor wash rack, polo field, three miles of trails, cross-country and stadium jumps, turnout paddocks, pasture, separate guest barn and paddocks, three-bedroom bed-and-breakfast in antebellum farmhouse, carriage sales barn with marathon and pleasure vehicles, and carriage repair shop.

Number of stalls: 25.

Board: $$$. Includes daily stall cleaning, hay all day, grain twice a day, daily supplement, turnout, access to 11 pastures and paddocks, small-group turnout, personalized feeding programs (upon request). The owner has a degree in animal nutrition.

Lessons: Private, semiprivate, group, adult. Minimum age is 7.

School horses: 10

Requirements: Safety equipment.

Shows/clinics: Driving and dressage clinics hosted regularly.

Transportation: Will provide transportation to shows.

Other: Owner provides high-quality carriage sales and service for marathon and pleasure driving.

Hoofbeat Ridge
Mazomanie

Hoofbeat Ridge in Mazomanie is a kids' paradise. With summer camps and year-round lesson programs, Hoofbeat has been instrumental in developing lifelong horse lovers for more than 40 years.

Started by John and Betty Bennett and their 11 children, the farm is now owned and operated by the Bennetts' daughter Mary and her husband, Ted Marthe. The Marthes run a number of programs, most notably their summer resident and day camps, which are accredited by the American Camping Association. Their riding programs are accredited by the Horsemanship Safety Association.

The environment at Hoofbeat is noncompetitive and learning based. Instructors teach children as young as seven the basics of not only English and western riding, but of good horsemanship.

The farm is 20 miles west of Madison on 250 scenic acres overlooking the Wisconsin River Valley, and offers an indoor riding arena plus several outdoor rings. The property has numerous groomed riding trails, which are used regularly for camps and lessons.

Polo players in a practice match at Hickory Knoll Farm.

Older children are given the opportunity to jump in specialized camps. Beyond the camps, which run from June through August, Hoofbeat offers specialized programs for Girl Scouts and Boy Scouts, as well as programs during Christmas and spring breaks.

Location: 5304 Reeve Road, Mazomanie, WI 53560.

Phone: (608) 767-2593; (608) 767-2590 (fax).

E-mail: Hoofbeat@midplains.net

Web site: http://www.hoofbeat.org

Year founded: 1962.

Owner(s): Mary and Ted Marthe.

Hours: Varies. Call ahead.

Specialization(s): Western pleasure, English pleasure, jumping for older children.

Facilities: Lounge, indoor arena, trading post, classrooms, bunkhouses, dining room, three outdoor arenas, miles of trails.

Number of stalls: n/a.

Board: n/a.

Lessons: n/a.

School horses: 65+.

Requirements: Riders must wear a helmet and boots with a 1-inch heel.

Shows/clinics: Schooling shows at the end of some sessions.

Other: Hoofbeat hosts a resident adult dressage camp each year and offers other programs, including mother/daughter weekends, group retreats for up to 100 people, Girl Scout and Boy Scout programs, and youth programs from September through May during spring and Christmas vacations, over some weekends, and on other days when school is not in session. Most staff members are certified in Red Cross First Aid and CPR. A camp nurse is available during the day. Horses are occasionally for sale.

Hoofer Riding Club and Equestrian Center
Belleville

The Hoofer Riding Club is the official riding club of the University of Wisconsin–Madison and is the parent organization of the UW Equestrian Team. But members do not have to be UW students, faculty, or alumni. Anyone can join, and members are eligible to join all UW Hoofer Riding Club activities.

The Hoofer Riding Club has its boarding facility in Belleville, which comes complete with an indoor and outdoor riding ring, 40 acres of pasture, four tack rooms, and a heated lounge with full bath. Board is very reasonable for the area.

Members are also eligible to take lessons from Hoofer Riding Club instructors. The club offers lessons in hunt seat and dressage, with occasional eventing and western instruction.

While the UW Equestrian Team is a member of the Intercollegiate Horse Show Association and travels to recognized shows, the Hoofer Riding Club hosts low-key member shows two to three times a year. The organization also hosts trail rides, clinics, and educational events throughout the year.

Note: new riders are required to ride under supervision at all times. Intermediate and advanced riders are allowed to ride Hoofer horses without supervision, and advanced riders are encouraged to become trip leaders, who guide trail rides and study to become Hoofer instructors.

People wishing to join Hoofers should attend the executive committee meeting at 6:30 p.m. on the first or third Wednesday of each month at the UW Memorial Union, or check the organization's Web site for current information.

Location: 1008 Severson Road, Belleville, WI 53508.

Phone: (608) 424-1301.

Web site: http://www.hoofers.org

Year founded: The Hoofer Riding Club was founded in the 1920s as the University Hunt Club for Women. The facility was based in Shorewood Hills, near the UW–Madison campus.

Owner(s): UW–Madison Hoofer Riding Club.

Hours: 7:00 a.m.–10:00 p.m. daily.

Specialization(s): Hunter/jumper, eventing, dressage, trails, some western.

Facilities: Numerous stalls in two barns, four pastures on 40 acres, an 80 x 120-foot indoor arena, an 85 x 160-foot outdoor arena, a 4-acre jump field, a cross-country course, and 300 acres of trail access. There are two full-time residents who live on the property.

Number of stalls: 45.

Board: $$. Includes daily turnout (mares and geldings are turned out separately), three feedings per day, regularly scheduled vet visits, regular farrier visits, and equine chiropractor, massage therapist, and myofacial release visits. Blanketing is free of charge.

Lessons: Private, semiprivate, group. Members sign up for books of lessons, six or seven at a time, to be taken over the course of the semester. Each semester (there are three—spring, summer, and fall), is made up of two six- to-seven-week sessions. Call for details.

School horses: 10 (on average).

Requirements: Boots with a heel, helmet.

Shows/clinics: Hoofers hosts several shows and clinics each year, and members also travel to shows.

Transportation: Available to some shows.

Other: Horses for sale and lease. Hoofers also accepts donations of horses and tack.

Kickapoo Valley Ranch
La Farge

Located between Richland Center and La Crosse, Kickapoo Valley Ranch (KVR) is a unique find in the Midwest. Nestled in the beautiful Kickapoo Valley, the ranch is more like something you would find in Colorado than Wisconsin, complete with wranglers, trail rides, and overnight lodging.

Riders from the Kickapoo Valley Ranch on a leisurely ride through the Kickapoo Valley Reserve. Photo courtesy of Kickapoo Valley Ranch.

The focus of KVR, which opened in 2003, is guided trail rides. These can range from one-hour rides on the ranch's 30 acres to four-hour trips in the Kickapoo Valley Reserve. The owners of KVR stress that their horses are not the "nose to tail" type, but real western-trained mounts.

What makes KVR unique is that it is more like a dude ranch than a trail-riding facility. The ranch has eight cabins, all with kitchenettes. In its short history, KVR has been home to marriage proposals and family reunions. While the ranch does not currently offer meals (cabins are set up for self-catering), a dining facility may be added in the future.

"There are folks who come here just for a getaway; they don't even ride," says co-owner Joe Rogan. And why not? The facility is bordered on three sides by the Kickapoo Valley Reserve, an 8,600-acre playground that offers fishing and hunting, horseback riding, biking and hiking trails, cross-country skiing, snowshoeing, camping, and canoeing. It should be noted that the reserve's horseback-riding trails are closed November 15 to May 1 to protect the ecosystem. During that time, riding takes place on the ranch, which has plenty of natural beauty of its own.

Location: E11761 County Road P, La Farge, WI 54639.

Phone: (608) 625-6222 (office); (608) 625-6226 (fax).

E-mail: cowboyjoe@kvranch.com

Web site: http://www.kvranch.com

Year founded: 2003.

Owner(s): Joseph Rogan and David Nordstrom.

Hours: 9:00 a.m.–5:00 p.m. daily, with longer hours for overnight guests.

Specialization(s): Overnight dude ranch that offers guided trail rides to guests and the general public. Children must be six years old to ride.

Facilities: Facility has eight cabins on 30 acres. Property is surrounded on three sides by the Kickapoo Valley Reserve, which boasts trails on 8,600 acres. All cabins have kitchenettes. Guests bring their own food.

Number of stalls: n/a.

Lessons: Western pleasure, plus guided trail rides.

Trail horses: 25.

Requirements: KVR recommends protective headgear (available), long pants, and boots with a heel.

Shows/clinics: n/a.

Transportation: n/a.

Other: Facility is located in the beautiful Driftless Area of southwestern Wisconsin.

Little Hill Top Ranch, LLC
Tomah

Little Hill Top Ranch is a relatively new facility that is making a name for itself among riders starting out in the western show world. Located in Tomah, Little Hill Top is dedicated to bringing along beginning and intermediate riders in western pleasure and speed events, including pole bending, barrel racing, and roping. Owners Stacy and Jon Tormoen offer barrel-racing and pole-bending classes every Wednesday night, and roping instruction on Sundays. The Tormoens host 2D pole-bending events, as well as 3D and 4D barrel-racing shows, once a month. "Most of our students are western pleasure riders," Stacy says. "I'm teaching a lot of people the basics of horsemanship," and whether they go on to compete is up to them.

Stacy is known for her patience with young riders. The owners work with Boy Scouts and Girl Scouts earning merit badges for horse activities, and they offer birthday parties and camps for other kids. "We accept all the different aspects of horse lovers," she says, describing how they attract such a diverse group of riders.

The people who come to Little Hill Top are rewarded with a nice facility and owners with more than 20 years of experience in the industry.

Location: 16694 Holiday Road, Tomah, WI 54660.

Phone: (608) 372-0894.

Year founded: 2003.

Owner(s): Stacy and Jon Tormoen.

Hours: Call for appointment.

Specialization(s): Pole bending, barrel racing, and roping. Also offers summer camp and birthday parties on-site.

Facilities: Remodeled barn, 80 x 200-foot indoor arena, pastures, paddocks, trails on 10 acres with access to trails on 20 additional acres.

Number of stalls: 22 box stalls and 4 tie stalls.

Board: $–$$. Includes daily turnout, daily stall cleaning, two feedings per day, safe fencing, and scenic riding routes. Pasture board is also available.

Lessons: Private, on your horse or theirs, with reasonable rates.

School horses: 7.

Requirements: Helmets are required. Owners prefer that riders wear boots with a heel. Some boots are available.

Shows/clinics: Little Hill Top hosts a 4D barrel-racing, 2D pole-bending, and 3D pole-bending show the third Sunday of every month at 11:00 a.m. (January excluded). Shows have junior and tiny tot classes.

Transportation: Boarders provide own transportation to shows.

Other: Offers practice night for barrels and poles on Wednesday nights at 6:30. Offers roping one Sunday per month. Horses for sale and lease.

OK Corral
Wisconsin Dells

As trail riding facilities go, the OK Corral in the Wisconsin Dells is top-notch. This family-oriented barn caters to novice riders and families, exposing first-timers to riding in a safe and enjoyable manner.

The OK Corral was established in 1980 and has been serving vacationing families ever since. Their emphasis is on safety, and they offer good saddle horses—primarily quarter horses—to carry riders through a scenic canyon trail.

The OK Corral is family-owned and run, and utilizes more than 100 of its own horses. During the summer months, guides are available to take groups of one to 12 riders out every 10 minutes. All horses follow the same route through Devil's Canyon, a winding sandstone gorge, and up to an area surrounded by American Indian tepees, a graveyard, and a large horse pasture, where you can see horses grazing on their days off.

Trail rides average 55 minutes, depending on the pace of the group. It should be noted that, like most places in the Dells, the OK Corral does not allow riders to run their horses. The owners say that they maintain a slow pace so that a typical family with little or no riding experience can enjoy themselves.

While the OK Corral does not take reservations, the maximum wait is usually 30 minutes during the peak months of July and August. Management does, however, appreciate advance notice if you plan to come out with a large group (more than 12 riders). The facility offers a free petting zoo, a gift shop, and an air-conditioned snack bar to make the wait go faster. Families can also visit the petting zoo and check out the facility, free of charge, without signing up for a ride.

New to the OK Corral is the moonlight ride, a great way to unwind after a day at the Dells or an afternoon on the links. At $25 an hour, the cost is just slightly more than a day ride.

Location: One mile east of Wisconsin Dells on Highway 16 East.

Phone: (800) 254-2811.

E-mail: info@okcorralridingstable.com

Web site: http://www.okcorralridingstable.com

Year founded: 1980.

Hours: Spring season: 10:00 a.m.–3:00 p.m.; summer season: opens at 9:00 a.m. daily. Moonlight rides available. Inquire at office. Opens as early in the spring as weather permits—May 1 at the latest. The season runs through October and beyond, weather permitting. Horses are boarded at home during the winter.

Specialization(s): Western trail riding for the entire family.

Facilities: n/a.

Number of stalls: n/a.

Board: n/a.

Lessons: n/a.

Trail horses: 100–120 (primarily quarter horses).

Requirements: Absolutely no running of horses.

Shows/clinics: n/a.

Transportation: n/a.

Other: Some horses for sale after Labor Day.

Red Ridge Ranch
Mauston

It is hard to say what kids like more about Red Ridge Ranch: the horse trails or the kittens and foals that are in abundance at the farm. To be sure, the horse trails are enjoyable. The basic ride lasts approximately one hour and travels a well-worn railroad grade past the Lemonweir River. Riders are likely to see deer and wild turkeys, but the horses are accustomed to sharing the land with the surrounding wildlife. The goal at Red Ridge is to provide a safe, fun experience for the novice horseperson. Owners Cindy and Lyle Peterson run a family business and are involved in all phases of the rides. Hard hats are optional and available to all riders, and shoes with a heel are preferred.

Although Red Ridge is open year-round (call ahead during gun season), things really get hopping in the summer, when the ranch offers Horse Wishes Day Camp for young horse lovers, and roundups for kids and adults.

The day camp offers a fun way for kids to learn about horse care and ownership. Each child is assigned a horse on the first day that they care for and ride all week. Camp runs 9:00 a.m. to 5:00 p.m., Monday through Friday, and is limited to 10 students at a time. Campers study the parts of the horse, learn how to tack and untack, and ride every day. On Friday, students make a presentation to parents, and a reception follows.

The roundups are fun for the whole family. Families camp (primitive), enjoy cookouts and meals, and spend plenty of time in the saddle.

Location: W4881 State Highway 82, Mauston, WI 53948.

Phone: (608) 847-2273.

E-mail: redridgeranch@hotmail.com

Web site: http://www.redridgeranch.com

Year founded: 1999.

Owner(s): Cindy and Lyle Peterson.

Hours: Hours vary with the season. Please call ahead.

Specialization(s): Guided trail rides, summer day camp, ranch roundups (overnight camping for kids and adults).

Facilities: Barn, indoor arena (available during winter months), trails, round pen.

Number of stalls: 16.

Board: $. Includes use of facility, daily feedings, and overnight stabling if requested.

School horses: 30 used as both trail and school horses.

Requirements: Day campers must wear helmets. Helmets are offered for adult/group trail rides.

Shows/clinics: n/a (most boarders are trail riders).

Transportation: n/a.

River Ridge Stables
Platteville

River Ridge Stables is located conveniently off Highway 18/151 just south of Platteville. Opened in 2001, River Ridge caters to hunter/jumper equestrians, eventers, dressage riders, and western pleasure riders.

Owner Stephanie Field (who leases the property) has been riding and showing for years; she has years of experience getting people ready for the show ring. "We have a real mix of people here," says Field, including kids, students from the University of Wisconsin–Platteville, and adults learning how to ride. Some want to show and some do not, and Field and her crew of trainers seem adept at handling both types of riders.

Field hosts natural horsemanship clinics on an irregular basis and travels to shows, both in the area and in neighboring Illinois. "There are plenty of open shows in this area," says Field, for those who want the exposure. Even though the facility is large, it has an intimate feeling. "There aren't people fighting over the indoor, and there's plenty of room to spread out," Field notes. River Ridge also specializes in sale horses.

Location: 5753 Highway 151 South, Platteville, WI 53818.

Phone: (608) 348-2497.

E-mail: sfield78@aol.com

Web site: http://www.riverridgestable.net

Year founded: 2001.

Owner(s): Stephanie Field.

Hours: 8:00 a.m.–9:00 p.m. daily.

Specialization(s): Hunter/jumper, eventing, dressage, western pleasure.

Facilities: Barn, 180 x 80-foot indoor arena, hot/cold indoor wash rack, outdoor wash rack, 160 x 70-foot outdoor arena, small cross-country course, dressage ring, jump field, spacious turnout paddocks, pasture, tack room, lights for night riding, hunt course, indoor working round pen, and outdoor working round pen.

Number of stalls: 23.

Board: $$–$$$$. The rate depends on the training package. Board includes two feedings a day, turnout, twice daily cleaning of stalls, and feeding of supplements. Extra boarding services are available, including grooming, mane pulling, clipping/trimming, and bathing.

Lessons: Private, semiprivate, group, adult.

School horses: 3.

Requirements: Boot with a heel, hard hat (provided).

Shows/clinics: Hosts natural horsemanship and hunter/jumper clinics.

Transportation: Transportation can be provided to other shows and events.

Other: Horses for sale to both recreational and competitive riders.

Shenandoah Riding Center
Galena, Illinois

Yes, this guide is about stables and barns in Wisconsin, and yes, Shenandoah Riding Center is in Illinois, but the facility is too close to Wisconsin—and too good—to leave out of this book.

Owned by the Galena Territory Association, the Shenandoah Riding Center is located inside Eagle Ridge Resort, about five miles southeast of Galena, Illinois, and approximately 10 miles south of the Wisconsin border. Shenandoah offers more than 40 miles of groomed trails, a large indoor and outdoor arena, more than 90 acres of pasture, lessons, clinics, and shows.

One of the beautiful things about Shenandoah is its flexibility. If you are visiting Galena, you can stop by for a one-hour trail ride (call for an appointment), or you can bring your horse and see the sights of the Galena Territory (part of the Driftless Area) by horseback.

Lessons are available to Shenandoah boarders and members. The facility does not have schooling horses, but does rent horses for guided trail rides. During the summer, Shenandoah offers five-day camps that run from 8:00 a.m. to noon, Monday through Friday. Students are grouped by riding ability, not age, and may be required to take riding tests so instructors can make assessments of each rider's ability. The minimum age is 8.

Location: 200 North Brodrecht Road, Galena, IL 61036.

Phone: (815) 777-2373.

E-mail: src@galenalink.net

Web site: http://www.shenandoahridingcenter.com

Year founded: 1973.

Owner(s): Galena Territory Association.

Hours: 8:30 a.m.–4:30 p.m. daily.

Specialization(s): Western pleasure, English pleasure, dressage, hunter/jumper, gaited/saddle seat, driving, guided trail rides, summer day camps for kids. Offers overnight/short stay and lay ups.

Facilities: Barn, indoor and outdoor arenas, turnout paddocks, pasture, clubhouse/viewing area, lights for night riding, security system, indoor and outdoor wash racks, hunt course, cross-country course, tack shop, more than 40 miles of trails.

Number of stalls: 48.

Board: $–$$$. Pasture and stall board. Stall board includes two feedings per day, daily stall cleaning, turnout, blanketing, unblanketing, and vet and farrier records. Pasture board includes two feedings per day, grass turnout in the spring, summer, and fall, blanketing service, and farrier and vet records. Other services (bathing, clipping, exercising) available for an additional cost.

Lessons: Private, semiprivate, group, adult for boarders and members. Minimum age is 8.

School horses: None (some rental horses available for guided trail rides).

Requirements: ASTM-approved riding helmets (facility can provide), boots or paddock shoes.

Shows/clinics: Shenandoah offers clinics throughout the year. See Web site for postings. The facility is also host to two Illinois Dressage & Combined Training Association (IDCTA) dressage schooling shows per year, hunter/jumper schooling shows, open shows, and driving shows. The facility also hosts mini-events, fun shows, and drill team. There is a Professional Rodeo Cowboys Association (PRCA) rodeo on-site each year over the Fourth of July weekend, featuring fireworks and a dance. Call for information.

Transportation: Boarders trailer themselves to shows.

Other: Boarders are required to have Coggins and interstate health certificates. Guided trail rides are offered year-round on more than 40 miles of groomed trails.

Thistle Downs Sport Horses
Verona

Established in 1969, Thistle Downs is a mainstay in the Madison area. Located just off Highway 69 in Verona, its instructors have been teaching dressage and basic horsemanship for so long that almost every area rider has heard of the facility.

Former host to dressage shows and events, Thistle Downs no longer hosts shows (they do however, travel to them). That does not seem to bother the boarders, many of whom have been there a decade or more. Asked why boarders stay so long, owner Virginia Sanborn answers, "I think it's because we take care of horses like they're pets and companions, not just animals. Most of the horses here are integral parts of their owners' lives, and we understand that."

About a third of Thistle Downs boarders travel to shows. Boarders provide their own transportation, but there is a trainer on-site who coaches students on request.

Location: 7771 Riverside Road, Verona, WI 53593.

Phone: (608) 845-7719.

Year founded: 1969.

Owner(s): Virginia and Edwin Sanborn.

Hours: 8:00 a.m.–9:00 p.m.

Specialization(s): Dressage, English pleasure.

Facilities: Two barns, indoor arena with lights for night riding, outdoor arena, turnout paddocks, pastures, outdoor wash rack, tack room.

Number of stalls: 30 in two barns.

Board: $$. Includes daily stall cleaning, box stall, feed two times a day, limited turnout; extra turnout available for an additional fee.

Lessons: Dressage.

School horses: 3.

Requirements: Boot with a heel and a hard hat.

Shows/clinics: None. Travels to dressage shows.

Transportation: Boarders have their own trailers. Dressage coach will accompany students to shows.

Other: Horses occasionally for sale and lease.

Enjoying the best that Thistle Downs has to offer.

Three Gaits, Inc.
Stoughton

Three Gaits is a therapeutic riding facility that was established more than 20 years ago. Started by two women who loved horses and had an interest in therapeutic riding, Three Gaits offers the only program of its kind in Dane County (there are approximately 20 therapeutic riding facilities in Wisconsin). Three Gaits was designed to use riding and horse interaction to help riders channel their cognitive and physical disabilities into something physical, challenging, and rewarding.

Three Gaits caters to children, youth, and adults who have special physical and cognitive needs. The founders, Gail Brown and Lorrie Renker, started their backyard program in 1983 and have watched it grow every year. By the year 2000, Brown, Renker, and more than 100 volunteers were serving over 250 students a year on a 20-acre facility outside Stoughton.

Three Gaits offers a bevy of activity. First and foremost, there is the therapeutic riding program, around which "everything at the farm revolves," says one employee. Schooling dressage and jumping shows are held on Three Gaits' grounds each year, and all proceeds benefit the therapeutic riding program. Board is available and able-bodied students can bring their trainers to the barn for lessons.

All of Three Gaits' volunteer riding instructors are certified by the North American Riding for the Handicapped Association (NARHA). The stable and program are fully accredited by NARHA, which is the national association responsible for establishing safety standards and quality control.

Three Gaits enjoys an excellent reputation throughout Dane County, and the facility is supported by many in the area. Donations of goods, services, and horses are always welcome. Please inquire with the program manager for specific guidelines.

Location: 3741 Highway 138, Stoughton, WI 53589.

Phone: (608) 873-1929.

E-mail: 3gaits@mailbag.com

Web site: http://www.3gaits.org

Year founded: 1983.

Owner(s): Gail Brown and Lorrie Renker.

Hours: Call for schedules. Therapeutic riding classes are held evenings Monday through Thursday and on Saturday mornings. Most sessions run 10 weeks.

Specialization(s): Therapeutic riding for those with disabilities and special needs. Riders use English saddles. The facility also hosts dressage shows and combined tests for able-bodied riders, which benefit the therapeutic riding program. See Web site for details and show dates.

Facilities: Indoor riding arena, one-third-mile trail, outdoor arena, wash rack, picnic pavilion, indoor bathrooms, grass turnout.

Number of stalls: 26.

Board: $$. Boarding available to those outside the program. Includes box stall, three hay and two grain feedings a day, and turnout. Stalls are cleaned six days a week. There is an indoor arena available for year-round lessons and riding.

Lessons: Therapeutic riding, hippotherapy, unmounted horsemanship activities.

School horses: 12.

Requirements: Boarders and horse-owners from the general public can bring horses and trainers for schooling on Three Gaits property, but must receive prior permission. Therapeutic riding lessons always take priority.

Shows/clinics: Three dressage schooling shows per year, proceeds to benefit therapeutic riding program.

Transportation: n/a.

Other: Most lessons are taught by volunteers, who are trained on-site. If interested in volunteer opportunities, contact program director.

Three Gaits accepts donations. Three Gaits is a nonprofit 501(c)3, tax-exempt corporation that accepts barn supplies, funding, and horses. All horses are accepted on a trial basis.

Timeless Farm
Arena

Timeless Farm is a facility born of determination and the sheer love of horses. Located 27 miles west of Madison, the operation came about when "A" show hunter/jumper Stephanie Veloff-Histed decided that it was time for a place of her own. She had run shows and lessons out of other facilities, but she had a vision of what a local barn could be.

She purchased a former goat farm in Arena and now, several years later, she has Timeless Farm, a hunter/jumper facility that is host to eight schooling shows a year. She and her group of students, who all speak fondly of her, travel to rated shows, but learning at her place is all about camaraderie, and yes, hard work.

"When I started," Veloff-Histed says, "I had a bunch of green students with green horses, and I realized there was nowhere to show." Always entrepreneurial, Veloff-Histed organized and hosted her first show within a year, and a tradition was born.

Although you do not have to show to be at Timeless Farm, most of her students have show aspirations, be they local schooling shows or the "A" show circuit. Board includes a lesson requirement, although students are not required to jump.

"I gear my lessons toward the 'A' circuit," says Veloff-Histed, "but that's just because that's where I come from." The reality is, she says, that it has to stay fun. While she encourages competition in the ring, she insists that her students respect each other.

Location: 7431 Village Edge Road, Arena, WI 53503.

Phone: (608) 753-2295 (office) or (608) 753-2201 (barn); (608) 753-9066 (fax).

E-mail: Timeless@merr.com

Web site: http://www.timelessfarm.com

Year founded: 1999.

Owner(s): Stephanie Veloff-Histed.

Hours: Flexible. Open daily.

Specialization(s): Hunter/jumper.

Facilities: Barn, 60 x 140-foot indoor arena, paddocks, pasture, 200 x 400-foot outdoor arena.

Timeless Farm owner Stephanie Veloff-Histed showing how it's done.

Number of stalls: 18 in main aisle, 28 in annex (used for shows).

Board: $$$ (with lesson requirement). Includes turnout, two feedings per day, blanketing and unblanketing, supplements, regular farrier and vet schedules.

Lessons: Private.

School horses: 1 horse, 1 medium pony, 1 small pony.

Requirements: Proper lesson attire, hard hats required and available.

Shows/clinics: Facility hosts 8–9 shows per year.

Transportation: Provided to shows for students.

Other: Horses occasionally for sale and lease. Owner is member of Western Wisconsin Horse Show Association.

Uff-Da Farm
Stoughton

Uff-Da Farm is a small, centered-riding facility that caters to dressage and western pleasure enthusiasts. With six to seven steady schooling horses, Uff-Da is a good place for beginners and intermediate riders to learn the art of natural horsemanship and centered riding.

"I seem to get a lot of riders who have been scared or hurt around horses," says co-owner and trainer Pat Vogel. "I start all my horses with natural horsemanship, and they're very calm." Vogel breeds Hungarian Sport Horses, which average 16 hands and are known for their calm dispositions. She is a patient trainer, having worked in therapeutic riding with emotionally abused children, and she has a way of bringing people back to horses. "Some say I'm in the rehab business," she says with a laugh.

Vogel has been breeding horses for 18 years, and is partial to the Hungarians because "they're nice movers and they like to learn." Uff-Da is not nicknamed the Home of the Heavenly Hungarians for nothing.

The facility is located outside Stoughton where the Yahara River leaves Lake Kegonsa. It is a pretty setting with a traditional red barn and green arena.

Location: 2144 Williams Drive, Stoughton, WI 53589.

Phone: (608) 873-8956.

E-mail: uf-dafarm@itis.com

Year founded: 1975.

Owner(s): Pat and David Vogel.

Hours: No curfew.

Specialization(s): Dressage, centered riding, natural horsemanship, hunt seat, western pleasure.

Facilities: Barn, 66 x 120-foot indoor arena, pasture, tack room, lights for night riding, outdoor dressage arena, trails.

Number of stalls: 13.

Board: 250, includes turnout, personalized feeding programs.

Lessons: Private, semiprivate, group, adult. Minimum age is 5.

School horses: 6–7.

Requirements: Boot or paddock shoe, ASTM-approved helmet.

Shows/clinics: Clinics regularly held on-site.

Transportation: Can provide transportation to clinics and shows.

Other: Foals and started horses for sale.

More Stables and Barns

American Standardbred Adoption Program (ASAP)
S6039A Pedretti Lane
De Soto, WI 54624
(608) 637-8045
E-mail: asapinc@mwt.net
Web site: http://www.4thehorses.com
Specialization(s): Rescue, lessons in harness and ground driving,
saddle seat, English pleasure, western pleasure. By appointment only.

Beat Road Farm Bed and Breakfast and Stable
2401 Beat Road
Verona, WI 53593
(608) 437-6500
Specialization(s): Overnight stabling and bed-and-breakfast. Four stalls
available, space for trailers. Approximately 30 minutes from Governor
Dodge State Park and five minutes from Donald Park. Call for prices
and availability.

Beaver Springs Horseback Riding Stable
615 Trout Road
Wisconsin Dells, WI 53965
(608) 254-2707
Web site: http://www.beaverspringsfun.com/Riding_Stable.cfm
Specialization(s): Guided trail rides year-round, weather permitting.

Buck-N-Horse Ridge
4817 Ridgeview Road
Barneveld, WI 53507
(608) 924-3029
E-mail: dcoyne@mhtc.net
Specialization(s): Therapeutic riding with registered
occupational therapist.

Canyon Creek Riding Stable
60 Hillman Road
Lake Delton, WI 53940
(608) 253-6942
Web site: http://www.dells.com/horses/canyoncreek.htm
Specialization(s): Year-round guided trail rides, weather permitting.

Champion Valley Training Center
3073 County Trunk F
Barneveld, WI 53507
Phone/Fax: (608) 437-3912

E-mail: champvalley@mhtc.net
Web site: http://www.champvalley.com
Specialization(s): Western pleasure, English pleasure, hunt seat, saddle seat, horse safety. 40 acres of trails on-site, other trails available. Birthday parties on-site or will travel.

Domino Stables, Inc.
S4049 Old Highway 33
Baraboo, WI 53913
(608) 356-4701
E-mail: dominostbl@baraboo.com
Web site: http://www.cosmosmorgans.com
Specialization(s): Boarding facility that can be rented for mini-events, carriage-driving events, dressage, and other shows. Facility has been in business since 1972 and was the first facility to host mini-events for the Wisconsin Dressage and Combined Training Association (WDCTA). Trainers are welcome.

Dreams Therapeutic Riding Center
S2417 Hegge Road
Westby, WI 54667
(608) 634-4315
E-mail: Tiadreamer@yahoo.com
Web site: http://www.angelfire.com/stars3/dreamsridingcenter
Specialization(s): Offers therapeutic and recreational horsemanship to children and adults with physical, cognitive, or emotional challenges. Day camps are offered. NARHA certified.

Farraaway Ranch
47990 State Highway 171
Gays Mills, WI 54631
(608) 735-4128
Specialization(s): Basic horsemanship for English and western riders. Trainers get horses started under saddle for trail.

Francis Farm
7635 West State Highway 11
Janesville, WI 53545
(608) 876-6698
Specialization(s): Guided trail rides, wagon rides, pony rides (will travel off-site with ponies), lessons in western pleasure and English pleasure. Facility hosts four "fun" open horse shows per year, Halloween rides, and public horse auctions twice a year.

Friendship Farm
N3046 County Road FA
La Crosse, WI 54601
(608) 785-1222

E-mail: gottaridem@hotmail.com
Specialization(s): Hunter/jumper lessons and training.

GlenWillow Farm
E10102 Haugrud Hollow Road
La Farge, WI 54639
(608) 625-2510
E-mail: glenwillow@mwt.net
Specialization(s): Hunter/jumper, hunter under saddle, equitation.

Hilltop Farm Appaloosas
2959 County Road E
Mineral Point, WI 53565
(608) 987-3290
E-mail: sandy@paintshorses.com
Web site: www.paintshorses.com/hill_top_farm.htm
Specialization(s): Private lessons in western pleasure, English pleasure, and halter.

Huntington Farms
S4240 Haugen Road
Viroqua, WI 54665
(608) 637-2936
E-mail: ashunterus@yahoo.com
Web site: http://huntington-dhrojafarms.lfchosting.com
Specialization(s): Hunter/jumper. Huntington Farms is a member of the
Western Wisconsin Horse Show Association. Co-owner Amy Hunter is a
Grand Prix-level rider.

Lois Heyerdahl and Liz Lamm
17341 Hammer Road
Sparta, WI 54656-3454
(608) 269-7272
E-mail: crheyerdahl@iname.com
Specialization(s): Quality dressage instruction from training level through
Grand Prix. Heyerdahl is also a Senior USAE dressage judge. Both trainers
travel to give clinics.

Hylee Farm
3460 County Road JG
Mount Horeb, WI 53572
(608) 437-5530
Specialization(s): Saddle seat, hunt seat, western pleasure, driving; travels to
Class-A Morgan shows.

The Interstate Horse Center (IHC)
2655 County Road BN
Stoughton, WI 53589

(608) 873-0572
E-mail: ihchorse@aol.com
Specialization(s): Beginning horsemanship, English pleasure,
western pleasure, driving.

LaFleur Van Ess Stables

3440 Meadow Road and 7415 Valley View Road
Verona, WI 53593
(608) 833-3635
Specialization(s): Saddle seat for children and adults, age 4 years
and up. Horse lovers' day camp for ages 7–17.

Taking a break from dashing through the snow on a two-horse open sleigh at Redrock Trails.

Liberty Stables

2796 White Crossing Road
Verona, WI 53593
(608) 848-RIDE (7433)
E-mail: Mandys@libertystables.com
Web site: http://www.libertystables.com
Specialization(s): English pleasure, western pleasure, hunt seat,
jumping, dressage. One of the newer barns in the Madison area,
off County Road PD.

Lindinhof Equine Sports Zentrum

4246 Schneider Drive
Oregon, WI 53575
(608) 835-9819
E-mail: lindinhof1@aol.com
Specialization(s): Dressage and classical dressage clinics.

Little Tamarack Ranch

W23712 Little Tamarack Road
Galesville, WI 54630
(608) 539-2910
E-mail: LTHorseRanch@aol.com
Specialization(s): Western pleasure, barrels, poles, breaking young horses;
experience with all western disciplines. Located 22 miles north of La Crosse.

Lost Canyon Tours

720 Canyon Road
Lake Delton, WI 53940
(608) 254-8757
Specialization(s): Horse-drawn tours through canyons. Each wagon holds
15 people, and tours last 30 minutes. Call for reservations for large groups.

Madison Dressage Lesson and Training Center

8512 Highway 19
Cross Plains, WI 53562
(608) 798-4020
Specialization(s): Dressage lessons and training.

Madison Polo Club

3402 Sugar Maple Lane
Verona, WI 53593
(608) 829-1929
Specialization(s): Year-round polo lessons; owned by Ruth Dumesic.
Eight school horses. Hickory Knoll Farms (see description earlier in this
section) hosts Madison Polo Club games.

Notara Farms

7732 Riverside Road
Verona, WI 53593
(608) 845-7490
Specialization(s): English pleasure, western pleasure, driving. Also offers
sleigh rides and carriage rides.

Opagon Farm

272 Edgerton Road
Edgerton, WI 53534
(608) 884-2005

E-mail: opagonfarm@yahoo.com
Specialization(s): General horsemanship, English pleasure, western
pleasure, limited jumping, dressage, by appointment only. Open May
through October. Owner judges open and 4-H shows.

Parkhaven Private Boarding Stable

3258 South Gammon Road
Madison, WI 53719
(608) 271-1587 or (608) 441-8948
Specialization(s): Trainer Michelle Wilther will travel to barns in the
Madison area to teach lessons in basic English and western pleasure.

Peck's Farm Market

E3217 Highway 14/60
Spring Green, WI 53588
(608) 583-4977
Specialization(s): Free horse-drawn wagon rides during the summer.
Pony rides available in the fall. Complete farm market with zoo.

Pioneer Valley Stables

W7225 Hustad Valley Road
New Glarus, WI 53574
(608) 527-2566
Web site: http://www.pvalley.net
Specialization(s): Dressage, jumping, and eventing. Hosts
international-caliber clinicians, including Denny Emerson and Vitor Silva.

Prairie Sport Horses

3145 County Road T
Sun Prairie, WI 53590
(608) 241-4251
E-mail: felixj@merr.com
Specialization(s): Hunter/jumper, lessons, training, and show coaching.

Quad D Ranch Riding Stable

1841 Deerborn Avenue
Friendship, WI 53934
(608) 339-6436 or (800) RANCH-75
Specialization(s): Guided trail rides on more than 300 acres. Regular
ride is approximately one hour, and the pace is based on that of the
least-experienced rider. Open year-round, call for appointment.

Rabuck Ranch

1830 County Road C
Arkdale, WI 54613
(608) 564-7104
Specialization: Horse-drawn wagon rides; open year-round.
Call for appointment.

Ramblin B Arabians

E11230 Moon Road
Baraboo, WI 53913
(608) 356-7533
E-mail: ramblinb@baraboo.com
Web site: http://www.homestead.com/ramblinbarabians
Specialization(s): Western pleasure, English pleasure, hunter/jumper.

Redrock Trails

13597 Katydid Avenue
Sparta, WI 54656
(608) 823-7865
Specialization(s): Guided trail rides are offered spring through fall,
horse-drawn bobsled rides in the winter. More than 40 horses on-site.

Richwood Bed and Breakfast

6332 Highway 78 North
Gratiot, WI 53541
(608) 922-6402
E-mail: richwood@mhtc.net
Specialization(s): A bed-and-breakfast for horse owners, with a
three-bedroom house for guests, plus 12 stalls for horses and
55 acres off the Cheese Country Trail.

Saddle Ridge

1273 Judd Road
Oregon, WI 53575
(608) 835-2075 or (608) 835-9591
Specialization(s): English pleasure, hunt seat, dressage, eventing, jumping,
western pleasure. Boarders have access to miles of trails.

Sandy Meadows Quarter Horse Farm

W3647 Highway 16
Rio, WI 53960
(920) 992-5623
Email: UndunWind@CenturyTel.net
Web site: http://www.sandymeadowsfarm.com
Specialization(s): Reining, western pleasure, and lead-line lessons and
training for show-minded individuals; breeds top-quality quarter horses.

Show Horse Training Center

3671 Windsor Road
De Forest, WI 53532
(608) 846-4232
E-mail: shwhrs@cs.com
Specialization(s): Beginning through show-level lessons in hunt seat
and saddle seat. Trains Arabians and half-Arabians for breed circuit
and travels to recognized breed shows. Open year-round.

Silent Hollow Farm

7642 Ames Road
Darlington, WI 53530
(608) 776-4590
Web site: http://www.silenthollowfarm.com
Specialization(s): Reining.

Southwind Farm

1970 15th Avenue
Friendship, WI 53934
(608) 339-9606
Specialization(s): Western pleasure, English pleasure, dressage,
Parelli natural horsemanship; private and public trails for riding.

Stone Ridge Stables

W7508 Military Road
Portage, WI 53901
(608) 742-6815
E-mail: awschl@aol.com
Specialization(s): Western pleasure, hunter/jumper, dressage,
eventing; offers overnight and short stay with negative Coggins.

Sunburst Farm Boarding Stable and Kennels

E9674 County Road SS
Viroqua, WI 54665
(608) 629-5544
Email: sunburst@mwt.net
Specialization(s): Overnight and short-stay stabling; near Wildcat
Mountain State Park, Kickapoo Valley Reserve, and LaRiviere Park.

Sunrise Stables

4320 State Highway 138
Oregon, WI 53575
(608) 835-5656
E-mail: sunrisestables4@aol.com
Web site: http://www.members.tripod.com/sunrisestableswi/index.htm
Specialization(s): Western pleasure, English pleasure, dressage. Indoor
arena with lights for night riding, reasonable board. More than five
miles of trails.

Sunset Stables

W4803 Meyer Road
La Crosse, WI 54601
(608) 788-6629
Specialization(s): Western pleasure lessons, guided trail rides,
hayrides, and sleigh rides. Open year-round.

Triple K Stables

4721 Schneider Drive
Oregon, WI 53575
(608) 835-7285
Specialization(s): Beginning western pleasure, horsemanship;
does some commercial hauling.

Touchstone Farm

W1619 King Road
Brooklyn, WI 53521
(608) 455-2208
E-mail: Touchstn@chorus.net
Specialization(s): Dressage clinics with internationally recognized
trainers. Owner is president of the Wisconsin Dressage and
Combined Training Association.

Wildflower Stables

N7566 Marshall Bluff Road
Monticello, WI 53570
(608) 938-1675
E-mail: wildflowerstables@yahoo.com
Specialization(s): Western pleasure, English pleasure.

Willow Spring Farm

W4935 County Road B
La Crosse, WI 54601
(608) 781-6688
Specialization(s): Dressage, eventing, hunter/jumper, western
pleasure. Three school horses available. Open year-round.

York Farm Stables

3299 McMillan Road
Poynette, WI 53955
(608) 635-9916
Specialization(s): Guided or unguided trail rides over 3.5 miles of
trails (ride takes just over one hour). Open year-round except
during hunting season, weather permitting. Call to confirm.

Riding Trails

Castle Rock Trails
Adams County

Castle Rock, found in the heart of Adams County, offers 20 miles of gently winding trails in six loops. Great for riding horses and driving carriages (hikers and cross-country skiers share the same trails), Castle Rock Trails meander through pine plantations, marshes, past the Wisconsin River, and back through prairies. Open areas are great for driving, but there are plenty of wooded trails for riders as well. Driving trails are marked with wagon wheels on the trail signs.

There are no garbage cans at the parking lot; Castle Rock has a strong "pack it in, pack it out" policy, so please be conscientious. There is no camping, and there are currently no restrooms. Bring your own food, water, and other provisions. For those who want to ride back-to-back days, the Ukarydee Equestrian Campground is located just southeast of the main trails (see description in the More Riding Trails section of this chapter), and with 30 sites that can handle big rigs, they have room for just about everyone.

The Castle Rock Trails are owned by the Wisconsin River Power Company. The Castle Rock Trails Club and Glacial Drumlin Horse Trails Association were instrumental in securing and maintaining these trails for trail riders. These groups, along with the Wisconsin State Horse Council and other saddle clubs, often put in hard work and long hours to secure our trails, so if you come upon them, be sure to say thanks.

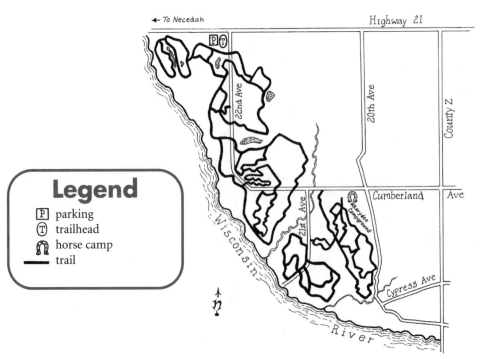

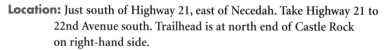
Location: Just south of Highway 21, east of Necedah. Take Highway 21 to 22nd Avenue south. Trailhead is at north end of Castle Rock on right-hand side.

Contact(s): Castle Rock Trails
P.O. Box 782
Friendship, WI 54943

Phone: (608) 575-8604.

E-mail: castlerocktrails@yahoo.com

Trails: Twenty miles of marked trails, divided into six loops. Terrain is gently rolling with creek crossings, ponds, and winding trails. Some trails are wide enough for wagons and buggies, and these trails are marked with small wagon wheels on the bottom corner of the trail signs.

Shared use: Shared with hikers during the summer, snowshoers and cross-country skiers during the winter. Do not ride during gun deer season.

Horse rentals: n/a.

Camping: Day use only. Camping is available at Ukarydee Equestrian Campground (see description in the More Riding Trails section of this chapter), which can be found on the southeast border of the horse trails.

Reservations: n/a.

Dates of use: Open year-round. Do not use during deer gun season.

Passes: n/a. Donations accepted online and at the trailhead.

Other: Castle Rock Trails are privately owned by the Wisconsin River Power Company. Please stay on marked trails.

Maintaining a brisk pace on the Castle Rock Trails.

Cheese Country Trail
Lafayette and Iowa Counties

The Cheese Country Trail, between Monroe and Mineral Point, follows 47 miles of a former railroad corridor that offers beautiful vistas of the Pecatonica River. There are dozens of bridge crossings, including a long one over the river near Browntown, about six miles west of Monroe.

The Cheese Country Trail is known for its beautiful scenery. Unfortunately, because it is a relatively flat, packed trial and is open to motorized vehicles, the trail is also known as a place where you need to exercise extreme caution when riding or driving your horse. If you choose to ride the Cheese Country Trail, the best time to do so is on weekdays and before the snow falls (snowmobiles use the trails in winter).

The trail, which appropriately advertises itself as multi-use, is open to ATVs, off-road motorcycles, bicycles, horses, and hikers. The Green County Welcome Center, located at the Monroe trailhead, advises users to be "cautious and courteous of the many trail-users traveling at different speeds along this scenic, back road view of southern Wisconsin." Although the trail is patrolled by the sheriff's department, there have been accidents involving horses and motorized vehicles. If riding, bring your most level-headed horse, and keep your eyes and ears open.

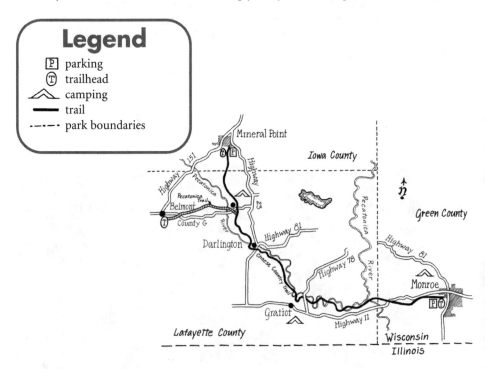

Location: The Cheese Country Trail runs parallel to the Pecatonica River from Mineral Point to Monroe. Trailheads are located in Mineral Point at Old Darlington Road and in Monroe at 4th Avenue west near Highway 69 south.

Contact(s): Green County Welcome Center (Monroe trailhead)
   1016 16th Avenue
   Monroe, WI 53566

   Mineral Point Chamber of Commerce (Mineral Point Trailhead)
   225 High Street
   Mineral Point, WI 53565

Phone: (608) 328-9430 (Green County) or (608) 987-3201(Mineral Point).

Web site: http://greencounty.org/tourism/cheesemappage.htm or
   http://www.lafayettecounty.org/tourrec/trailsandscenicd.html

Trails: Former railroad corridor that runs 47 miles through scenic woods, fields, river valleys, and fields. The trail is shared with motorized vehicles that do not always respect posted speed limits. Use caution at all times. Trail intersects with the Pecatonica Trail at Calamine. The best time to use the trail is weekdays and in the winter, before the snow falls.

Shared use: Trail is multi-use and shared with ATVs, off-road motorcycles, bicyclists, and hikers, as well as snowmobilers and cross-country skiers in winter.

Horse rentals: n/a.

Camping: Day use only. See listing for Richwood Bed and Breakfast, which offers lodging for you and your horse. Located in Gratiot, Richwood has trail access and private riding facilities for use.

Dates of use: Open from April 1 to November 15. Closed during hunting season. Open again December 1 for riders, snowmobiles, skiers, hikers, and bikers.

Passes: State trail pass required for riders 16 and older.

Children's Ranch
Crawford County

   Children's Ranch offers board and other "stable" amenities, but also draws hundreds of trail riders each year. (Because of its dual purpose, the facility is also described in the "Stable and Barns" section of this chapter.)

   Children's Ranch opened in 1996 as a free facility to help at-risk kids and to attract equestrian activities to the area. It has become a very popular destination for trail riders, who are granted access to miles of Children's Ranch trails and 20 miles of LaRiviere Park trails, all at no cost. Even the camping is free.

   Children's Ranch does not rent horses for trail rides, but with a negative Coggins, riders are welcome to bring their own and stay overnight in primitive campgrounds (primitive showers are available). Reservations are not necessary, but occasional shows fill the campground, so cal ahead to ensure there will be room for you and your horse. Space permitting, overnight boarders are welcome to use the 135 x 340-foot arena and round pen.

Note: Children's Ranch is a 501(c)3 organization and accepts donations as riders see fit. Please see the Web site for more information.

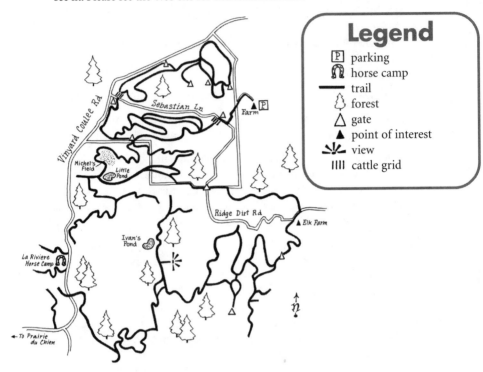

Location: Children's Ranch is on the south side of Prairie du Chien along Highway 18/35/60. When you reach Dick's Supermarket, turn east (toward the bluffs) onto Vineyard Coulee Road. Drive two miles and follow the signs to the ranch.

Contact(s): Sarah Tarjeson
Children's Ranch
38371 Highway 18 South
Prairie du Chien, WI 53821

Phone: (608) 326-5362 or (800) 946-7262.

E-Mail: youthranch@yahoo.com

Web site: http://www.childrensranch.org

Trails: Miles of hilly trails that connect with LaRiviere Park trails; in total, the ranch offers more than 100 miles of excellent horseback riding. Trails are open year-round.

Shared use: Some light hiking.

Horse rentals: n/a.

Camping: Free overnight camping. Primitive showers available.

Reservations: Please call for availability.

Dates of use: Open year-round. Please be respectful during the spring thaw.

Passes: None. All activities at Children's Ranch are free.

Other: Children's Ranch is always in need of volunteers and donations. Children's Ranch is a 501(c)3 organization, and donations are tax-deductible to the extent of the law.

Donald Park
Dane County

Located in the southwestern corner of Dane County near Mount Vernon, Donald Park is one of Wisconsin's newest horse parks. It started with a donation of 105 acres from Delma Woodburn in 1993, and the area recently opened for equestrian use.

Coupled with 10 miles of nearby trails, Donald Park offers 14 miles of trails. Hikers share the trails (dogs are allowed on-leash). The trails are an easy complement to the more rugged trails at nearby Governor Dodge State Park. The trails are mowed grass over rolling hills with some steep, but not extreme, grades. Many people like Donald Park for its ease of access and its "dayride" feel. It is a friendly place where people enjoy the outdoors and each other. Donald Park is a welcome addition to the equestrian trails of Dane County.

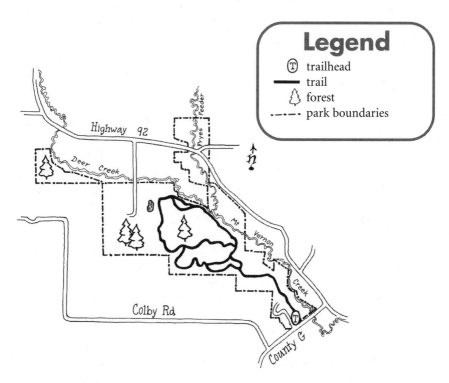

Location: The equestrian trailhead is off County Road G in Mount Vernon. Note: This is separate from the Pop's Knoll picnic area.

Contact(s): Dane County Parks
4318 Robertson Road
Madison, WI 53714
or Friends of
Donald Park

Phone: (608) 246-3896 (Dane County Parks).

E-mail: ralthous@execpc.com (Friends of Donald Park)

Web site: http://www.co.dane.wi.us/parks/parkhome.htm (Dane County Parks) or http://www.donaldpark.org (Friends of Donald Park)

Trails: Approximately 14 miles of bridle trails over mowed grass. Terrain is rolling but not extreme. Trails are closed when conditions are wet.

Shared use: Shared with hikers and dogs (on-leash).

Horse rentals: n/a.

Camping: Day use only.

Dates of use: Spring/summer/fall. Winter riding available on adjoining land. Call for dates. Trails are closed when conditions are wet.

Passes: Dane County trail pass required.

Endless Valley Stables
Sauk County

While many facilities cater to people interested in lessons or trail riders, Endless Valley does both. While Endless Valley rests on 200-plus acres, the owners lease and maintain the trails on 3,000 acres owned by a Madison family. Presently, Endless Valley offers 30 miles of trails that begin in a valley and climb into the hills around Spring Green. The facility hopes to establish another 10–20 miles of trails by 2005, and what spectacular trails they will be.

The scenery in Spring Green, which rests in the Driftless Area of southwestern Wisconsin, is rugged and beautiful. The land is wooded, and the landscape in the fall is nothing short of spectacular. The trails are well maintained and well marked, and riding on them involves lots of climbing. Riding at Endless Valley is a great way to get your horse fit. Owners control the number of horses on the trails at any given time, so the trails never get too crowded. Camping is available. For those who do not like roughing it, Endless Valley offers a three-bedroom cabin (sleeps eight) attached to the barn. The cabin includes a kitchenette and a bath.

Endless Valley trails are closed during hunting season for safety reasons. Please call ahead for reservations, and remember to bring your negative Coggins. (See also the description of Endless Valley Stables in the "Stables and Barns" section of this chapter.)

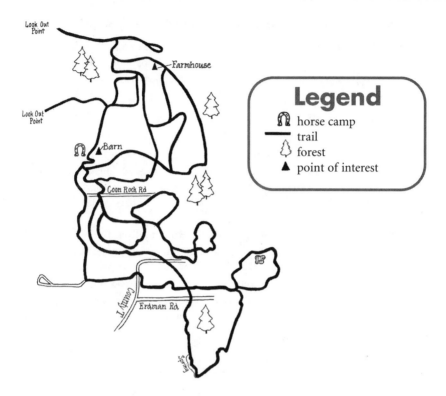

Location: On County Road T between Highway 23 and County Road H.

Contact(s): 5975 County Road T
Spring Green, WI 53588

Phone: (608) 753-2887.

E-mail: lsmurphy@execpc.com

Web site: http://www.endlessvalleystables.com

Trails: More than 30 miles of trails that start on the valley floor and wind into the hills around Spring Green. Terrain is rolling but not difficult. Trails are well marked and maintained.

Shared use: None

Horse rentals: Not currently available. Guided trail rides may be offered in the future. Call for more information.

Camping: Primitive campsites with fire pit and corral. There is also a three-bedroom cabin with kitchenette, which sleeps eight (two-night minimum stay).

Reservations: Required. A limited number of riders are allowed on the trails at any given time.

Dates of use: Open year-round, except during deer hunting season.

Passes: Reasonable trail-use fee, payable to Endless Valley Stables.

Other: Please bring original Coggins with a copy for the facility. If from out of state, you will need interstate health papers. Those not having the proper paperwork will be asked to leave the property, as mandated by state law.

400 State Trail
Juneau and Sauk Counties

The equestrian portion of the 400 State Trail runs seven miles from Wonewoc to La Valle, just a portion of the entire trail, which runs 22 miles from Elroy to Reedsburg. The trail, which is open during the spring, summer, and fall (trails are used for snowmobiling in the winter), has trailheads and parking for horse trailers at both Wonewoc and La Valle.

This former railroad corridor runs along the Baraboo River. The equestrian trails run parallel to the bike path, and riders must stay on their designated trail. There are several bridge crossings along the way. Wildlife is common in the area, including muskrats, turtles, sandhill cranes, and blue herons. Bluffs can be found on both sides of the trail, and fall is a particularly beautiful time to ride. Between the colors, the river, and the wildlife, a ride on the 400 State Trail is a super way to spend your day.

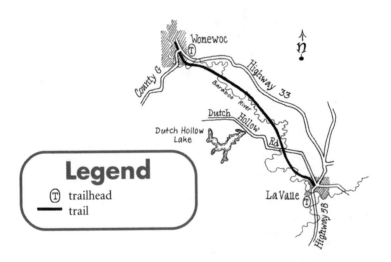

Location: Trailheads are located in Wonewoc and La Valle, between Elroy and Reedsburg (see map).

Contact(s): 400 Trail Headquarters
P.O. Box 142
Reedsburg, WI 53959

Phone: (608) 337-4775 (DNR) or (800) 844-3507 (trail headquarters); (608) 337-4362 (fax).

E-mail: reedsbrg@mwt.net

Web site: http://www.400statetrail.org

Trails: The equestrian portion runs 7 miles from Wonewoc to La Valle. The terrain is relatively flat.

Shared use: The equestrian portion of the trail runs alongside the hiking and biking trail.

Horse rentals: n/a.

Camping: Day use only.

Reservations: n/a.

Dates of use: Spring, summer, and fall.

Passes: State trail pass required for riders 16 and older.

Governor Dodge State Park
Iowa County

Governor Dodge State Park, located north of Dodgeville in the Driftless Area of southwestern Wisconsin, is made up of more than 5,000 acres of rolling land peppered with caves, steep sandstone bluffs, rock formations, natural hollows, dells, and valleys. As a result, horseback riding here is an exhilarating experience. The terrain is varied and rugged in some places, but the park's trails are suitable for all riders.

There are 21 miles of horseback-riding trails at Governor Dodge. The outer 15.3-mile loop winds through some of the most scenic and remote parts of the park. Average ride time is 3.5 hours. Inside the loop, there is a shorter 6.7-mile trail that connects the horse camp and horse day-use areas. The inner and outer trails intersect near the horse camp. The trails pass by Cox Hollow Lake, a favorite for canoeists, kayakers, and swimmers in the summer. The atmosphere at Governor Dodge is laid-back, and riders like it for the variety of terrain and the longer length of the trails. Governor Dodge State Park is one of the nicest places to ride a horse in the state.

Location: About 3 miles north of Dodgeville; take Highway 23 to the main entrance.

Contacts(s): 4175 State Highway 23 North
                 Dodgeville, WI 53533

Phone: (608) 935-2315; (608) 935-3959 (fax).

E-mail: gruenka@dnr.state.wi.us

Web site: http://www.dnr.state.wi.us/org/land/parks/specific/govdodge

Trails: 21 miles in two loops. Terrain is variable, and includes flat areas and wooded hillsides. Note that horses must stay on bridle trails.

Shared use: Some trails are shared with hikers and mountain bikers.

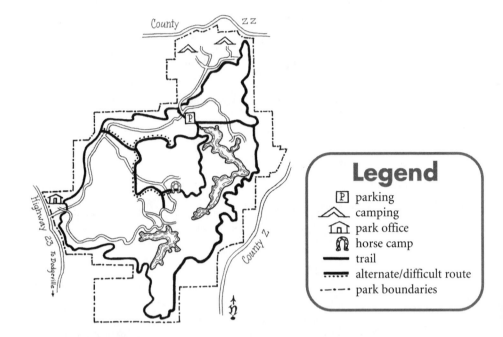

Horse rentals: Guided tours are available from Doby Stables, which is across Highway 23 and accesses the park via an underground tunnel. See the listing in the Stables and Barns section of this chapter.

Camping: Seventeen campsites are available for horse campers. Electricity is not available. Fees are $10 per night for Wisconsin residents and $12 per night for nonresidents. Small discounts apply for the off-season and for Sunday through Thursday nights. Vehicle admission sticker and trail passes are required. Advance reservations are recommended.

Two small group sites are also available in the horse campground on a first-come, first-served basis. Contact the park office for more information.

Hitching posts are provided at each campsite. It is important that you bring your own lead line, as none are available at the park. Please contact the park office for information about the use of fencing or other stabling devices.

Reservations: Call ReserveAmerica (888) 947-2757 or visit www.reserve america.com. Campers can register at the park office during regular office hours, space permitting.

Dates of use: Horse campground and trails are open from May 1 to November 15, unless otherwise posted. Hours are 8:00 a.m.–11:00 p.m. daily from June through August. The same hours apply for spring and fall weekend nights. Hours for September through May are 8:00 a.m.–4:00 p.m.

Passes: Vehicle sticker and trail passes are required.

Other: Doby Stables, which has been in business since the 1970s, is located across Highway 23 and rents horses for guided trail rides through the park. Riders enter the park through an underground tunnel separating the facility from Governor Dodge trails. Governor Dodge is in the state's Chronic Wasting Disease eradication zone. Use caution when riding around hunters.

Taking it slow over a bridge in the Kickapoo Valley Reserve. Photo courtesy of Kickapoo Valley Ranch.

Kickapoo Valley Reserve
Vernon County

Ask anyone what they think of the Kickapoo Valley Reserve, located between La Farge and Ontario, and the answer is sure to be "beautiful," "awesome," "spectacular," or something similar. What makes the reserve even more appealing is that rarely will you find 8,600 acres of such unspoiled land anywhere else in Wisconsin's Driftless Area (the area spared by the most recent glaciers).

The Kickapoo Valley Reserve is host to many sports, but horse enthusiasts love it because ATVs and other motorized vehicles are not allowed on the trails. The terrain can range from flat to downright mountainous, providing something for everyone.

The Kickapoo Valley Reserve is not a state park, so it is not marked as well as nearby Wildcat Mountain. The terrain can be challenging, and beginners can easily find themselves on trails better suited to experienced riders. A good trail map, widely available at the reserve office, should keep you on course.

If you ride on the valley floor, you will likely see towering rock outcroppings above, from which the Kickapoo River and its tributaries can be seen.

Of the reserve's 20 campsites, four are available for horseback riders. These are Willow, Mule, Ma & Pa's, and Rockton, with Willow and Mule being the most pop-

49

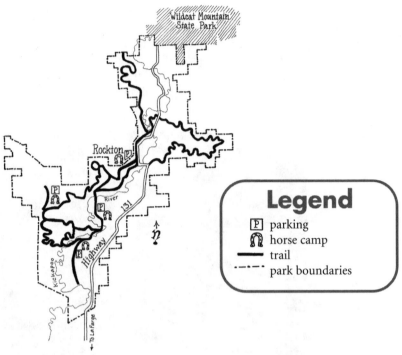

ular. All camping is first come, first served, and requires a visitor's permit, available at the reserve office and seven self-registration stations on the land. Trails are open to riders from May 1 to November 15.

Location: Just south of Wildcat Mountain State Park, between
La Farge and Ontario.

Contact(s): Kickapoo Valley Reserve Office
505 North Mill Street
La Farge, WI 54639

Phone: (608) 625-2960; (608) 625-2962 (fax).

E-mail: kickapoo.reserve@krm.state.wi.us

Web site: http://kvr.state.wi.us/home

Trails: Almost 37 miles of trails over varied terrain. Riders will experience towering rock outcroppings, some flatland, river crossings, and steep hills.

Shared use: Some equestrian trails are shared with bicycles.

Horse rentals: n/a. There are several nearby stables, including the Kickapoo Valley Ranch (see the Stables and Barns section of this chapter), that offer guided trail rides through the reserve.

Camping: Four sites, including Mule, Willow, Ma & Pa's, and Rockton.

Reservations: First come, first served.

Dates of use: May 1 through November 15.

Passes: Can be purchased at the reserve office or at one of the seven self-registration stations on the reserve.

Other: Absolutely beautiful scenery. Not all trails are suitable for beginners.

Pointing the way to LaRiviere Park.

LaRiviere Park
Crawford County

LaRiviere Park in Prairie du Chien is one of the state's more popular riding parks. LaRiviere (pronounced la-vee-ay) has more than 20 miles of marked trails and adjoins the Children's Ranch (see separate descriptions in this section and the Stables and Barns section of this chapter). Together, they offer 100 miles of trails through the bluff country near the Mississippi River.

Eagles, hawks, and other birds of prey are abundant during the fall, and can easily be seen from the trails. Other wildlife abounds, and the park's hilly trails, which travel over 320 acres, offer plenty of sightseeing opportunities. LaRiviere is situated where the Wisconsin and Mississippi rivers join, and the scenery is breathtaking.

Trails at LaRiviere are well-marked with yellow posts. There are 18 horse campsites, some with electricity and some without, and two shelters. There is a horse barn on-site, which is available for indoor activities. Corrals are also available. Camping is free, but donations, which help pay for maintenance and trail upkeep, are accepted but not required. Donation boxes are located at the campground. If the LaRiviere campsites are full, there is usually room for camping at Children's Ranch (call ahead).

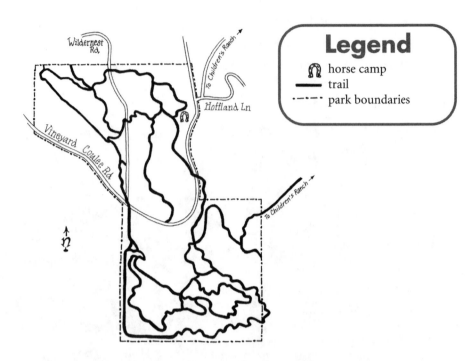

Location: LaRiviere Park is on Vineyard Coulee Road, 1 mile south of Prairie du Chien in Bridgeport. There is a Dick's Supermarket on the corner of Vineyard Coulee Road.

Contact(s): LaRiviere Park
Vineyard Coulee Road
Prairie du Chien, WI 53821

Dan Boom
1915 East Brunson Street
Paririe du Chien, WI 53821

Phone: (608) 326-6114.

Trails: There are 20 miles of trails at LaRiviere Park, which adjoins Children's Ranch and its additional 80 miles of trails. The park overlooks the mouth of the Mississippi and Wisconsin rivers, affording riders beautiful scenery. Trails vary between prairie and woods, and the terrain is hilly, but not extreme. Take bug spray in the summer. Maps are not currently available. Both LaRiviere and Children's Ranch get high marks for ample parking and camping space.

Shared use: Shared with hikers.

Horse rentals: n/a.

Camping: LaRiviere has 18 free camping sites, some with electricity. When these fill, campers can try Children's Ranch (also free), provided they call in advance. LaRiviere offers two shelters at the horse camp, one with electricity, one without. There are Porta-Potties, fire rings, and picnic tables available. Drinking water is available at the park barn.

Reservations: First come, first served.

Dates of use: Trails are open year-round. Bring your own provisions, as water is shut off during the winter. If you pack it in, pack it out. Use caution during gun hunting season.

Passes: n/a. Donations accepted at the campground.

Lower Wisconsin State Riverway, Black Hawk Unit
Dane County

The state of Wisconsin owns more than 43,000 acres in the Lower Wisconsin State Riverway, and while some of the acreage is closed to protect endangered species, the vast majority is open to the public. There are horse trails at three units of the state riverway: Black Hawk, Millville, and Muscoda.

The Black Hawk Unit of the Lower Wisconsin State Riverway between Sauk City and Mazomanie has 12 miles of equestrian trails, about half of which are wide enough for carriages. The Black Hawk Unit has a large covered pavilion available for equestrian-related events, and can be reserved by calling (608) 588-2116. Parking for this pavilion can be found in the middle of the park, off Wachter Road and south of Highway 78.

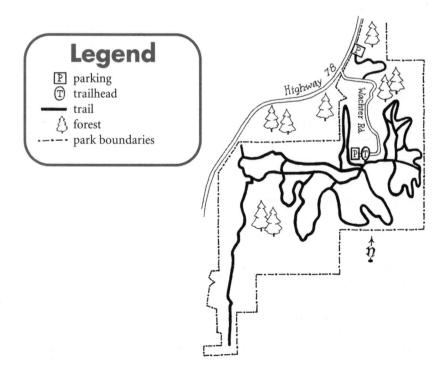

Legend

P parking
T trailhead
— trail
forest
·—·—· park boundaries

Location: Parking for the riverway is available off Highway 78 between Sauk City and Mazomanie. Horse trailers can also be parked at Cedar Hills Campground (private) on Dunlap Hollow Road, a quarter mile east of Highway 78 in Mazomanie. Call (608) 795-2606 for directions and camping reservations.

Contact(s): Tower Hill State Park
Department of Natural Resources
Attn: Mr. Wayne Schutte
Riverway Recreation Specialist
5808 County Road C
Spring Green, WI 53588

Phone: (608) 588-2116.

E-mail: schutw@dnr.state.wi.us

Web site: http://lwr.state.wi.us/home/landrec.htm

Trails: The Black Hawk Unit has 12 miles of equestrian trails, seven of which are suitable for horse-drawn vehicles. The trails vary between open prairie and woods, and are hilly in some areas. The terrain is user friendly. Horses must stay on designated trails.

Shared use: Shared with hikers and cross-country skiers.

Horse rentals: n/a.

Camping: Horse camping is available at the nearby Cedar Hills Campground, near the southern parking lot.

Reservations: Call (608) 795-2606.

Dates of use: Open year-round. Use extreme caution during hunting season. The Black Hawk Unit is in the Chronic Wasting Disease intensive harvest area, and extended gun seasons apply. The Black Hawk Unit gets more hunters than either the Millville or Muscoda Units.

Passes: n/a. Call campground for fees, if any.

Lower Wisconsin State Riverway, Millville Unit
Grant County

The trails on the Millville Unit of the Lower Wisconsin State Riverway include seven grass-and-gravel trail miles over rolling hills. The Millville Unit, made up of more than 3,600 acres, lies east of the Wisconsin River, southeast of Prairie du Chien. Like its cousins, the Black Hawk and Muscoda Units, Millville is full of wildlife, including deer, turkeys, and grouse. Unlike the other units, Millville trails are too hilly for horse-drawn carriages.

The equestrian trail begins with a steep climb to a ridge overlooking the Wisconsin River. The trail follows the ridge, then descends into a valley, only to rise to another ridge. It makes a loop through an area recently planted with trees, crosses back through the valley, and returns to the beginning of the loop through a beautiful gorge.

The mostly wooded landscape (with some agricultural fields) is beautiful, but it also creates the most difficult of the Riverway rides. Still, the trail is user friendly. Maps are available at the parking area off County Road C or by contacting the Riverway Recreation Specialist at Tower Hill State Park.

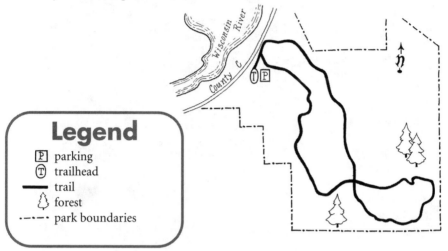

Legend

P parking
T trailhead
— trail
🌲 forest
·—·—· park boundaries

Location: Off County Road C, just north of Millville. There is a parking lot at the trailhead on C, across from the Millville Town Park.

Contact(s): Tower Hill State Park
Department of Natural Resources
Attn: Mr. Wayne Schutte
Riverway Recreation Specialist
5808 County Road C
Spring Green, WI 53588

Phone: (608) 588-2116.

E-mail: schutw@dnr.state.wi.us

Web site: http://lwr.state.wi.us/home/landrec.htm

Trails: Seven miles of grass trails in a figure eight.

Shared use: Shared with hikers.

Horse rentals: n/a.

Camping: Day use only.

Reservations: n/a.

Dates of use: May 15 through October 15.

Passes: n/a.

On the trail along the Lower Wisconsin State Riverway.

Lower Wisconsin State Riverway, Muscoda Unit
Grant County

The Muscoda Unit of the Lower Wisconsin State Riverway runs eight miles along the Wisconsin River between Muscoda and Blue River. While horses can drink from the river, there is no water for human consumption, so bring your own. The trail, which is made up of open prairie, wetlands, and some woods, is flat and soft, but it is firm enough for good riding and driving. The trails are open from May 15 through October 15.

The Muscoda Unit is made up of 2,291 acres, all state-owned. Riders will be treated to sandhill cranes, deer, and plenty of squirrels and rabbits. This is a popular area for bird-watching, so watch out for pedestrians during your ride.

Location: Two miles west of Muscoda on West Pine Road. Parking on the Blue River (west) end is off Highway 133 on Jones Lake Road.

Contact(s): Tower Hill State Park
Attn: Mr. Wayne Schutte
Riverway Recreation Specialist
Department of Natural Resources
5808 County Road C
Spring Green, WI 53588

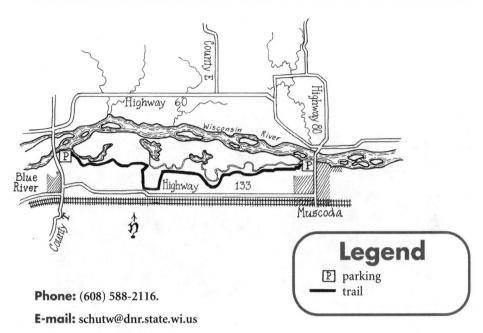

Legend

P parking
— trail

Phone: (608) 588-2116.

E-mail: schutw@dnr.state.wi.us

Web site: http://lwr.state.wi.us/home/landrec.htm

Trails: Eight miles of flat trail with a sand-and-gravel base. The trail runs just south of the Wisconsin River, from Muscoda to Blue River. The entire trail is wide enough for horse-drawn vehicles.

Shared use: Shared with hikers and hunters.

Horse rentals: n/a.

Camping: Day use only.

Reservations: n/a.

Dates of use: Open year-round. Use extreme caution during hunting season.

Passes: n/a.

McCarthy Youth and Conservation Park
Dane County

Opened in September 2003, McCarthy Youth and Conservation Park, near Cottage Grove, has four miles of equestrian trails. Divided into several loops, the mowed-grass trails, which vary between flat and gently rolling, are rider friendly. McCarthy Park is great for green horses and/or green riders. The land is open and gentle; none of the terrain is threatening. The facility, which began with a 180-acre donation by Russ and Ella McCarthy to Dane County, is designated for kids with access to horses. There are plans for an arena where 4-H groups and others can practice their riding, and a campground is also in the works.

The Friends of McCarthy Park, an incorporated and nonprofit group, operates to ensure that these goals and other future developments will come to fruition. They depend on donations of time and money to help meet these objectives.

McCarthy Park—designed with youthful riders in mind.

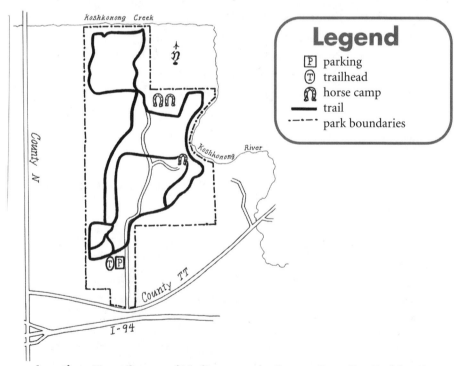

Location: Five miles east of Madison near the Cottage Grove/Sun Prairie exit (County Road N) of Interstate 94. Entrance is on County Road TT, just east of its intersection with County Road N.

Contact(s): Friends of McCarthy Park
4658 Pierceville Road
Cottage Grove, WI 53527
Dane County Parks
4318 Robertson Road
Madison, WI 53714

Phone: (608) 246-3896 (Friends of McCarthy).

Web site: http://www.mccarthypark.org

Trails: Four miles.

Shared use: Shared with hikers.

Horse rentals: n/a.

Camping: Day use only. Camping may be available in the future.

Reservations: n/a.

Dates of use: Call for exact dates.

Passes: Dane County trail pass required.

Pecatonica Trail
Lafayette County

Like the Cheese Country Trail (see description earlier in this section), the Pecatonica Trail is a multi-use trail. Running for 10 miles between Belmont and Calamine, the trail follows the valley of the Bonner Branch of the Pecatonica River. It ends in Calamine, where it connects with the Cheese Country Trail.

The floor of the Pecatonica Trail is composed of limestone and offers secure footing. The trail is traveled frequently by motorized vehicles, including ATVs and motorcycles, so extreme caution is urged. Motorcycles and ATVs are not allowed on the trail during the winter months, so if there is no snow (snow-mobiling and skiing are permitted), the colder months may offer quieter (and safer) riding.

Location: Trailheads in Belmont and Calamine, the latter of which intersects the Cheese Country Trial.

Contact(s): Green County Welcome Center (Monroe trailhead)
1016 16th Avenue
Monroe, WI 53566

Phone: (608) 328-9430.

Trails: Ten miles of multi-use trails from Belmont to Calamine. Intersects with the Cheese Country Trail in Calamine. The Pecatonica Trail is on the former branch line of the Milwaukee Road Railroad. Parking is available in both Belmont and Calamine. The trail is surfaced in

limestone and follows the Bonner Branch of the Pecatonica River. Use caution when riding near motorized vehicles on this trail.

Shared use: Like the Cheese Country Trail, the Pecatonica Trail is multi-use and is shared with motorcycles, ATVs, hikers, and bikers in the summer months and with hikers, bikers, snowmobilers, and skiers during winter months.

Camping: Day use only. Overnight accommodations available for horses and riders at the Richwood Bed and Breakfast in Gratiot, off the Cheese Country Trail.

Reservations: n/a.

Dates of use: Open year-round for equestrian use, except during deer gun season and from November 15 to December 1, when the trail is closed for maintenance.

Passes: State trail pass required for riders 16 and older.

Token Creek Park
Dane County

Token Creek Park, just north of Madison, is best known for its extensive shelters and group facilities, but it is also home to 3.5 miles of equestrian trails, which are shared with hikers. The terrain is mostly flat with some very gently rolling hills.

The trailhead is near the end of the main drive (follow the signs for bridle trails), and offers several hitching posts and a handicapped mounting area. Trails are well marked and easy to navigate. This is a great trail for beginners or horses being exposed to trails for the first time. The grassy land is relatively flat, and the parking is both ample and easily accessed. For an easy and enjoyable day ride, check out Token Creek.

Legend

P parking
── trail
🌲 forest
·—·—· park boundaries

Location: Just north of Madison and the Highway 51 exit from I-90/94. Follow main drive to the southern end of the park. Directions are well marked.

Contact(s): Dane County Parks
4318 Robertson Road
Madison, WI 53714

Phone: (608) 246-3896 or (608) 242-4576 (information line).

E-mail: dane-parks@co.dane.wi.us

Web site: http://www.co.dane.wi.us/parks/parkhome.htm

Trails: 3.5 miles over mostly flat terrain. Some gently rolling hills. Trail starts and finishes at the trailhead at southern end of the park. Trails are mowed grass and are mostly one-way.

Shared use: Shared with hikers.

Horse rentals: n/a.

Camping: Day use only. Groups passing through the area have been allowed, on rare occasions, to camp overnight with their horses. This is considered a special event and requires a permit from the Dane County Parks Department.

Reservations: n/a.

Dates of use: Spring, summer, and fall. Call for exact dates.

Passes: Dane County trail pass required. Pay at trailhead.

Walking Iron County Park
Dane County

The horse trails at Walking Iron County Park measure 3.5 miles, rolling through restored prairies and woods. The trails may be short, but the terrain is varied enough to keep things interesting.

Walking Iron is north of Mazomanie. Archery clinics often take place in the park, but these are held away from the horse trails. As Walking Iron is bordered by private land, caution is urged during bow- and gun-hunting seasons.

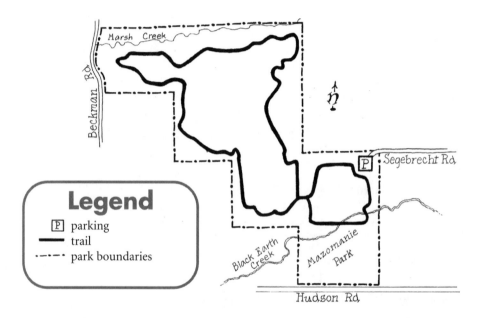

Legend

P parking
— trail
----- park boundaries

Location: From Madison, take Highway 14 to Mazomanie and exit right onto County Road Y (there is a gas station on the corner), which takes you into historic Mazomanie. Go left on Hudson Street, right on Bridge Street, and left on Segebrecht Road. Trailer parking will be down the road on your left.

Contact(s): Dane County Parks
4318 Robertson Road
Madison, WI 53714

Phone: (608) 246-3896 or (608) 242-4576 (information line).

E-mail: dane-parks@co.dane.wi.us

Web site: www.co.dane.wi.us/parks/parkhome.htm

Trails: Most of the horse trails at Walking Iron Park are one-way, and they are clearly marked. There are nearly four miles of horse trails. Trailers can be parked at the end of Segebrecht Road just northwest of Mazomanie (note: the lot is small and may be full). Trails are rated for difficulty at the trailhead. No bikes or motorized vehicles (except snowmobiles in winter) are permitted in the park, making this an especially horse-friendly park.

Shared use: Shared with hikers.

Horse rentals: n/a.

Camping: Day use only.

Reservations: n/a.

Dates of use: Spring, summer, and fall. Park trails are used for snowmobiling in the winter. Call for exact dates.

Passes: A Dane County trail pass is required.

White Mound County Park
Sauk County

White Mound County Park is regarded as one of the best-kept secrets of Sauk County. Fewer riders visit here than the larger Wildcat Mountain State Park, but White Mound's trails are beautiful and challenging nonetheless.

Located between Spring Green and Reedsburg, the park encompasses 1,100 acres with a 104-acre lake in the middle. The eight miles of horse trails include a main loop around the lake and a few small loops off the main trail. The site has a dedicated horse campground, which includes restrooms, picnic tables, hitching posts, fire rings, and pump water. A hot water shower at the main campground is open to riders at the horse campground. Camping reservations can be made by fax, by mail, or at the park, and fees are minimal. A registration form is required; you can download the form online at http://www.baraboonow.com/parks/whitemound.asp, or call (608) 546-5011 to have one mailed to you.

White Mound is best for horses that are conditioned or are in a conditioning program. The trails can be steep, and there are a few stream crossings. White Mound does not have a volunteer maintenance group, so if you are out riding and see something that needs attention, please contact the park management. They are friendly and helpful, and they will tend to your needs as soon as possible.

Location: Off Highway 23 on County Road GG, between Spring Green and Reedsburg.

Contact(s): White Mound County Park
S7995 White Mound Drive
Hillpoint, WI 53937

Phone: (608) 546-5011; (608) 546-5022 (fax).

E-mail: slkoenig@co.sauk.wi.us

Web site: http://www.baraboonow.com/parks/whitemound.asp
or http://www.co.sauk.wi.us/dept/parks/description.html

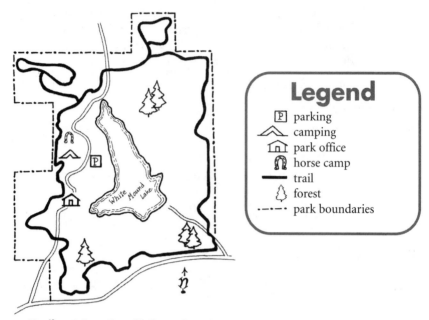

Trails: Eight miles of hilly trails with stream crossings. Best for horses in good condition.

Shared use: Designated horse trail sees some hikers. Runs along snowmobile trail part of the way.

Horse rentals: n/a.

Camping: A horse campground is at the northern end of the park. Facilities include restrooms, picnic tables, hitching posts, trailer parking, pump water, and fire rings.

Reservations: You can register at the office, by fax, or by mail. If no one is in the office, please register using the yellow registration envelopes.

Dates of use: May 15 through November 1.

Passes: Minimal parking fee applies.

Other: White Mound is one of the few county parks that does not have a volunteer trail group or riding club performing maintenance on the equestrian trails. Trails are generally well maintained by park staff. Offer to help if you can.

Wildcat Mountain State Park
Vernon County

Wildcat Mountain is home to some of the most popular equestrian trails in the state. Although it only has 15 miles of trails (as opposed to the Southern Unit of the Kettle Moraine State Forest, which has around 50), Wildcat's varied and sometimes difficult terrain is part of what makes it so popular. Complete with hills, valleys, water crossings, and scenic overlooks, Wildcat Mountain offers breathtaking trails, especially during the fall.

"We've been described as a mini Black Hills," says one park employee. Riders have been flocking to Wildcat Mountain for years, and the place, though not over-crowded, is well used.

Wildcat Mountain, just east of the town of Ontario, shares a border with the Kickapoo Valley Reserve to the south, but there are currently no trails connecting the two. This will change in the future, say park personnel, but for the time being, you will need to ride each one separately. Both share the same rugged terrain and beautiful scenery, but the trails at Wildcat are better marked than those at the reserve.

While the entire Wildcat Mountain area is striking, it is the horse trails that traverse some of the most beautiful property. Wildcat Mountain is a gem for trail riders, so get out there and enjoy.

Lodging for humans is available at the nearby Kickapoo Valley Ranch in La Farge, which also offers guided trail rides into the Kickapoo Valley Reserve on their horses. They are not currently set up to board other horses. If you find yourself in the area without a horse of your own, call the Kickapoo Valley Ranch (see the description earlier in this chapter in the Stables and Barns section). Then come back to Wildcat with a horse of your own.

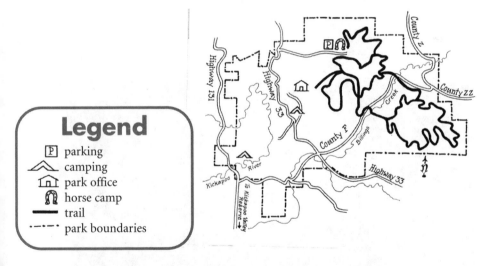

Legend
- P parking
- 🏕 camping
- 🏠 park office
- 🎠 horse camp
- ▬ trail
- ·--·-- park boundaries

Location: Wildcat Mountain State Park is off Highway 33 on Taylor Valley Road, approximately two miles east of Ontario.

Contact(s): Wildcat Mountain State Park
P.O. Box 99
Ontario, WI 54651

Phone: (608) 337-4775; (608) 337-4362 (fax).

E-mail: CampbR@dnr.state.wi.us

Web site: http://www.dnr.state.wi.us/org/land/parks/regions/ wcr/wildcat.html

Trails: Fifteen miles of trails on four hilly loops. The terrain can be rugged, so shoes are recommended for soft-footed horses. The trails are home to stream crossings, hills, valleys, and scenic overlooks. Not recommended for beginning riders or green horses.

Shared use: Horse trails are generally restricted to riders. Riders may see some hiking activity.

Horse rentals: Available nearby at Kickapoo Valley Ranch (see the description earlier in this chapter in the Stables and Barns section)

Camping: Twenty-four primitive horse-camping sites with high lines, clean pit toilets, posts for picket lines, hitching rails, and safe outside stalls. There is a modern bathroom with clean showers, which equestrians are welcome to use, at the non-horse campground. Campsites fill early in the summer and fall, so be sure to call for reservations.

Reservations: Strongly recommended. Call (888) 947-2757 or log onto http://www.reserveamerica.com. Specify horse campground.

Dates of use: Horse trails and camping are open from May 15 to November 15. Other sections of the park are open year-round.

Passes: State park vehicle sticker and state trail pass required for riders 16 and older.

A stop at the "Johnny Cake" rest area in Wildcat Mountain State Park.

More Riding Trails

Bremer Creek
Buffalo County

Bremer Creek is a privately owned ranch near Arcadia in Buffalo County, offering 18 miles of mapped trails on 700 acres of land.

Bremer Creek offers three lodging options: a furnished bunkhouse, a furnished cabin, or primitive camping. Photos of all buildings can be viewed on the Bremer Creek Web site listed below.

Horses can stay with their owners in primitive campsites or stay in covered pens. Owners can clean the pens themselves or have them cleaned for a small fee. Feed can be purchased for a minimal price. All horses must have a negative Coggins, and only well-behaved stallions will be allowed on-site.

Location: Bremer Creek is in the center of Buffalo County, 40 miles south of Eau Claire, 60 miles north of La Crosse. Call for directions.

Contact(s): Bremer Creek
S1421 County Road U
Mondovi, WI 54755

Phone: (608) 323-3092.

E-mail: brian@bremercreek.com

Web site: http://www.bremercreek.com

End of the Trail Equine Campground
Vernon County

End of the Trail is a privately owned campground that rests between Wildcat Mountain State Park and Kickapoo Valley Reserve in Ontario. End of the Trail hosts 18 campsites (reservations are recommended) with high-line posts and permanent line, fire pits, free firewood, water near the campsites, picnic tables, electricity at some sites, Porta-Potties and a flush toilet, and a shower house. Inexpensive box stalls are available for an additional fee. Most sites are big enough to accommodate two rigs. Dogs are welcome, but must be kept at individual campsites.

End of the Trail was designed with the horse person in mind, so you will find many of the items on your camping wish list already on-site. There is a minimum two-night stay on weekends (Friday, Saturday, and Sunday) and a three-night minimum on holiday weekends, including Memorial Day, the Fourth of July weekend, and Labor Day.

Both Wildcat Mountain and the Kickapoo Valley Reserve are accessible from the property. Wildcat Mountain boasts 15 miles of marked trails over hilly terrain with moderate stream crossings. Kickapoo Valley Reserve has 37 miles of rugged trails. Riders find these some of the most challenging and rewarding trail systems in the state, so be sure your horse is in condition and take plenty of breaks.

Note: End of the Road does not rent horses. Bring your own, and do not forget your negative Coggins test paperwork.

Location: South of Wildcat Mountain State Park on Cass Valley Road. Take Highway 33 west until it turns into County Road F. Go south on Cass Valley Road to End of the Trail.

Contact(s): Jan and Moose Tassler
End of the Trail Equine Campground
E13722 Cass Valley Road
Ontario, WI 54651

Phone: (608) 337-4738.

E-mail: equineexpress@centurytel.net

Experimental Forest
La Crosse County

Experimental Forest is unusual in that there are no marked trails for horseback riding, and riding is permitted throughout the entire forest.

The Experimental Forest encompasses 3,000 acres in the Driftless Area of southwestern Wisconsin filled with upland oak forests, experimental plantings, open fields, rock outcroppings, and a few "goat" prairies on steep hills. The purpose of the forest is to take an ecosystem approach to land management, combined with wood production. You will run into other horse people, but the trails are relatively quiet, and no motorized vehicles are allowed in the forest other than work vehicles.

Located northeast of La Crosse and south of West Salem, the Experimental Forest offers excellent views. The terrain is varied, with steep hillsides, valleys, and woodlots. Parking is available off of Russian Coulee Road, just south of Interstate 90.

Location: Take I-90 to County Road M south to Barre Mills. Take M three quarters of a mile to Russian Coulee Road. Turn left. Russian Coulee Road will dead end. Parking is allowed in the fields on the left where the road ends. Note: All manure must be removed from parking lots.

Contact(s): Wisconsin Department of Natural Resources
3550 Mormon Coulee Road
La Crosse, WI 54601

Phone: (608) 785-9007.

E-mail: james.dalton@dnr.state.wi.us

Hoeth Forest
La Crosse County

There are no designated riding trails at Hoeth Forest, but horses are allowed on the fire lanes throughout the 400-acre area. The park is free from motorized vehicles; horses can move freely throughout the forest. The trails are generally flat with a few ridges and gullies. Trails have been largely created by the riders who use them most often. There are a few areas where horses are not permitted (steps have been built into some of the hillsides), so use caution and keep your eyes open.

The eastern and western sections of Hoeth Forest are divided by Radcliffe Road, which runs between Lockington Road to the north and Davis Creek Road to the south. The Black River runs through the northeastern section of the forest, a lovely place to ride. The forest is a bit of a drive from La Crosse, but you will feel like you are in the middle of the wilderness when you are there. The forest is lightly traveled, so, for safety, take a friend if you head out.

Location: The forest is south of North Bend off Highway 54. Take Highway 54 to County Road VV. Go east on Lockinton Road until you come to Radcliffe Road. Turn right (south). Radcliffe Road runs through Hoeth Forest.

Contact(s): La Crosse County Facilities Department
400 Fourth Street North, Room 208
La Crosse, WI 54601

Phone: (608) 785-9770.

Ukarydee Equestrian Campground
Adams County

Ukarydee Equestrian Campground is just southeast of the Castle Rock Trails (described in the Riding Trails section of this chapter) in Adams County. The campground, which is privately owned, has 30 large campsites in two loops, and it is loaded with amenities. Each campsite has its own picnic table, corral, and fire pit. Sites are large enough to pull a big rig in and pitch a tent. All sites have access to water.

Campsites in the upper loop have water and electricity (available in the center of the loop). Only those campsites close to the center can use electricity.

Campsites in the lower loop have three electricity outlets and three sites for water. Ukarydee is a popular camping ground for those riding Castle Rock, so be sure to call ahead and reserve your spot, especially in the spring and fall.

Location: Just south of Highway 21, east of Necedah. Take Highway 21 to 22nd Avenue South. Follow 22nd Avenue until it turns into Cumberland Avenue. Follow Cumberland to the end.

Contact(s): 2047 Cumberland Avenue
Arkdale, WI 54613

Phone: (608) 564-2233.

Yellowstone Wildlife Area Horse Trails
Lafayette County

Yellowstone Wildlife Area has approximately 33 miles of horse trails in four loops. Each of the loops is similar, but they vary slightly in terrain, the views that they offer, and length. Generally, the terrain is gently rolling and lined with wildflowers. Riders can expect to see deer, rabbits, and the occasional fox.

The wilderness area runs along Yellowstone Lake State Park, which offers almost 1,000 acres of recreation space.

Note: Trails are open to horse riders from noon to dusk, May 1 to May 19. Trails are open to equestrians full-time from May 20 through October 31.

Location: Located on County Road D, just north of Fayette. Trailer parking is available near the old Fayette School building.

Contact(s): Wildlife Manager
Yellowstone Wildlife Area
2514 Morse Street
Janesville, WI 53545

Phone: (608) 743-4831
Lafayette County Zoning Administrator
627 Washington Street
Darlington, WI 53533

Phone: (608) 776-4830.

E-mail: ldc@mhtc.ne

Web site: http://www.lafayettecounty.org/tourrec/trailsandscenicd.html

The convenient—and very popular—Ukarydee Equestrian Campground near the Castle Rock Trails.

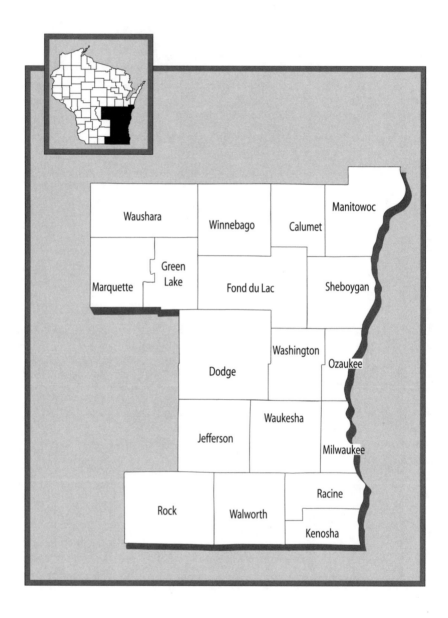

Southeast

Wisconsin

Stables and Barns

Amos Acres
Whitewater

If you are looking for a small barn with a family atmosphere, Amos Acres is a place to check out. Although the facility does not offer an indoor riding arena, it is open year-round and runs an eight-week unmounted class for beginners on basic horsemanship during what owner Patti Mirsky calls the "dead of winter." This class teaches soon-to-be riders the basics of horse care, how to handle a horse on the ground, how to work with veterinarians and farriers, and how to choose a boarding facility.

"Horses are a little more complicated than dogs," Mirsky says with a laugh, "and a bit more expensive." Her goal is to teach people not only how to ride, but how to be responsible owners.

Although Amos Acres caters to children and adults, it is the kids who benefit most. Mirsky is a 4-H leader, and she takes on one or two 4-H kids and their projects per year. Her facility is close to the University of Wisconsin–Whitewater, for students who want to ride.

Her lessons are geared toward English and western beginners, although the facility appeals to a wide variety of riders, some of whom travel three miles down a two-lane road to access 40 miles of Kettle Moraine trails.

Location: W2861 Highway 59, Whitewater, WI 53190.

Phone: (262) 473-7515.

E-mail: amosacres@yahoo.com

Year founded: 2001.

Owner(s): Patti and Carl Mirsky.

Hours: 9:00 a.m.–9:00 p.m. daily.

Specialization(s): Beginning English pleasure, western pleasure, overnight/short stay, lay-ups; trails available at Kettle Moraine three miles down the road.

Facilities: Barn, outdoor arena, turnout paddocks and pasture, lights for night riding, outdoor wash rack, tack room, parking for horse trailers.

Number of stalls: 20.

Board: $–$$. Includes daily turnout, daily stall cleaning, fresh water, grain, and home-grown hay. Private paddocks available. Pasture board available. Overnight/short stay with private stall and paddock.

Lessons: Private and group.

School horses: Currently has two school ponies and several horses.

Requirements: Boots with a heel, helmet.

Shows/clinics: Facility hosts 4-H training events and benefit shows for the American Standardbred Adoption Program (ASAP).

Transportation: Available to other shows.

Apple Ridge Stable
Mequon

Apple Ridge is a hunter/jumper barn located deep in the horse country of southeastern Wisconsin. It is a family-oriented, fun place to ride, but it also caters to serious horse people, plenty of whom train and show on the "A" hunter/jumper circuit.

The enthusiastic trainers here teach adults, but they do an especially good job with kids. They host two summer day camps per year, one for beginners that involves grooming and horse care in addition to riding, and one for students who are already jumping.

There are four schooling shows for those who ride or board at Apple Ridge, and these are low-key events. Students are required to wear boots and helmets, but need not dress for show. For those who are more serious about competing, Apple Ridge trainers travel to an average of two rated shows per month nearby or in surrounding states.

Trainers can help those who have been taking lessons and want to buy a horse of their own. Apple Ridge has something for beginners as well as seasoned competitors.

Location: 7230 West Highland Road, Mequon, WI 53092.

Phone: (262) 242-1110.

Year founded: 1985.

Owner(s): Mr. and Mrs. Joseph Patton.

Hours: 8:00 a.m.–8:30 p.m., Tuesday through Thursday; 8:00 a.m.–8:00 p.m., Friday; 8:00 a.m.–4:30 p.m., Saturday and Sunday; closed Mondays.

Specialization(s): Hunter/jumper lessons and training, summer day camp, family fun.

Facilities: Heated barn, indoor and outdoor arenas, turnout paddocks, pastures, club room, viewing area, wash racks, and tack rooms.

Number of stalls: 32.

Board: $$$$. Includes feed, bedding, stall cleaning, and daily individual turnout, weather permitting.

Lessons: Private, group (2–6 students) for children and adults. Minimum age is 6.

School horses: 15.

Requirements: Helmet, boots or shoes with a heel, long pants.

Shows/clinics: Hosts four in-barn schooling shows for students and boarders per year. Travels to rated shows twice a month. All levels of competition.

Transportation: Transportation is provided to shows.

Other: Horses leased to students only. Horses for sale.

Bounds Showtime Arena
Deerfield

If you are involved in the western show world, then you have probably been to Bounds Showtime Arena in Deerfield. A top-ranked show facility with two heated indoor arenas and one outdoor arena, Bounds hosts events and clinics every month, and has hosted the Badger State Games horse events on several occasions.

Owner Pam Bounds is no stranger to showing. The daughter of Will Holmes (of Holmes Rodeo renown), Bounds has been riding and showing since she was a child. It seemed a natural extension that she would open a show facility and help bring others along.

Bounds offers boarding and lessons, and teaches others who trailer in. She specializes in horsemanship, barrels, and mounted shooting, but caters to a wide variety of riders. There are no school horses here, so if you are interested in studying with Bounds, you must have your own.

The Showtime facility is available to cross-country travelers with horses. Overnight boarding requires a negative Coggins and advance reservations. One of the few places that can handle tractor-trailers (Show Time is on the Clydesdale circuit), it will be quickly apparent that the facility was built with the serious horse person in mind. Even if you are not showing yet, you should check out some of their shows, which run year-round. Bleachers are available and the arenas are heated, so winter events can be held comfortably.

Location: 845 Oak Park Road, Deerfield, WI 53531.

Phone: (608) 764-5555.

E-mail: showtimear@aol.com

Web site: http://hometown.aol.com/showtimear

Year founded: 1991.

Owner(s): Pam Bounds.

Hours: 8:00 a.m.–9:00 p.m. daily.

Specialization(s): Barrel racing, horsemanship, cowboy mounted shooting.

Facilities: Two heated indoor arenas, outdoor arena, lights for night riding, outdoor wash rack, turnout paddocks, pasture with shelters, bleachers for viewing, plenty of parking with electric hookups for those staying overnight. The facility is on the Clydesdale circuit and can handle semis. Short-stay and overnight boarding is available.

Bounds Show Time Arena.

Number of stalls: 95 permanent.

Board: $–$$ for pasture or stall boarding. Pasture board includes morning grain and hay as needed. Stall boarding includes daily private turnout, stall cleaning, and two feedings daily.

Lessons: Private, semiprivate, group. By appointment only.

School horses: None. Those taking lessons are either boarders or trailer in from other facilities.

Requirements: Proper attire.

Shows/clinics: Clinics and shows are hosted on the grounds year-round.

Transportation: Boarders transport their own horses to other shows.

Breezewood Farm
Muskego

Breezewood Farm, located 15 miles southwest of downtown Milwaukee, offers a multitude of activities, from English and western pleasure lessons to carriage and sleigh rides. The owners, Lisa and Pete Heck, raise Haflingers (a small horse, 13.5–15 hands tall, with chestnut coloring, and a light tail and mane. For more information, check out http://haflingerhorse.com).

The lesson program at Breezewood offers a range of riding styles, but all focus on good horsemanship and having a good, balanced seat. The Hecks run an exceedingly popular 10-week basic horsemanship course in the summer for 100 children ages 8–16. Owner/instructor Lisa Heck got her equine education in England (she is a graduate of the British Horse Society's Horsemaster Course) and brings her strong equine knowledge to the States, benefiting numerous students. She also helps Scout groups that are working on their badges.

The Hecks are interested in showing and have several students who show, but Lisa says that the majority of her students are pleasure riders. With more than 100 acres of trails to ride and explore, it is easy to understand why.

Location: S87 W13205 Priegel Drive, Muskego, WI 53150.

Phone: (414) 425-2276.

E-mail: llhcatz@aol.com

Year founded: 1988.

Owner(s): Lisa and Pete Heck.

Hours: 8:00 a.m.–10:00 p.m., daily.

Specialization(s): Horse management lessons, balanced seat lessons (both English and western), jumping, dressage, carriage and sleigh rides, hayrides with or without cookout, birthday parties, and pony rides. Owners breed and show Haflingers.

Facilities: Indoor arena, heated lounge, indoor hot-water wash stall, outdoor ring, turnout paddocks, pasture, tack room, 100 acres of trails.

Number of stalls: 40.

Board: $–$$ for pasture and indoor board. All horses are fed twice daily. Stalls are cleaned once a day. All stabled horses are turned out daily.

Lessons: Group, private, or semiprivate. Minimum age for group lessons is 8. Minimum age for private lessons is negotiable.

School horses: 25.

Requirements: Long pants and hard-soled shoes or boots with a heel are strongly recommended. Helmets are provided.

Shows/clinics: Annual fun-day show on grounds. Some horses are available for showing off-grounds.

Transportation: Owner(s) can transport students to shows.

Other: Haflinger horses for sale, other horses for lease.

Cheska Farm
Waukesha

Although Cheska Farm advertises expert instruction for all levels, it is best known as a hunter/jumper lesson and sale facility that caters to serious show people. Located outside Waukesha on 45 acres of rolling pasture, Cheska Farm is family owned and operated.

The owners, Dick and Gloria Cheska, are best known for finding up-and-coming horses for riders and trainers. While they used to buy most of their horses off the track, they are increasingly turning to Europe, where they buy and export primarily thoroughbreds and warmbloods for the Milwaukee and Chicago areas.

The Cheskas have a top-notch facility, with sprinkler systems throughout the property to cut down on dust. Their indoor facility is 72 x 200 feet and filled with jumps. Although all kinds of students ride and board at Cheska, the facility's main clientele are people who show or are interested in learning enough to show on the "A" circuit. The Cheskas hold a few schooling shows on-site for students and travel extensively to "A" shows. They are willing to customize lesson and training programs, so it is best to work with them one-on-one. The same holds true for boarding. Horses are fed two to three times a day, depending on the horse, and stalls are cleaned daily. Turnout and blanketing are not included with board, but those services can be purchased for an additional fee. Boarders are welcome to turn their own horses out in Cheska's many private paddocks.

Location: S58 W22114 Glengarry Road, Waukesha, WI 53186.

Phone: (262) 547-5454.

E-mail: rcheska@wi.rr.com

Web site: http://cheskafarm.com

Year founded: 1980.

Owner(s): Dick and Gloria Cheska.

Hours: 9:00 a.m.–8:00 p.m., Tuesday through Sunday; closed Mondays.

Specialization(s): Hunter/jumper.

Facilities: Heated barn, indoor and outdoor arenas, lights for night riding inside, turnout paddocks, pastures, security system, club room, viewing area.

Number of stalls: 65 permanent.

Board: $$$$. Board includes two to three feedings per day, stalls cleaned daily, turnout is extra and comes with blanketing services. Boarders are welcome to turn their own horses out in private paddocks.

Lessons: Private, semiprivate, group, adult group, training programs for boarders. Minimum age is 6.

School horses: 6.

Requirements: Long pants, boots with a heel, approved safety helmet.

Shows/clinics: Schooling shows on-site. Frequent trips to "A" rated hunter/jumper shows.

Transportation: Transportation to shows and clinics is provided.

Other: Horses for sale and lease.

Crossroads Farm
Hartford

Established in 1977, Crossroads Farms is one of the older hunter/jumper barns in Wisconsin. Offering lessons from the beginning to Grand-Prix level, Crossroads is a barn that can cater to a wide range of students who are interested in jumping and showing. A show barn itself, Crossroads hosts up to eight schooling shows a year and two Wisconsin-rated "B" shows. They regularly travel throughout the country to "A" shows.

Lessons take place year-round in the large indoor arena. The facility also offers two outdoor arenas and a 3.5-acre hunt field. Owner Nancy Maloney said her primary students are people who want to learn to ride well noting that they draw a strong show clientele. The caliber of students and horses is high, including her school horses. Maloney currently has one green school horse that is used in schooling shows, but notes that any of her remaining horses could be shown well in rated shows.

"We have a strong one-on-one program," says Maloney, "despite our size. I'd say our biggest strength is the individualized attention each rider receives."

Location: 1671 County Road K, Hartford, WI 53027.

Phone: (262) 673-7007.

E-mail: Nmaloney@nconnect.net

Owner(s): Nancy Maloney.

Year Founded: 1977.

Hours: 9:00 a.m.–9:00 p.m., Tuesday through Friday; 9:00 a.m.–5:00 p.m., weekends; closed Mondays.

Specialization(s): Hunter/jumper.

Facilities: Barn, 56 x 172-foot indoor arena, two outdoor arenas, 3.5-acre hunt field, large turnout paddocks, heated viewing area, outdoor wash rack, tack room.

Number of stalls: 30.

Board: $$$$. Includes three feedings per day, daily stall cleaning, turnout.

Lessons: Private, semiprivate, group, and adult; minimum age is 5.

School horses: 4–5.

Requirements: Helmet, paddock boots or boots with a heel.

Shows/clinics: Up to eight schooling shows per year. Three Wisconsin-rated "B" shows. Regular travel to "A" shows.

Transportation: Will transport students to shows.

Other: Horses for sale and lease.

Gymnastics—a good way for horses and riders to learn to balance over fences.

Elkhart Lake Equestrian Center
Elkhart Lake

Elkhart Lake Equestrian Center is an impressive facility. The indoor arena, which is 65 x 198 feet, is meticulously maintained for dressage, with professionally installed footing, angled kick-walls, and mirrors. When the facility was built in 2002, owners Richie and Lisa Morris wanted a place where dressage riders could train properly. Lisa, who is the main instructor at Elkhart Lake, follows the Classical Training Pyramid and what she calls the tried, tested, and true methods of the masters. Training students through fourth level, Morris regularly brings in clinicians who can teach the FEI levels, including Olympic hopeful Jessica Jo Tate (see Wyngate Dressage Center) and Portuguese riding master Frank Grelo.

Her board and training fees are reasonable. Dressage training and basic riding fundamentals are taught 5–6 days per week, and lunge-line lessons are available for all students. The facility has several school horses, which have been trained classically.

In case you are thinking Elkhart Lake is all work and no play, Elkhart Lake also offers a quadrille team and hosts the Elkhart Lake Stablemates, a Sheboygan County 4-H club. Boarders regularly take trail rides on the facility's 145 acres and meet for a ladies book club, where the favorite topic is, of course, horses.

Location: W6721 County Road A North, Elkhart Lake, WI 53020-1827.

Phone: (920) 876-3534 (barn); (920) 876-3765 (fax).

E-mail: richieandlisa@earthlink.net

Year founded: 2002.

Owner(s): Richie and Lisa Morris.

Hours: 8:00 a.m.–10:00 p.m. daily.

Specialization(s): Dressage and classical training.

Facilities: Barn, 65 x 198-foot indoor arena, outdoor arena, pasture, paddocks, viewing area, laundry, hot and cold indoor wash rack, tack room, lights for night riding, security and fire system, 145 acres of trails.

Number of stalls: 28; pasture board also available.

Board: $–$$ for pasture and stabling. Includes turnout, two feedings per day, vitamins, daily stall cleaning.

Lessons: Private, semiprivate, group.

School horses: 8.

Requirements: Boots or paddock shoes. Helmets are required for students under 18.

Shows/clinics: Dressage schooling shows on-site. Clinics held regularly.

Transportation: Can be provided to off-site shows and events.

Other: References and résumé happily provided. Horses offered occasionally for sale, half-lease, and lease.

Did You Know?

The Paso Fino breed was developed in Puerto Rico in the sixteenth century. The Paso Fino has five distinct gaits, including the paso fino (a slow gait where the feet move up and down very quickly), the paso corto (about as fast as a trot but much more comfortable), and the paso largo (between the canter and gallop in terms of speed).

Emerald Creek Stable, LLC
West Bend

Emerald Creek Stable is a state-of-the-art equine boarding and training facility that specializes in eventing and dressage. The facility has 49 stalls, a 70 x 180-foot indoor arena, two outdoor arenas, a heated wash stall, heated tack rooms, and a heated and air-conditioned observation lounge. Built in the late 1990s, Emerald Creek has proven to be a popular place for boarders and students alike.

"I think the best part about Emerald Creek is that it manages to be both a serious and a fun place to ride at the same time," says one trainer. "There are not many barns that can pull that off."

Boarders will tell you that it is one of the friendliest places around. Owner Julie Zak takes excellent care of the horses, providing multiple feedings throughout the day. Horses are turned out in paddocks, either individually or in groups of three or four. The Zaks own 40 acres and have access to an additional 80 acres, for those who like to ride outside.

One of the reasons for Emerald Creek's success is its laid-back atmosphere, where riders are not expected to adhere to rigid standards. Indeed, there is a lot of learning going on, but the students are also having fun.

Location: 1896 County Road NN, West Bend, WI 53095.

Phone: (262) 334-3003.

E-mail: Julie@EmeraldCreekStable.com

Web site: http://www.EmeraldCreekStable.com

Year founded: 1998.

Owner(s): Julie and Gregg Zak.

Hours: 9:00 a.m.–10:00 p.m. daily.

Specialization(s): Eventing, dressage.

Facilities: Barn, indoor arena, viewing area, indoor wash rack, heated tack room, security system, two outdoor arenas, pasture, paddocks, hunt course, three-mile cross-country course.

Number of stalls: 49.

Board: $$$–$$$$. Includes individual and small group turnout, blanketing and unblanketing, and multiple feedings per day. Stalls are cleaned daily.

Lessons: Private. Minimum age is 7.

School horses: 1.

Requirements: Paddock boots with a heel, hunt cap for juniors and all adults who are jumping.

Shows/clinics: Mini-events and clinics held on-site.

Transportation: Available to off-site shows and clinics.

Other: Horses occasionally for sale and lease.

Fantasy Hills Ranch
Delavan

Located just north of the Beloit and Lake Geneva corridor, Fantasy Hills Ranch is nestled onto 70 acres near the beautiful Kettle Moraine State Forest, which provides 25 miles of horse trails.

Fantasy Ranch prides itself as being a family-friendly facility, and its many clients confirm this. The ranch, which offers lessons in addition to trail rides on the facility's property and in the state forest, is multifaceted and succeeds on many levels.

Fantasy Hills ranch has been ranked one of the top horseback riding facilities in the *Midwest by Action Adventure Unlimited* magazine, and the reasons are clear. Fantasy Hills caters to a diverse group of riders. Riders can go on a one-hour guided trail ride on the property, or the owners will transport horses 25 miles to the state forest for a 5–6 hour ride. Not for the feint of heart, the latter ride takes all day.

The ranch's prices are on the low side, and Fantasy Hills is able to keep them low due to the facility's large volume of business. The people who work there are mature and responsible, and they strive to make sure that their customers are well cared for.

Fantasy Hills offers carriage rides, and hay and sleigh rides in the winter. The ranch also offers a carriage for weddings; it is available for travel to certain off-site functions.

Location: 4978 Town Hall Road, Delavan, WI 53115.

Phone: (262) 728-1773.

E-mail: greyston@vbe.com fhr_ron@Yahoo.com

Web site: http://www.fantasyhillsranch.com

Year founded: 1995.

Owner(s): Ron and Cathy Weiss.

Hours: Opens at 9:00 a.m. daily.

Specialization(s): Lessons in English pleasure, western pleasure, and jumping. Also offers guided trail rides, wedding carriage rides, pony rides, sleigh and carriage rides, a petting zoo, and host of private parties. Hosts many Scout and other youth groups.

Facilities: Insulated barn and indoor arena, outdoor arena, turnout paddocks, pasture, round pen, clubhouse, viewing area, indoor wash rack, outdoor wash rack, tack room, lights for night riding, 70 acres of trails.

Number of stalls: 25.

Board: $–$$. Includes alfalfa grass hay and sweet feed grain in the morning and afternoon, stalls cleaned daily, turnout (weather permitting). Pastured horses have shelters and automatic waterers.

Lessons: Private, semiprivate, group, adult.

School horses: 3 lesson horses, 60 trail horses.

Requirements: Helmets are offered to all trail riders.

Shows/clinics: Occasional shows and clinics hosted on-site.

Transportation: Boarders make own arrangements for transportation to shows and clinics. Fantasy Hills will transport livery horses to Kettle Moraine State Forest for all-day guided trail rides.

Other: Horses occasionally for sale and lease.

GreyStone Equestrian Center
Omro

Horse owners are hard-working people. Those who work with horse owners have to work doubly hard, just to stay ahead of the game. Nobody knows this better than GreyStone owner Susan Tank, who, with husband Dan, bought a dairy farm and turned it into an equestrian center in the late 1990s. The Tanks did most of the work themselves, turning GreyStone into a shining example of what hard work and a love of horses can create.

These days, GreyStone is a full-service facility specializing in (but not limited to) Arabians. Offering boarding, showing, training, lessons, equine psychology, and seminars, GreyStone has become a popular fixture in the Omro area. The area is surrounded by state land, and is quiet and peaceful, with a lot of wildlife. Located just west of Oshkosh in Winnebago County, GreyStone caters to riders who want to understand horses, not just ride them.

Susan is a patient teacher and trainer who believes in helping riders learn to train their own horses, even after she is done teaching them. She has more than 20 years of experience training English pleasure, western pleasure, trail, and halter horses. She owns several horses and treats boarders' horses as well as she treats her own. The owners of GreyStone have gone to great lengths to make sure the horses in their care are safe and secure.

Location: 9457 Haase Road, Omro, WI 54963-9601.

Phone: (920) 685-7318.

E-mail: greyston@vbe.com

Web site: http://www.greystoneec.com

Year founded: 1998.

Owner(s): Susan and Dan Tank.

Hours: Call for appointment.

Specialization(s): Western pleasure, English pleasure, beginning jumping, trail, halter, showmanship, equine management, horse psychology.

Facilities: Barn, outdoor arena, pasture, indoor/outdoor wash racks, large tack room, lights for night riding, trails, 60-foot-round pen, obstacle/trail courses.

Number of stalls: 15.

Board: $–$$. Includes 12 x 12-foot matted stall with window, daily turnout, stall cleaning, and three feedings per day. Personalized care. Each boarder gets two saddle racks and two bridle racks.

Lessons: Private. Can be bought as single lessons or in packages of 10–20. Minimum age is 6. Will travel for lessons.

School horses: 4.

Requirements: Boot/paddock shoes. Helmets required for juniors and recommended for adults.

Shows/clinics: Fun shows and obstacle courses on-site.

Transportation: Owner will rent her two-horse trailer to responsible boarders and students.

Other: Owner sometimes has horses for sale and knows of others with sale horses. GreyStone has fresh artesian water on-site. Many boarders bring their own jugs to take some home.

Ledges Sporting Horses
Roscoe, Illinois

The Ledges, just south of Beloit in Roscoe, Illinois, falls into the "too good to be excluded category." Although not officially a Wisconsin facility, so many Wisconsinites frequent the Ledges for its show grounds and lessons that it would be foolish not to include it in this guide.

The Ledges, owned by Stan Mannino, has been an important show facility for Wisconsin riders since it opened in 1970. The facility sports a heated barn, a heated indoor arena, outdoor arenas, lights for night riding, turnout paddocks, a security system, clubroom, and viewing area. Ledges trainers tend to stay here for a long time. They offer hunter/jumper lessons for beginners and experienced riders, but riders must be 7 years of age to take lessons.

One of the facility's biggest draws is its accessibility from Interstate 90. Its covered viewing area spans the width of two outdoor riding arenas, which are lit for night riding. Spectator bleachers are built into the side hill behind the arenas.

The Ledges hosts up to 15 hunter/jumper shows each year, including its famed Winter Series. The shows, which offer classes at the "A" and "B" levels, are open to the public and are well attended by those who live and show in southern Wisconsin. The Ledges is a great place to go and watch a show if you are interested in showing at the "A" level and want to see the workings of a well-run event.

The Ledges offers private, semiprivate, group, and adult group lessons throughout the week.

Location: 12250 Love Road, Roscoe, IL 61073.

Phone: (815) 623-2700 or (815) 624-2200.

Web site: http://www.ledgesstables.com

Year founded: 1970. Stan Mannino bought and renovated the facility in 1987. His daughter, Jennifer Davenport, now manages the Ledges.

Owner(s): Stan Mannino.

Hours: Call for appointment.

Specialization(s): Hunter/jumper. Facility can be rented for other events.

Facilities: Barn, four outdoor arenas with complete sound system, 86 x 200-foot indoor arena with lights and indoor watering system, eight indoor restrooms (one with a shower), five hot/cold wash stalls, 86 x 100-foot indoor warm-up area, tack rooms, heated viewing room, open viewing area. There are two tack shops and vending areas available during shows.

Number of stalls: 40 for boarders and 275 for shows; all wood with doors and concrete aisles. Water easily accessible.

Board: $$$$. Includes feed, stall cleaning, bedding, and use of arena. Turnout, body clipping, lunging, exercising, and trimming are extra.

Lessons: Call for details.

School horses: 7.

Requirements: Riders must have boots or paddock boots and wear a hunt cap, as well as riding pants, or chaps.

Shows/clinics: More than 15 shows held on-site per year, including the winter series.

Transportation: Transportation can be provided to other shows.

Other: Horses for sale and lease.

Legacy Dressage Center
Burlington

If you are serious about dressage, you should check out Legacy Dressage Center. Owner and trainer Galina Shelepov has made dressage a mainstay in her life, and it shows, both in her riding and that of her clients.

Shelepov's credentials are impressive. She schooled in classical dressage for 10 years with the Russian Riding school at Gomel in the former Soviet Union, where she showed and trained to the Grand Prix level. While still in Russia, Shelepov received scores of 65 percent and above from five different judges to qualify for the "Master of Sport" title at age 18. She has been in America for more than a decade and continues to grow, taking clinics with international instructors and adding to her classical education.

"I continue to learn and grow as a trainer, rider, and teacher," Shelepov says, reflecting how she values lifetime learning. She likes to teach like-minded students, and only teaches children if they are serious about learning and working hard at their sport. She passes her professionalism on to her students, who ride and show throughout the Midwest and beyond.

"I was fortunate to have the opportunity for a proper beginning," says Shelepov, who started riding when she was nine. She's clearly dedicated to her horses and her clients' well-being, and tries to give them the same good beginning she had.

The facility at Legacy is older, but is professionally run and well-built. It sits on a hill and has excellent ventilation, with doors at 90-degree angles. The place is run more like a training facility than a lesson barn, but Shelepov has excellent school horses for those who do not have their own. She is willing to teach anyone, provided they are willing to work hard and have a true appreciation for horses.

Location: W782 Highway 11, Burlington, WI 53105.

Phone: (262) 767-2883.

Year founded: 1999.

Owner(s): Galina Shelepov and Matthew Konichek.

Hours: Open Monday through Saturday. Call for appointment.

Specialization(s): Dressage. Specializes in clinics, training, lessons, and sales.

Facilities: Insulated 20-stall barn, 60 x 200-foot heated indoor arena with Fibar-mix footing, heated lounge with air conditioning in the summer, heated indoor wash rack, tack room, heated restroom, large outdoor dressage arena, private and semiprivate turnout paddocks.

Number of stalls: 20.

Board: Please call for boarding and training rates.

Lessons: Private, adult. Lessons for children only if they show a serious interest.

School horses: 2–3 horses from training to FEI levels.

Requirements: Proper riding attire, including boots or paddock shoes. Helmets are recommended.

Shows/clinics: No shows on-site. International clinicians visit two to three times a year. Owner travels to shows.

Transportation: Some transportation to shows available.

Other: Quality dressage horses for sale.

Nimrod Farm
Oconomowoc

Nimrod Farm is one of Wisconsin's oldest family-owned riding facilities. Owned by Doty and Homer Adcock since 1967, the facility has long been a mainstay for hunter/jumper riders in southeastern Wisconsin.

Nimrod Farm has 42 beautiful, fenced acres with turnout pastures and paddocks. Nimrod was set up as a show facility and has been hosting hunter/jumper shows for years. The Adcock's mission has been to prepare both horses and riders for the show ring, a goal they met long ago and continue to meet.

Every barn attracts a certain kind of rider, and show-oriented people who like to have qualified professionals meeting their training needs tend to be Nimrod's clientele. The farm's trainers can teach beginners and advanced riders, children and adults; the common denominator being people who want to show and want to show well. Nimrod has trained horses and riders that have won local, zone, and national championships, and the facility shows no sign of slowing down.

Location: 2208 North Summit Avenue, Oconomowoc, WI 53066.

Phone: (262) 567-3103.

E-mail: info@nimrodfarm.com

Web site: http://www.nimrodfarm.com/

Year founded: 1967.

Owner(s): Homer and Doty Adcock.

Hours: Open 9:00 a.m.–9:00 p.m., Tuesday through Thursday; 9:00 a.m.–6:00 p.m., Friday through Sunday; closed Mondays.

Specialization(s): Hunter/jumper. Also provides conditioning for racehorses.

Facilities: Heated barn with 12 x 12-foot stalls, indoor and outdoor arenas, heated lounge, viewing area, lights for night riding, turnout paddocks, pastures.

Number of stalls: 33.

Board: $$$$. Full and regular service. Call for details. Nimrod Farm also accepts broodmares and foals, and offers layups for racehorses. Extra services include body clipping, grooming, trimming, turnout, lunging, and exercising.

Lessons: Private, semiprivate, group, adult group.

School horses: 6–10 available at any time. Some jump, some are used on the flat.

Requirements: Hunt cap.

Shows/clinics: Regularly hosts clinics and shows on-site.

Transportation: Can transport students to shows.

Other: Quality horses for sale. Videotaping services also available.

Did You Know?

Transportation can be stressful on you and your horse. In cool weather, horses can lose two to five pounds of body weight for every hour they travel. It can take up to three weeks for a horse to gain that weight back.

Owner Anne Jennings of Pigeon Creek Farm.

Pigeon Creek Farm
Mequon

Horse lovers looking for a barn where the facilities are as well cared for as the horses should check out Pigeon Creek Farm. Pigeon Creek is an established and professional English riding facility located 20 miles north of Milwaukee.

Established in 1978 by nationally recognized rider and trainer Anne Jennings, Pigeon Creek offers lessons in hunt seat, eventing, and dressage six days a week. Jennings and her son Charles Zwicky (an accomplished trainer and hunter/jumper rider) cater to the beginner as well as the serious competitor. While it is not required, many students show on the hunter/jumper, dressage, and eventing circuits. Transportation to and from shows is available for a fee.

Pigeon Creek features a clean, airy barn with an indoor arena and viewing area for year-round lessons and riding. The facility also hosts an outdoor arena with stadium jumps and a cross-country course. For safety reasons, unsupervised jumping is not allowed, and trail riders are encouraged to go out in pairs. In addition to the training facilities, Pigeon Creek offers turnout paddocks, a pasture, a clubhouse, indoor wash rack, outdoor wash rack, and a spacious tack room.

For those who are serious about dressage, Florida clinicians are brought in several times a year. Clinics are open to students, boarders, and riders from other barns. Sign-up is on a first-come, first-served basis.

Jennings, who has bought and sold horses for many of her students, also offers training for young and inexperienced horses. She has ridden at the top levels of the hunter/jumper and eventing circuits, and her facility provides a fine opportunity for learning the basics correctly or getting serious about showing.

Location: 14001 North Thorngate Road, Mequon, WI 53097.

Phone: (262) 375-2964.

E-mail: Equinepcf@aol.com

Web site: http://www.pigeoncreekfarm.4t.com

Year founded: 1985.

Owner(s): Anne Jennings.

Hours: Open 9:00 a.m.–8:00 p.m., Tuesday through Thursday; 9:00 a.m.–5:00 p.m., Friday through Sunday; closed Mondays.

Specialization(s): Eventing, dressage, hunter/jumper, English pleasure.

Facilities: Barn, indoor arena, outdoor arena, clubhouse, viewing area, tack room, indoor wash rack, outdoor wash rack, turnout paddocks, pasture, cross-country course.

Number of stalls: 33 in two barns.

Board: $$$ in the small barn, $$$$ in the large barn. Includes use of the facility, two feedings per day, daily stall cleaning, and daily turnout. Pigeon Creek does not charge extra for blanketing services. "We do all the things that are necessary," says one of the trainers. Most boarders put their horse on a wellness program with a local equine clinic, paying twice a year for vaccinations, worming, teeth floating, and other health maintenance issues.

Lessons: Private, semiprivate, group.

School horses: 7.

Requirements: Boots or paddock boots. Helmet with chin strap for all riders. No unsupervised jumping. Trail rides must be taken with another rider.

Shows/clinics: Pigeon Creek hosts regular dressage clinics.

Transportation: Transportation to clinics and shows is available for boarders and students.

Other: Quality horses for sale and lease.

The Ranch Riding Center
Menomonee Falls

Ranch Community Services is the home of the Ranch Riding Center, one of Wisconsin's oldest and largest therapeutic riding centers.

Located just minutes from Milwaukee, the ranch has been in business since the mid-1970s. The facility caters to children and adults with developmental disabilities, head injuries, and emotional disorders. They also offer board for able-bodied riders, in addition to hayrides, bonfires, tiny tot and adult riding programs, and birthday parties. As if that wasn't enough, the Ranch Riding Center also offers field trips for school-aged children and badge opportunities for Scouts.

On the therapeutic riding side, the ranch has a staff of therapeutic riding instructors and licensed therapists who provide quality lessons, tailored to the needs of each student. The facility is heated and offers lessons year-round, which is beneficial to its disabled clientele, who benefit from continuity. The staff at the ranch is dedicated and has been there for some time, which speaks to the quality of the operation.

The Ranch Riding Center has 10 miles of trails on-site, and backs up to the Bugline Trail (see the description in the Trails section of this chapter). Boarders like the ranch because their horses receive high-quality care, and because they know they are supplying the ranch with revenue to support a good cause. The Ranch Riding Center is a nonprofit 501(c)3 organization and accepts monetary donations, as well as in-kind donations of horse equipment, supplies, and occasionally horses.

Did You Know?

Bridles were developed long before saddles. Most riders rode bareback until the Middle Ages.

Location: W187N8661 Maple Road, Menomonee Falls, WI 53051.

Phone: (262) 251-8670.

E-mail: hschanen@ranchwi.org

Year founded: mid-1970s.

Owner(s): Nonprofit organization.

Hours: No set hours. Open seven days a week.

Specialization(s): Therapeutic riding, boarding for able-bodied riders, hayrides, bonfires, birthday parties, and lessons for tiny tots through adults.

Facilities: Heated barn, indoor arena, viewing area, tack room, heated restrooms and classrooms, outdoor arena, paddocks, pasture, 10 miles of trails.

Number of stalls: 23.

Board: $$. Includes individualized feeding three times a day, daily turnout. Stalls cleaned six days a week.

Lessons: Private, semiprivate, group. Minimum age is 4.

School horses: 12.

Requirements: Helmets are required and available for use. Boots with a heel recommended.

Shows/clinics: The ranch hosts one equine-health clinic per year.

Transportation: Boarders provide their own transportation to shows.

Other: The facility retires old horses to homes and, as a general rule, does not sell horses. The ranch is always looking to build relationships with facilities that keep retired horses.

Silverwood Farm
Camp Lake

Located just north of the Illinois border, Silverwood Farm boasts more than 15 recognized dressage, eventing, and hunter/jumper shows per year. Owned by Lisa Froelig, an FEI-level dressage instructor, and Howard Nelson, a successful thoroughbred racehorse trainer, Silverwood is a competition- and boarder-friendly venue. The facility has 175 permanent stalls, which fill regularly during shows.

Located on more than 100 acres just west of Racine, Silverwood's terrain is flat. The cross-country course, which was built around a former training racetrack, runs counterclockwise, with a variety of fences to challenge horses from beginner-novice through training level. Eventers will find banks, a water complex, and ditches on-course. Dressage riders will be delighted with award-winning footing in the facility's four rings, and jumpers will be challenged by the narrow layout of the fenced jump ring.

Boarders at Silverwood do not have to show, but many do. The professional and fun environment successfully integrates events into Silverwood's business. Those showing at Silverwood will find it to be professional and rider-friendly. Competitors can now register online. All they have to do is get their health certificates in order, show up, and ride.

Location: 28426 98th Street (County Road AH), Camp Lake, WI 53109.

Phone: (262) 889-4700.

E-mail: dressage@silverwoodfarm.net

Web site: http://www.silverwoodfarm.net

Year founded: 1976.

Owner(s): Lisa Froehlig and Howard Nelson.

Hours: 7:00 a.m.–10:00 p.m. daily.

Specialization(s): Dressage, hunter/jumper, eventing, racehorses.

Facilities: Four barns with water in each barn aisle, indoor arena, four show rings, two warm-up rings, a lunging ring.

Number of stalls: 175.

Board: $$–$$$$. Stall board includes daily turnout, grain, and hay. Stalls cleaned daily. Pasture board includes daily feedings. Extra services include body clipping, lunging, exercising, and trimming.

Lessons: Private. Minimum age is 8. Parental supervision required for children.

School horses: None. Boarders ride their own horses in lessons.

Requirements: ASTM-SEI helmet with harness.

Shows/clinics: 15 recognized dressage, eventing, and hunter/jumper shows per year. Silverwood also hosts clinics.

Transportation: Boarders help other boards get to and from shows.

Other: Horses for sale and lease.

Signature Arabians, Ltd.
Union Grove

Signature Arabians is a midsized facility that specializes in Arabians but welcomes riders and horses of any breed. "We've got quarter horses, paints, appaloosas, national show horses, Hanoverians, and one paint/Percheron cross," laughs owner David Mann. Some boarders ride English, some western, and some drive on the facility's regulation half-mile track.

The Manns started Signature Arabians in 1995. David said he got tired of keeping his horses "in average places." He went out and created a facility that was "a little cleaner, with a little more pizzazz."

The facility is near the Kettle Moraine northern unit trails and just miles from the Richard Bong State Recreation Area. Mann and his wife Jill organize trail rides for their boarders on a regular basis, and regularly host special events on their farm. Signature Arabians is set on 35 beautiful acres just off Highway 20, 7 miles west of Interstate 94.

Location: 1117 North Britton Road, Union Grove, WI 53182.

Phone: (262) 878-9204.

E-mail: stable@signaturearabians.co

Web site: http://www.signaturearabians.com

Year founded: 1998.

Owner(s): David and Jill Mann.

Hours: 8:00 a.m.–9:00 p.m. daily.

Specialization(s): Hunt seat, dressage, western pleasure.

Facilities: Heated barn, indoor arena, clubhouse, viewing area, lights for
night riding, outdoor arena, 10 turnout paddocks, pasture, indoor
wash rack, outdoor wash rack, trailer parking, half-mile regulation
track for driving.

Number of stalls: 35.

Board: $$$. Includes turnout and feedings. Stalls cleaned daily. Daily Strongid
and quarterly paste wormer included.

Lessons: Private. Local kids who come out and help clean on Saturdays get a
free lesson.

School horses: Two, one western and one English.

Requirements: Helmet required.

Shows/clinics: Hosts several special events per year.

Transportation: Can transport students and boarders to shows.

Other: Horses occasionally for sale and lease.

Did You Know?

If you cannot stop to water horses every 2 to 3
hours when traveling, you can give them soaked
hay to keep them from getting dehydrated.
Feeding them carrots or apples will also help.

Sorensen Equestrian Park
East Troy

Sorensen Equestrian Park is a unique mix of down-home friendliness at a show
barn that consistently turns out quality students.

Sorensen Park hosts between 10 and 15 United States Dressage Federation
(USDF) shows per year, which are popular with those trying to qualify for regionals.
The Sorensens host back-to-back shows, meaning that you only have to travel once
to try to obtain two qualifying scores for regional competition.

Although the Sorensen facility looks low-key, owners Reid and Linda are serious
about their students and about hosting quality shows. Several students who started
with them as children are now competing at the national and FEI levels. It is a friendly
barn with an at-home feeling.

Location: W1700 Saint Peters Road, East Troy, WI 53120.

Phone: (262) 642-4111.

E-mail: reid@sorensenpark.com

Web site: http://www.sorensenpark.com

Year founded: 1981.

Owner(s): Reid and Linda Sorensen.

Hours: 8:00 a.m.–8:00 p.m., Monday through Saturday; closed Sundays.

Specialization(s): Dressage, some western, therapeutic riding. Linda Sorensen was one of the first three instructors in the United States certified by the North American Riding for the Handicapped Association (NARHA) to work with the handicapped.

Facilities: Barn, 80 x 80-foot indoor arena (there are plans for expansion), three outdoor riding arenas, turnout paddocks, pasture, outdoor wash rack, tack room.

Number of stalls: 44 permanent, 12 portable.

Board: $$. Includes daily turnout, hay, and basic grain. Stalls are cleaned daily. If your horse requires supplements, you provide the supplements and the staff will administer them daily.

Lessons: Private, semiprivate, group.

School horses: 6.

Requirements: Boots or paddock shoes, helmets.

Shows/clinics: Sorensen hosts 10 to 15 schooling and USDF-recognized dressage shows per year. Three of these are run back to back.

Transportation: Boarders are responsible for getting themselves to clinics and shows.

Other: Horses for sale and lease.

Kathy Emery of Spring Willow Farm.

Spring Willow Farm
Union Grove

Spring Willow Farm in Paris Corners (with a mailing address of Union Grove) is a classy yet delightful place, where hunter/jumper riders can go to train, or just to relax and enjoy the trails. Located 10 minutes north of the Illinois border, Spring Willow is a moderate-sized barn with 25 stalls and a beautiful layout.

The owner, Kathy Emery, has owned the facility with husband Bob since 1997. Spring Willow is 25 minutes from Lake Geneva and 30 minutes from Milwaukee, and draws boarders who live up to an hour away.

"They come here with their horses in mind," says Emery. The facility offers safe, all-day turnout and takes excellent care of its charges. "The common denominator," says Emery, "is that they all love their horses." While all boarders ride English, there is a mix of riders, and Emery has more than one trainer who comes to teach. Most of her riders travel to hunter/jumper shows, some going to Palm Beach, Florida, for the winter circuit. Others own retired show horses and come out for low-key rides. Still others are dressage riders who like the peace and quiet of Emery's place.

Location: 2002 200th Avenue, Paris Corners, WI 53182.

Phone: (262) 878-1288.

E-mail: boarder@springwillow.com

Web site: http://www.springwillow.com

Year founded: 1997.

Owner(s): Kathy and Bob Emery.

Hours: No set hours. Facility is open 365 days per year. Owners on premises.

Specialization(s): Hunter/jumper, dressage, English pleasure.

Facilities: Barn, 175 x 200-foot outdoor ring, new 70 x 150-foot indoor arena with great jumps, heated lounge and tack rooms, fly spray system, trails on 120 acres of varied terrain, including uplands, lowlands, woodlands, streams, ponds, and fields.

Number of stalls: 23.

Board: $$$–$$$$. Pasture and stall board. Stall board includes all-day turnout with large five-acre pastures and individual paddocks, blanketing and unblanketing, all worming, and two feedings per day. Stalls cleaned daily.

Lessons: Private, semiprivate, group. Minimum age is 12.

School horses: 2.

Requirements: Helmet, boot with a heel.

Shows/clinics: Hunter/jumper clinics hosted regularly.

Transportation: Owner can provide transportation to clinics and shows.

Other: Horses for sale and lease. Horses are usually available for share-boarding. Riders welcome to bring their own trainers for a small fee.

Stonehedge Farm
Union Grove

Equestrians serious about eventing or many of the other English disciplines will be right at home at Stonehedge Farm in Union Grove. Home to trainer and FEI-level eventer Eric Dierks, Stonehedge offers top instruction in dressage, jumping, and eventing.

Dierks, an advanced-level rider, gives several clinics annually and brings in two to three internationally regarded clinicians per year, including Captain Mark Phillips, Lucinda Green, Jimmy Wofford, and Denny Emerson. The facility sports a full cross-county course, complete with a water complex, and large indoor and outdoor arenas.

Although Stonehedge, built in 1998, is relatively new, the Dierks family has been involved with horses for decades. The facility includes a large viewing/meeting room for clinics.

Location: 935 172nd Avenue, Union Grove, WI 53182.

Phone: (262) 859-9397 or (262) 859-2852.

E-mail: KlsDrks@aol.com

Web site: http://www.stonehedgefarm.net

Year founded: Stonehedge Farm was founded in 1998, but the owners have been working with horses for more than 30 years.

Owner(s): Klaus and Erika Dierks.

Hours: 9:00 a.m.–9:00 p.m., Tuesday through Sunday; closed Mondays.

Specialization(s): Dressage, eventing, hunter/jumper.

Facilities: Barn, 80 x 200-foot indoor arena, viewing/meeting room, indoor wash rack, tack room, cross-country course with water complex, wood-fenced pastures, large outdoor arena, 175 acres of scenic rolling countryside, 15 acres of wooded trails, owners on premises.

Number of stalls: 30.

Board: Call for fees. Board includes daily turnout, daily cleaning, Purina Strategy Feed, and home-grown hay.

Lessons: Private, semiprivate, group, adult.

School horses: None.

Requirements: Boots or paddock shoes, hunt cap.

Shows/clinics: Facility hosts approximately three clinics per year with such prominent trainers as Captain Mark Phillips, Bruce Davidson, Jimmy Wofford, Ralph Hill, Lucinda Green, and Denny Emerson.

Transportation: Transportation can be provided to clinics and shows.

Other: Quality show horses and prospects for sale.

Sundance Farm
Plymouth

For people who want a professional place where they can learn hunt seat, dressage, or eventing, Sundance Farm is ideal.

Kelly Mahloch, who owns the facility with husband Steve, is a graduate of the Instructor Certification Program for hunt seat, dressage, stock seat, and combined training. Her students range in age from 7 to 80, but Mahloch admits that the barn's real strength is its connection with young riders. "I lead the County Mounties 4-H club, which has more than 50 members in the 4-H horse project," says Mahloch. "We have numerous speakers and clinicians who come in to educate the youth." Adults benefit from Mahloch's expertise as well. She has coached several students to championships in dressage, eventing, and hunt seat, not to mention stock seat equitation and showmanship.

Needless to say, Sundance is a busy place. Teaching between 70 and 90 students per year, Mahloch offers private, semiprivate, and group lessons. She holds a show for students and boarders every fall, and not everyone has to show.

Sundance students work hard, but when they are ready for some time off, they hit the trails at the nearby Kettle Moraine State Forest. (Note: Mahloch does not offer trail rides to the general public.) Sundance is just a mile from the trails as the crow flies, and boarders can cross state lands to enter the forest, where there are endless miles of trails. This is not a bad way to blow off some steam or just to end a good lesson.

Location: N6329 Branch Road, Plymouth, WI 53073.

Phone: (920) 893-0134.

E-mail: sundancfrm@aol.com

Year founded: 1990.

Owner(s): Kelly and Steve Mahloch.

Hours: 7:00 a.m.–9:00 p.m. daily.

Specialization(s): Hunt seat, dressage, eventing. Mahloch has also coached students to state championships in stock seat equitation and showmanship.

Facilities: Three barns (two are heated, one is not), 60 x 200-foot indoor arena, four tack rooms, wash rack, heated restroom, washing machine, 80 x 180-foot outdoor arena, pastures, cross-country course on 60 acres. There is a hunter course set up in the outdoor arena from May through October. Miles of trail access at nearby Kettle Moraine State Forest.

Number of stalls: 38.

Board: $$. Rates vary by barn. Board includes daily stall cleaning, feed, and turnout. Includes use of all facilities and trails. Owner makes own hay. Turnout is for a minimum of 8 hours per day.

Lessons: Private, semiprivate, group, ages 7–80. Owner is a nationally certified instructor with the American Riding Instructor Association.

School horses: 9.

Requirements: Helmets (no exceptions).

Shows/clinics: In-barn fun show every fall. Occasional dressage clinics. Owner is head of the County Mounties 4-H club, which has more than 50 members. Clinicians often come in to educate youth.

Transportation: Boarders help each other get to and from shows.

Other: Sundance does not offer trail rides to the public.

Swinging W Ranch
Eagle

Swinging W Ranch, located 30 miles southwest of Milwaukee, offers beautiful trail rides through the Kettle Moraine State Forest that last anywhere from one hour to four hours with bonfires and overnight stays.

Billed as one of the largest riding facilities in southeastern Wisconsin, Swinging W has been in business since 1968. It is a place that can accommodate all levels of riders, and the ranch can even entertain the nonriders in your group. Kids age five and under are steered toward the half-hour pony rides. Older kids can join their parents on Kettle Moraine trail rides, and nonriders are welcome to take tractor-drawn hayrides. Riders walk and trot through the forest, and all rides are geared toward the rider with the least experience. Groups of six or more can sign up for overnight stays in the forest, complete with campfires. All activities require a deposit, which will vary depending on the size of the group.

Swinging W is a popular place for Girl Scout troops, which often go there to meet their badge requirements. Western pleasure riding lessons are available. All activities at Swinging W require advance reservations, so be sure to call ahead.

Location: S75 W36004 Wilton Road, Eagle, WI 53119.

Phone: (262) 594-2416.

Year founded: 1968.

Owner(s): Swinging W, Inc.

Hours: 9:00 a.m.–5:00 p.m. daily, April 1 through November 30; call for an appointment.

Specialization(s): Western pleasure, trail rides, hayrides, pony rides, Girl Scout badge work.

Facilities: Barn, indoor arena, outdoor arena, pasture, trails (Kettle Moraine State Forest).

Number of stalls: Pasture board available.

Board: $–$$. Includes hay, shelter, and water.

Lessons: Private. Minimum age is 6.

School horses: 60 trail and school horses.

Requirements: Helmet, boots with half-inch heel, long pants.

Shows/clinics: n/a.

Transportation: Can transport to shows and clinics for a fee.

Other: Horses occasionally for sale.

Wyatt's Bunkhouse Inn at Ugly Horse Ranch
Palmyra

Situated next to the southern unit of the Kettle Moraine State Forest, Wyatt's Bunkhouse Inn has become a traditional getaway site for trail riders, who can bring their horses and enjoy almost 100 miles of trails.

"The thing that makes us unique," says co-owner Andrea Arnow, "is that people can spend days riding, but not have to trailer their horse all over." Indeed, you can trailer in on Friday (although many come on Thursday) and stay until Sunday, enjoying continental breakfasts, trail rides, campfires, and at times, team penning and cattle-working seminars (call ahead for schedule).

Although they have seen their share of women's getaway weekends and family reunions, Wyatt's is also a destination for couples celebrating anniversaries or just wanting to put some quality back in their time. Many riders also come solo. Wyatt's is unique in that you are surrounded by state parks, but close to the city; the facility is four blocks from Palmyra and about 10 miles from two "sit-down" restaurants.

Horses stay in indoor or outdoor stalls, which the horse owners clean. Feed is also provided by individual owners. Wyatt's offers you a place to sit down, put your feet up, and share some company, all while staying close to nature and your horse.

Location: N830 Tamarack Road, Palmyra, WI 53156.

Phone: (262) 495-2718; (262) 495-2718 (fax).

E-mail: UglyH@cni-usa.com

Web site: http://www.bbonline.com/wi/bunkhouse

Year founded: 1999.

Owner(s): John and Andrea Arnow.

Hours: All hours, May through October.

Specialization(s): Ranch lodging for those wishing to ride or play in the Kettle Moraine State Forest

Heading out on the trail from Wyatt's Bunkhouse Inn.

Facilities: For People: Motel-style bunkhouse with seven private rooms. All have private baths. There is also a bunkroom with shared baths, a lounge, and a breakfast room. Outdoors, there is a campfire ring and chuck wagon for evening campfires, plus covered porches with tables and chairs.

For Horses: Private indoor or outdoor stalls, a 100 x 200-foot outdoor sand arena, lights for night riding, and access to 100 miles of trails.

Number of stalls: 8 indoor, 16 outdoor.

Board: Small fee. Owners bring own feed and clean own stalls.

Lessons: Available by appointment for team penning, working horse, reining, and western pleasure.

School horses: None.

Requirements: Must have negative Coggins.

Shows/clinics: Cattle-working seminars and team-penning practice May through October.

Transportation: n/a.

Other: If you cannot bring your own horse, Wyatt's will make reservations for you at one of two local facilities, Swinging W Ranch or Kettle Moraine Ranch. Both places offer guided trail rides for a fee.

Wyngate Dressage Center instructors Jessica Jo Tate and Greta Larson Pell, with Donovan.

Wyngate Dressage Center
Walworth

Home to FEI-level instructors Jessica Jo Tate and Greta Larson Pell, Wyngate Dressage Center is a dressage facility for beginners and serious riders, but the general clientele is committed to showing. Located near Lake Geneva, Wyngate is a beautiful facility with an 80 x 200-foot indoor arena, 28 matted stalls, and exceptional instruction. Owned by Van and Greta Larson Pell, along with Jessica Jo Tate and Candace Tate, Wyngate is a relatively new facility with owners that have been involved in the dressage industry for decades, both in Wisconsin and on a national level.

With Olympic aspirations, Jessica Jo is schooled in classical dressage, having studied in Germany for two years. Greta Larson Pell has shown to the FEI levels and is a gifted instructor. "We teach correct horsemanship and classical dressage," says Candace Tate. "We finally started breaking young horses, because then we could guarantee that they'd been started properly."

Wyngate's prices are steep, but include a lot of instruction and personalized care. Their premier package includes board, turnout, individualized feeding programs, and six hours of training or instruction per week. A smaller package can be purchased that includes boarding services plus one lesson per week. Some riders trailer in for lessons, and those are charged on a lesson-by-lesson basis.

For students looking to move up, Wyngate has three to four FEI-level school masters available at any time. They train mostly warmbloods, but have also had success with thoroughbreds, Morgans, and other breeds.

Location: W5101 Cobblestone Road, Walworth, WI 53184.

Phone: (262) 275-8595.

Year founded: 1999.

Owner(s): Candace and Jessica Jo Tate, Greta and Van Larson Pell.

Hours: 9:00 a.m.–7:00 p.m. daily. Call to confirm.

Specialization(s): Dressage.

Facilities: Barn, 80 x 200-foot indoor arena with Permaflex footing, pasture, heated lounge and viewing area.

Number of stalls: 28.

Board: $$$$. Board and training programs at Wyngate are combined. Full training includes board and 6 hours of training or instruction per week. Partial training includes board and one lesson per week. Riders can also trailer in. School horses are available. Board includes individualized feeding programs and daily turnout. Stalls are cleaned daily.

Lessons: Lessons are part of training packages or may be purchased separately. Call for rates.

School horses: 3–4 FEI-level schoolmasters.

Requirements: Boot with a heel, helmets for juniors. All riders must sign waivers.

Shows/clinics: Facility hosts six clinics annually with internationally renowned riders and trainers.

Transportation: Transports clients to clinics and shows.

Other: Horses occasionally for sale.

More Stables and Barns

Aledos Riverside Ranch
W6953 Abbott Drive
Random Lake, WI 53075
(920) 994-1128
Email: lovehorses6@aol.com
Specialization(s): Western pleasure, English pleasure, dressage, speed events. All disciplines welcome.

A.N.D. Stables
1640 Highway 12/18
Deerfield, WI 53531
(608) 764-8549
E-mail: anitanik@chorus.net
Web site: http://www.showbarns.com/andstables.html
Specialization(s): English pleasure, hunt seat, dressage, western pleasure, barrel racing, gaited/saddle seat, eventing. Offers half-leases with tack. Specializes in getting people where they need to be able to show.

Applewood Farms
12126 39th Avenue
Pleasant Prairie, WI 53158
(262) 694-8565
E-mail: applewood@acronet.net
Web site: http://www.geocities.com/asbapplewood/Stallion.html
Specialization(s): English pleasure, western pleasure, introduction to dressage, saddle seat, birthday parties, day camps for Girl Scouts/Boy Scouts and others.

Arbor Lane Farm
7330 Botting Road
Racine, WI 53402
(262) 639-8500
Specialization(s): Hunter/jumper Pony Club camp, clinics, several miles of trails for boarders and Pony Clubbers.

Avalon Therapeutic Equestrian Center
N9368 Green Valley Road
Watertown, WI 53094
(920) 206-1148
E-mail: Avalontec@gdinet.com
Web site: http://www.globaldialog.com/~avalontec/photos2.html
Specialization(s): Therapeutic riding for children and adults with physical, emotional, and developmental disabilities. Avalon is a member organization of NARHA, and all of its instructors are certified registered

level North American Riding for the Handicapped Association (NARHA) instructors. Avalon has a dedicated staff, including an occupational therapist (OT), an OT assistant, a registered psychiatric nurse, and a certified special education teacher. Avalon is a nonprofit 501(c)3 organization and accepts tax-deductible donations. Past donations have included scholarships for students, hay, and equipment. Avalon occasionally accepts horses.

Black Star Farms, Ltd.

1971 Granville Road
Cedarburg, WI 53012
(262) 375-3844
E-mail: bkstr1@wi.net
Specialization(s): Hunt seat, western pleasure. Hosts 1–2 clinics per year.

A typical scene at Avalon Therapeutic Equestrian Center.

Blue Spring Farm

W220 N9110 Town Line Road
Menomonee Falls, WI 53051
(262) 502-3584
E-mail: questions@bluespringfarm.com
Web site: http://www.bluespringfarm.com
Specialization(s): Hunt seat; can trailer students to shows.

Bridlewood Equestrian Center
6500 East Highway 50
Lake Geneva, WI 53147
(262) 248-6131
Specialization(s): English pleasure, hunter/jumper, western pleasure, driving, and basic horsemanship. Located just outside Lake Geneva. Bridlewood's long-term plan includes therapeutic riding, lay up, and holistic horse care for aged horses.

Brighton Acres Guest House
26425 52nd street
Salem, WI 53168
(866) 537-4567
E-mail: jmp26425@aol.com
Web site: http://bbonline.com/wi/brightonacres
Specialization(s): Short stay and overnight bed-and-breakfast for you and your horse. Located close to Richard Bong State Recreation Area.

Cedar Ridge Ranch
W14471 Dartford Road
Ripon, WI 54971
(920) 748-8405
E-mail: MEAvery@powercom.net
Web site: http://CedarRidgeRanch.net
Specialization(s): English pleasure, western pleasure, basic horsemanship, driving. Guided trail rides on 250 acres following instruction in basic horsemanship. Low student-to-guide ratios. All riders wear protective headgear. Surry, carriage, and wagon rides on-site; surrey, carriage, and wagons for hire at your location. Call for rates. Hosts corporate retreats. Also attends 4-H and speed shows.

Cornerstone Stables
600 Rusk Road
Watertown, WI 53098
(920) 925-3391
Specialization(s): English pleasure, dressage, western pleasure. Specializes in beginners but works well with intermediate riders in dressage and other English disciplines. Helps all riders (children and adults) find a balanced seat. No trail rides.

Corrus Equine Center
2392 Highway 164
Richfield, WI 53076
(262) 628-1624
E-mail: scorrus@strong.com
Specialization(s): New facility, teaching western pleasure and hunter under saddle. Open year-round.

Country Retreat Bed & Breakfast, LLC
N4589 Primrose Lane
Juneau, WI 53039
(920) 386-2912
Specialization: Bed-and-breakfast for you and your horse, near the Wild
Goose State Recreational Trail.

Dan Patch Stable
Highway 50 East
Lake Geneva, WI 53147
(262) 215-5303
E-mail: stablesggrs@yahoo.com
Specialization(s): Guided trail rides offered year-round. Also offers hay rides,
sleigh rides, and bonfires. Located at the Grand Geneva Resort and Spa.
Resort guests and the general public are welcome. Please call for appointment.

De Equus Stable
11816 Morgan Road
Cato, WI 54206
(920) 775-4088
E-mail: brandllandfarm@yahoo.com
Specialization(s): Horse management, saddle seat, and hunt seat for kids
and adults; will transport riders to shows.

Dori-Lou Farms
N44W26098 Lindsay Road
Pewaukee, WI 53072
(262) 691-1162
Specialization(s): English pleasure, western pleasure.

Dream Haven Stables
7901 352nd Avenue
Wheatland, WI 53105
(262) 537-4481
E-mail: xenad63@hotmail.com
Specialization(s): English pleasure, western pleasure, dressage basics,
hunter/jumper trainers on-site.

Dreams to Reality Stable
4508 Grandview Road
Larsen, WI 54947
(920) 836-9967
E-mail: dreamstorealitystable@yahoo.com
Specialization(s): Eventing, hunter/jumper, dressage. Co-owner is a
certified equine massage therapist and national-level competitor. Also
runs strong consignment sales business for dressage, eventing, and
hunter/jumper horses.

El-Lor-Ru Stables

23510 Durand Avenue
Kansasville, WI 53139
(262) 878-1711
E-mail: ellorru@wi.rr.com
Web site: http://home.wi.rr.com/ellorru
Specialization(s): English pleasure, western pleasure, saddle seat; specializes
in Tennessee walking horses. Will transport students to shows.

Enchanted Oaks Stables, Inc.

W11687 State Highway 21
Coloma, WI 54930
(715) 228-2360
Specialization(s): Western pleasure, English pleasure, guided trail rides.
Open spring through fall.

4J's Stables

S63W17271 College Avenue
Muskego, WI 53150
(262) 679-1388
Specialization(s): English pleasure, western pleasure, limited dressage.

The Farm

9736 Serns Road
Milton, WI 53563-9120
(608) 868-5432
E-mail: thefarm@ticon.net
Web site: http://www.tracy-porter.net/index.html
Specialization(s): John Lyons-certified trainer. See Web site for
more information. Paso Fino horses for sale.

Fieldstone Farm

N120W14709 Freistadt Road
Germantown, WI 53022
(262) 255-9611
E-mail: Steelskies@yahoo.com
Web site: http://www.fieldstonefarm.com
Specialization(s): Lessons/training for the working hunter, hunter under
saddle, and western events, all for show enthusiasts. Show-quality horses
for sale. No trail rides.

Field Stone Farm Carriage and Pony, LLC

Burlington, WI 53105
(262) 539-3620 or (262) 539-3504
E-mail: caroline@fsfcarriage.com
Web site: http://www.fsfcarriage.com
Specialization(s): Horse-drawn carriage rides available within a 75-mile

radius of Burlington for engagements, weddings, birthdays, or any special occasion. Seasonal and hourly rates. Call for more information.

Fireside Farm
28130 98th Street
Camp Lake, WI 53109
(262) 889-8967
Specialization(s): Dressage.

First Class Horse Complex, Ltd.
11607 60th Street
Kenosha, WI 53144
(262) 857-7348
Specialization(s): English pleasure lessons on Paso Finos bred and raised on the farm.

Flying S Ranch
2331 Lake Shore Road
Grafton, WI 53024
(262) 284-2938
Specialization(s): Several trainers, teaching English pleasure, western pleasure, hunter/jumper, and eventing. A lot of acreage with lovely views of Lake Michigan.

Forest Rich Stables
N6439 Pioneer Drive
Fredonia, WI 53021
(262) 692-9894
E-mail: tvanhorn@wi.rr.com
Specialization(s): Western pleasure; English pleasure; speed events. Hosts open horse/speed shows throughout summer months.

Four Suns Ranch
W5185 Blackhawk Road
Wild Rose, WI 54984
(920) 787-0026
Specialization(s): Basic western horsemanship, barrels.
Lessons available by appointment.

Fox Hollow Farm, Inc.
7926 East County Road W
Clinton, WI 53525
(608) 676-5224
E-mail: foxhlw@aol.com
Web site: http://www.foxhollowfarm.net/main.html
Specialization(s): Western pleasure, hunt seat, saddle seat. A very successful training facility specializing in Arabians, half-Arabians, and national show horses.

Freedom Ridge Stables

2980 Jay Road
Belgium, WI 53004
(920) 994-9631
Specialization(s): Saddle seat, western pleasure, driving. Specializes in
Morgans. Can break stallions.

Free Spirit Riders, Inc.

P.O. Box 1291
W3950 Highway 23
Fond du Lac, WI 54936-1291
(920) 924-9920; (920) 533-3659 (fax)
E-mail: info@FreeSPIRITRiders.org
Web site: http://www.freespiritriders.org
Specialization(s): Therapeutic riding for children and adults with
physical and emotional disabilities. Free Spirit is a premier accredited
center affiliated with North American Riding for the Handicapped
Association (NARHA) and is a Fond du Lac area United Way-funded
organization. Free Spirit was founded in 1987 and recently moved into
a beautiful new facility, which allows the program to run year-round.

Grafton Equestrian Center

970 Ulao Road
Grafton, WI 53024
(262) 375-3434
Specialization(s): Dressage. Full-sized arenas, used mainly for clinics.

Grand Geneva Resort and Spa

See Dan Patch Stable above for guided trail rides, hayrides, and sleigh rides.

Grand Prix Farms

15034 County Road X
Kiel, WI 53042
(920) 692-3367
E-mail: cvestor@aol.com
Specialization(s): Dressage.

Green Meadows Petting Farm, Inc.

P.O. Box 182
Waterford, WI 53185
(262) 534-2891
E-mail: info@greenmeadowsfarmwi.com
Web site: http://www.greenmeadowsfarmwi.com
Specialization(s): Two-hour petting farm tour that includes pony rides and
cow milking. Well attended by elementary and pre-school students. Located
three miles west of Waterford and seven miles east of East Troy on Highway
20. Follow signs.

Greenwood Stables
W 399 S 3996 Fox Hill Drive
Dousman, WI 53118
(262) 965-3312
E-mail: LGreenw218@aol.com
Web site: http://hometown.aol.com/Greenwoodstable
Specialization(s): Dressage, western pleasure, English pleasure, gaited saddle seat, On Target Training.

Harmony Horsemanship
3989 Oak Park Road
Deerfield, WI 53531
(608) 764-5224
Specialization(s): Western pleasure, natural horsemanship.

Hearthstone Farm
W381S5225 County Road ZC
Dousman, WI 53118
(262) 965-2066; (262) 965-2164 (fax)
E-mail: Jayne@dressagehorse.com
Web site: http://www.dressagehorse.com
Specialization(s): Dressage and eventing lessons and training. Occasionally hosts dressage clinics. Owner is an FEI-level judge and instructor who teaches adults and children age 5 and above. Quality German warmbloods always for sale.

Heritage Stables
812 North Griffith Road
Oconomowoc, WI 53066
(262) 965-3609
E-mail: jsweezey@lang.com
Web site: http://www.3dconnections.com/3gusa
Specialization(s): Eventing, jumping, dressage, hunter/jumper. Facility has indoor and outdoor arenas, a cross-country course, and trails for boarders. Instructors give lessons and coach at events. Horses for sale and lease. Family business in operation for more than 25 years.

Hickory Ridge Equestrian Center
W 8740 County Road B
Lake Mills, WI 53551
(920) 648-4221
E-mail: darla@hickoryridgeequestrian.com
Web site: http://www.hickoryridgeequestrian.com
Specialization(s): Eventing, dressage, hunter/jumper, English pleasure. Located 15 minutes east of Madison on 350 acres. Offers youth summer day camps for beginning and advanced riders. Minimum age is 7.

Hidden Lake Stables

1808 128th Street
Pleasant Prairie, WI 53143
(262) 942-9702
Specialization(s): English pleasure, western pleasure, hunter/jumper, driving, side saddle, speed events. Hosts 4-H events and day camps during the summer for children ages 4–18. Hidden Lake also owns livery horses and offers one-hour guided trail rides. Kid-centered facility with friendly horses and owners.

Jumping uphill strengthens a horse's hindquarters.

Hidden View Farm, LLC

8104 West Highland Road
Mequon, WI 53097
(262) 512-4162
E-mail: esher1@aol.com
Web site: http://www.hiddenviewfarm.com
Specialization(s): Dressage, jumping, eventing. Specializes in retirement boarding and care.

Hillcrest Dude Ranch

8000 Arrow Road
Manitowoc, WI 54220
(920) 682-0158
Specialization(s): Girls summer camp, guided trail rides year-round (weather permitting).

Hood's Creek Farm
8700 Gittings Road
Racine, WI 53406
(262) 884-0615
E-mail: dhalver@wi.net
Specialization(s): English pleasure, dressage.

Hoof Beat Stables Equestrian Center
14120-12th Street
Kenosha, WI 53144
(262) 859-1828
Web site: http://www.hoofbeatstables.com
Specialization(s): Dressage, hunter/jumper, English pleasure, hunter under saddle, Western pleasure. 4-H mini camps and clinics held throughout the year. Specializes in teaching children and beginners.

Horseshoe Springs Stables
N8054 U.S. Highway 151
Fond du Lac, WI 54935
(920) 921-9842
Specialization(s): English and western lesson programs.

Indian Summer Farm
7922 Highway 45
Larsen, WI 54947
(920) 836-3430
E-mail: indsumfm@athenet.net
Specialization(s): Centered riding, basic horsemanship, saddle seat, English pleasure, western pleasure, pre-dressage, girls' summer camp. Owners have been involved with horses for decades and formerly raised Morgans. Trainers use a centered riding approach for all disciplines.

Island Farm
W3673 County Road ES
Elkhorn, WI 53121
(262) 642-5412
Specialization(s): Hunter/jumper, dressage, eventing.

Jo-Don Farms
P.O. Box 331
Franksville, WI 53126
(262) 835-2777
Fax: (262) 835-2731
E-mail: jodonfarms@aol.com
Web site: http://www.jodonfarms.com
Specialization(s): Offering pony rides, birthday parties, petting zoos. Will travel to sites in southeastern Wisconsin.

John Willis Stables

20920 45th Street (County Road NN)
Bristol, WI 53104
(262) 857-3307
E-mail: johnwillis@nconnect.net
Web site: http://www.johnwillis.net/welcome.htm
Specialization(s): Training of American saddlebred show horses.

Jus-Ran Farm

530-264th Avenue
Kansasville, WI 53139
(262) 878-3151
Specialization(s): Dressage, hunter/jumper, western pleasure, training, and
lessons. Owner breaks young horses and works with problem horses.
Facility is bordered on two sides by Richard Bong State Recreation Area,
which has 13 miles of groomed equestrian trails. Transportation can be
provided to shows and events for students and boarders.

Karen's Trail Rides

N4378 State Highway 57
Chilton, WI 53014
(920) 439-1296
Specialization(s): Guided trail rides. Open year-round (weather
permitting). Call for appointment.

Karen's Quarter Horse and Buckskin Ranch

2604 280th Avenue
Salem, WI 53168
(262) 537-2262
E-mail: karen@kqhranch.com
Web site: http://www.kqhranch.com
Specialization(s): Western pleasure, English pleasure. Social environment
includes shows, parades, trail rides, clinics, and a holiday party. Owner
has degree in equine management and holds six judging cards. Barn
sits on one acre, under one roof. Facility has 80 acres, which back
up to 13 miles of horse trails. Horses occasionally for sale.

Knollwood Farm, LTD

2800 Oakwood Road
Hartland, WI 53029
(262) 367-9111, (262) 367-9535 (fax)
E-mail: info@knollwoodfarmltd.com
Web site: http://www.knollwoodfarmltd.com
Specialization(s): Saddle-seat training and lessons for children and adults.
Knollwood Farm has a Tiny Tot program for children ages 4–6 and works
with Scout troops on their badge requirements. Call or visit their Web site for
more information.

Lake Country Riding Stable
5065 State Highway 50
Delavan, WI 53115
(262) 728-6560
E-mail: lcstable@lakecountryridingstable.com
Web site: http://www.lakecountryridingstable.com
Specialization(s): English pleasure, western pleasure, basic horsemanship lessons. Lake Country also offers sleigh rides, wagon rides, carriage rides, and a petting farm. Their facility is large enough to accommodate large groups for weddings, birthday parties, and company outings. Call for details. Family owned and operated since 1981.

Lake Lawn Stables at Lake Lawn Resort
2400 East Geneva Street
Delavan, WI 53115
(262) 728-7950
Web site: http://www.lakelawnresort.com
Specialization(s): Trail rides, pony rides, petting zoo, sleigh rides, carriage rides, and wagon rides. Can accommodate weddings, picnics, and special events. Will travel to off-site events.

Did You Know?
A pony is any breed of horse that measures 14.2 hands or less (equivalent to 58 inches from the top of the horse's withers to the ground).

Lakefield Farm
1440 Lakefield Road
Grafton, WI 53024
(262) 375-4451
E-mail: Lakefield@gna.net
Web site: http://www.LakefieldFarm.com
Specialization(s): English pleasure, dressage, hunter/jumper, eventing, western pleasure; hosts 1–2 clinics per year.

The Lantana
8337 County Road T
Larsen, WI 54947
(920) 836-3516
Specialization(s): Saddle seat, English pleasure, hunt seat, and western pleasure; for boarders only.

Ledgewind Farm

N2888 County Road B
Oakfield, WI 53065
(920) 583-4648
E-mail: Ledge@thesurf.com
Specialization(s): Saddle seat equitation lessons and training.

Liberty Equestrian Training Center

N844 Old Highway 26
Fort Atkinson, WI 53538
(920) 563-7650
Specialization(s): Classical dressage, combined driving. Liberty
is a full training facility, and boarders must be in some kind
of training program. All dressage training is classical and
can be taught from training through FEI levels. School
horses available. The center is easily accessible from
Madison and Milwaukee.

Lorenz Quarter Horses (formerly Milkie Stables)

6715 Brever Road
Burlington, WI 53105
(262) 539-3987
E-mail: florenzl@wi.rr.com
Specialization(s): English pleasure, western pleasure, horses for sale; newly
renovated farm.

Maple Row Farm

2200 53rd Drive
Franksville, WI 53126
(262) 835-9169
E-mail: mustangtalk@hotmail.com
Specialization(s): Western pleasure; fun show every fall.

McFadden Farm

997 Lakefield Road
Grafton, WI 53024
(262) 377-7510
Specialization(s): "A" circuit hunter/jumpers.

M H Ranch ("McHugh's Miniature Horses")

N 7551 County Road Y
Westfield, WI 53964
(608) 296-2171
E-mail: mhranch@aol.com
Web site: http://www.mhranch.com
Specialization(s): Miniature horse tours and miniature horse shows.

Miller's Farm

2903 264th Avenue
Salem, WI 53168
(262) 537-2827
E-mail: thediettrichfarm@tds.net
Specialization(s): Natural horsemanship lessons, trail riding, centered-riding clinics, basic horsemanship. Located next to Richard Bong State Recreation Area, which has 13 miles of trails.

Milwaukee Polo Club

32183 West Highway K
Hartland, WI 53029
(262) 367-8227
Web site: http://www.milwaukeepolo.com
Specialization(s): The Milwaukee Polo Club features competitive matches every Sunday at 1:00 p.m. from mid-June to mid-September. The club also travels to play other teams. Matches are played at the polo grounds on County Road VV, two miles east of Highway 83 and three miles west of Merton.

Meadow Creek Stables

N 5090 Bowers Road
Elkhorn, WI 53121
(262) 723-1815
E-mail: SnowFlake1327@aol.com
Specialization(s): Western pleasure, team penning, shooting, and trails for boarders.

(Bob and Sue) Mohr Stables

202 East Jefferson Street
Elkhorn, WI 53121
(262) 723-4958
Specialization(s): Harness racing.

Mustang Manor Riding Stable

N1085 Groeler Road
Fort Atkinson, WI 53538
(920) 563-3232
Specialization(s): Guided trail rides, hay rides, and sleigh rides. Mustang Manor is the only stable in the United States that uses only (formerly) wild mustangs for its rides. Owner and trainer Dennis Stork currently has a string of 16, which he has trained himself. Horses come to Stork from the western United States, including Nevada, Oregon, Colorado, Wyoming, and California. "They're the best horses I've ever worked with," says Stork, who trains all his horses for riding and driving. He prefers small groups on his trail rides so that riders of like ability ride together. Facility is open year-round.

Norberg Farm Corporation
N49W20683 Lisbon Road
Menomonee Falls, WI 53051
(262) 252-3033
Specialization(s): English pleasure, western pleasure.

Nordic Training Center
W9544 County Road O
Wautoma, WI 54982
(920) 787-2220
Specialization(s): Arabian and national show horses, English pleasure, western pleasure, halter, driving, dressage.

Norris Sunset Stables
W4555 Golf Course Drive
Fond du Lac, WI 54935
(920) 922-4000
Specialization(s): Western pleasure, English pleasure. Kids' pony rides in the summer. Horses and ponies for sale.

Northshore Equestrian (Formerly Mary Lynn Stables)
1048 Lakefield Road
Grafton, WI 53024
(262) 377-0250
Specialization(s): Saddle-seat equitation, resident summer camp ages 7–17 (brochure available). Sixty-three acres of trails, filled with wildlife, open to the public.

Peace and Plenty Farm
2230 Washington Avenue
Cedarburg, WI 53012
(262) 675-0564
E-mail: cthiel@wi.rr.com
Specialization(s): Dressage; horses occasionally for sale.

Rancho Del Rio
S103W36093 State Road 99
Eagle, WI 53119
(262) 594-5131
Specialization(s): Saddle seat.

Rodger Cavanaugh Carriages
3910 W Fairview Road
Neenah, WI 54956
(920) 836-2013
Web site: http://www.cavanaughcarriages.com
Specialization(s): Offers on-site carriage rides using standardbred trotters,

horse-drawn carriage rentals for weddings, petting zoo, miniature horses for birthday parties, horse-drawn hayrides, campfire area, use of party room.

Trail guides—often the difference between a fun riding experience and an unpleasant one.

Russet Stables

1625 County Road V
Coloma, WI 54930
(715) 228-2132
E-mail: e-mail@kimdiercksreininghorses.com
Web site: http://www.kimdiercksreininghorses.com
Specialization(s): Professional training barn for reining horses. Trainers teach beginning reining lessons for those who want to show.

Rustic Road Ranch

P.O. Box 64
2227 Maple Road
Rochester, WI 53167
(262) 939-6134
E-mail: rusticroadranch@yahoo.com
Web site: http://www.geocities.com/rusticroadranch
Specialization(s): English pleasure, western pleasure, gymkhana and basic rodeo (barrels/poles), dressage. Centrally located between Kettle Moraine State Forest and Richard Bong State Recreation Area trails.

Shady Oaks Farms
24821 31st Street
Salem, WI 53168
(262) 878-1564
E-mail: shadyoksfrm@aol.com
Specialization(s): Dressage, jumping, western pleasure. Facility is one-half
mile from the Richard Bong State Recreation Area, which has 13 miles of
groomed equestrian trails.

Sherwood Arabian Farm
W8698 Perry Road
Cambridge, WI 53538
(608) 423-7408
E-mail: Sherwood@smallbytes.net
Specialization(s): Training programs for Arabians and half-Arabians.
Disciplines include English pleasure, dressage, hunt seat, western pleasure,
and driving. Heavily slanted toward the amateur rider. Quality horses
always for sale.

Special Methods in Learning Equine Skills, Inc. (SMILES)
N2666 County Road K
Darien, WI 53114
(262) 882-3470; (262) 882-5661(fax)
E-mail: smiles@smiles.nu
Web site: http://www.smiles.nu
Specialization(s): NARHA-certified therapeutic riding center for children
and adults. Provides recreational rides and individual sessions with a
physical therapist to individuals with disabilities. Open year-round and
has been in business for more than 20 years.

Spring Meadows Farm
550 124th Street
Franksville, WI 53126
(414) 427-5995
E-mail: Equas5@aol.com
Specialization(s): Western pleasure, trail riding.

Stone Gate Farm
923-312th Avenue
Burlington, WI 53105
(262) 539-2525
E-mail: kathybenjamin@genevaonline.com
Specialization(s): Hunt seat, dressage, stock/western, eventing.
Indoor arena. Minimum age is 5; school horses available. Facility
is across from Richard Bong State Recreation Area, which has
13 miles of equestrian trails.

Stoneridge Farm
S75 W24580 National Avenue
Mukwonago, WI 53149
(262) 662-5501
Specialization(s): Western pleasure, English pleasure, saddle seat.

Did You Know?
The Nez Perce Indians are credited with
developing the Appaloosa breed.

Stonewall Farm
N9029 Highview Road
Ixonia, WI 53036
(920) 206-0028
Specialization(s): Hunter/jumper; specializing in ponies and children; has
taken several teams to pony nationals. Good with all levels of riders.

Stoneybridge Stables
1485 County Road JJ
Neenah, WI 54956
(920) 725-8161
Specialization(s): English pleasure, western pleasure, hunt seat.

Sunflower Farm
19000 128th Avenue
Bristol, WI 53104
(262) 857-8555
E-mail: reinsman@aol.com
Specialization(s): New hunter/jumper and dressage barn in
Bristol, just north of the Illinois border. Started hosting
hunter/jumper and dressage shows in 2004. Also offers
some lessons in western pleasure.

Summit Show Stables
1327 North Golden Lake Road
Oconomowoc, WI 53066
(262) 593-2970
Specialization(s): Jumpers. Owned by Grand Prix-level rider Laura Kraut.

Sunset Ridge Training
W3143 County Road D
East Troy, WI 53120
(262) 939-3370
E-mail: sunsetridgetraining@earthlink.net
Web site: http://home.earthlink.net/~sunsetridgetraining

Specialization(s): Western pleasure, dressage. Kettle Moraine trails are 30 minutes away.

Sunshine Equestrian Acres

8C2 Box 401
Harris Lake Road
Winchester, WI 54557
(715) 686-2735
E-mail: horseisme@hotmail.com
Specialization(s): Dressage and vaulting. Buys and sells horses. Short stay or overnight stay with negative Coggins. Many trails available nearby.

Tuckaway Farms

23700 98th Street
Salem, WI 53168
(262) 843-3568
Specialization(s): Boarding facility that offers 24-hour emergency equine transportation and lay up.

Twilight Farms, Inc.

1171 Limerick Lane
Hartford, WI 53027
(920) 474-7529
E-mail: jalft@execpc.com
Web site: http://twilightfarm.vulcan-ltd.com
Specialization(s): Western pleasure and English pleasure for boarders.

Valley View Stables

W1195 Valley View Road
Burlington, WI 53105
(262) 642-7915
E-mail: valley_view@centurytel.net
Specialization(s): Western pleasure, hunt seat, showmanship, halter, basic horsemanship.

Weber Performance Horses

15815 12th Street (County Road E)
Kenosha, WI 53144
(262) 859-3027
Email: weberperformance@aol.com
Specialization(s): Western pleasure, reining, English pleasure. Trainers can start horses. Youth and adults compete locally; owners can transport students to select shows. Facility is 2.5 miles off the interstate.

Westwind Stables

S107 W25620 County Road L
Mukwonago, WI 53149
(262) 662-0448

Email: westwindstables5@aol.com
Specialization(s): Saddle seat, English pleasure, western pleasure, driving, more than 33 acres of wooded trails.

Whispering Oaks Farm
10400 400th Avenue
Genoa City, WI 53128
(262) 279-2075
E-mail: whisperingoak@westoshaonline.com
Specialization(s): Dressage, English pleasure, hunt seat, jumpers.

Whispering Winds Ranch, LLC
2019 67th Drive
Union Grove, WI 53182
(262) 878-9572 or (262) 989-9573
E-mail: whisperingwindsranch@msn.com
Web site: http://www.whisperingwindsranch.com
Specialization(s): Western pleasure, performance horses.

Whisperwood Acres Boarding Stables
4737 Jackson Drive
West Bend, WI 53095
(262) 677-2356
E-mail: whisperwoodacres@hotmail.com
Web site: http://www.whisperwoodacres.net
Specialization(s): Western pleasure, English pleasure, hunter/jumper, dressage. Hosts open, hunter/jumper, and speed shows on a regular basis. Owners also offer pony rides and birthday parties on-site.

Wild Wind Equine Center
W279 S5798 Point Drive
Waukesha, WI 53189
(262) 970-7700
E-mail: wildwindequine@aol.com
Specialization(s): English pleasure, hunt seat, hunter/jumper, saddle seat, western pleasure. Set on 200 acres with trails.

Wild Wood Farm
W282 N5799 County Road KE
Hartland, WI 53029
(262) 538-3984
E-mail: Wildwood1997@aol.com
Specialization(s): Hunter/jumper, dressage.

Willow Glen Farm
N5884 Willow Glen Road
Sullivan, WI 53178
(262) 569-9367

E-mail: mgoodell@execpc.com
Web site: http://my.execpc.com/~mgoodell/index2.html
Specialization(s): Dressage, jumping. Facility has large indoor and outdoor arenas and is building a cross-country course. Also breeds performance warmblood horses.

Wind Ridge Farm

4909 County Road K
Oshkosh, WI 54904
(920) 233-2075
Specialization(s): Boarding facility that has a dedicated clinic for rent. Facility has 21 stalls. Wind Ridge hosts clinics and seminars but does not offer trail rides. All disciplines welcome.

Breaking in a future equestrian.

Riding Trails

Bannerman Trail
Waushara County

The Bannerman Trail, which runs southwest for seven miles between Redgranite and State Highway 73 north of Neshkoro, is a popular place for running and cycling races. It is also a popular place for horseback riding (when the races aren't scheduled, of course).

The Bannerman Trail is a former railroad corridor, which was graded flat with gentle curves and elevation changes by the Chicago & North Western Railroad. A small stretch of the trail is rented to a farmer in the summer, so trail users must follow a town road for a distance before they rejoin the trail. Although the trail is wide enough for carriages, there are gates at each road crossing, and while a rider can get around them, carts cannot.

The trail is sand- and grass-covered and is mowed in the spring, summer, and fall. There are no motorized vehicles allowed on the trail, except in winter when the trail is used for snowmobiling. The trail is also popular among birdwatchers, so keep an eye out for pedestrians near the edges of the trail.

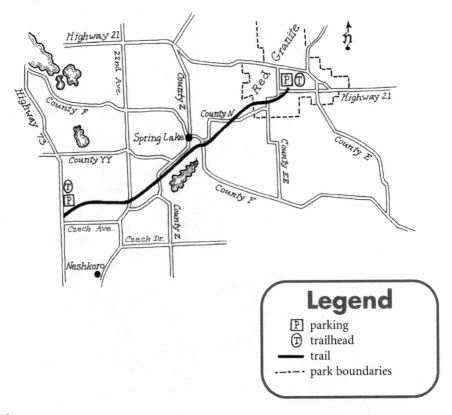

Legend

- P parking
- T trailhead
- — trail
- ·—·—· park boundaries

Location: Parking is available in Redgranite on the north side of Highway 21 and north of Neshkoro on the east side of Highway 73, just north of Czech Avenue (see map).

Contact(s): Waushara County Parks
N2402 South Town Road
Wautoma, WI 54982

Phone: (920) 787-7037; (920) 787-4608 (fax).

E-mail: wcparks@vbe.com

Web site: http://www.1waushara.com/Parks/default.htm

Trails: Seven miles of railroad grade that is well-maintained. The trail is grass-covered and is mowed in the spring, summer, and fall.

Shared use: Shared with hikers and bicyclists.

Horse rentals: n/a.

Camping: Day use only.

Dates of use: Spring, summer, and fall. Call for exact dates.

Passes: n/a.

Did You Know?

Horses do not have good vision, but they do have great depth perception. They cannot see below their nose, above their head, or to the rear. Horses can turn their ears to figure out where sounds are coming from, and they can hear high- and low-pitched sounds that humans cannot.

Black River State Forest
Jackson County

Black River State Forest is a beautiful woods that is geologically unique. It sits on the site of the glacial Lake Wisconsin on the edge of the Driftless Area, offering spectacular views that are only available in Wisconsin.

The horse trails at Black River traverse 35 miles in three loops. On the northern edge, near the horse camp, the forest runs along the east fork of the Black River, giving riders views of bald eagles, osprey, and other wildlife. Horses are not allowed in the Black River Wildlife Refuge within the forest, a haven for numerous wildlife species. But the refuge encompasses only 2,100 of the forest's 67,000 acres in the Black River Wildlife Refuge, and there is plenty of wildlife to see on the surrounding acreage.

The terrain is relatively flat, and almost all of the 35 miles of horse trails are dedicated, meaning they are not shared with hikers, bikers, ATV-drivers, or other potential trail users. There are short segments, over stream bridges and intersections,

127

where a rider might meet someone on an ATV, but this is rare. In addition to the designated trails, riders are allowed on all logging roads and areas not marked as closed to horses. The trails are open year-round (use caution during hunting season).

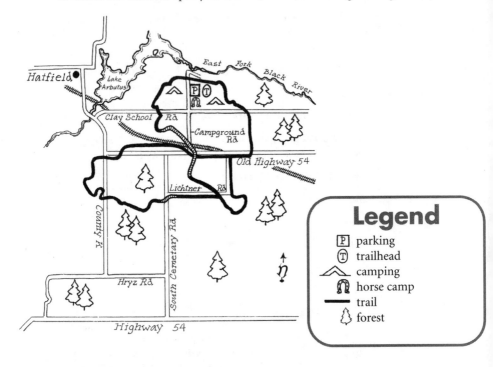

Location: Take I-94 to Highway 54 East. The northern edge of the park (where the horse campground and trailhead can be found) lies 4–5 miles east on Highway 54. A vehicle sticker is required.

Contact(s): Black River State Forest
910 Highway 54 East
Black River Falls, WI 54615-9276

Phone: (715) 284-4103 or (715) 284-1417; (715) 284-3153 (fax).

E-mail: BeyerT@dnr.state.wi.us

Web site: http://www.dnr.state.wi.us/org/land/Forestry/
StateForests/meet.htm#BlackRiver

Trails: Thirty-five scenic miles in three loops. The forest around the flat and gently rolling trails is filled with wildlife and waterfowl. Terrain is considered easy.

Shared use: Almost all trails are designated horse trails. Riders may see an occasional ATV at trail intersections. Hiking trails are separate. No horses allowed at beaches. Some horse trails are wide enough for carriages.

Horse rentals: n/a.

Camping: Twelve primitive campsites at Black River, which are available on a first-come, first served basis. The campground includes an overflow parking lot for day use and water. Campsites are primitive with pit-style toilets

Reservations: Campsites are first come, first served only.

Dates of use: Open year-round. Use caution during deer gun season. No hunting is allowed in campground areas.

Passes: State park vehicle sticker required.

Black River Trail
Sheboygan County

The Black River Trail is one of the shortest trails in this book, but its location, just west of Lake Michigan in Kohler-Andrae State Park, makes it well worth covering. Kohler-Andrae State Park runs along Lake Michigan, but the Black River Trail is separated from the beach by the Kohler Company Forest Preserve State Wildlife Refuge, which is private land. The Black River Trail is west of the reserve, in the northwestern section of the park just off County Road V. The trail winds back and forth through open prairie, woodlands, and a red-pine plantation, and it is shared with hikers and mountain bikers. For those planning more than one ride a day, the Kettle Moraine State Forest is a mere 30-minute drive to the west.

Trails are maintained by Neighbors for Trails, a group of riders from the Friends of Kohler-Andrae.

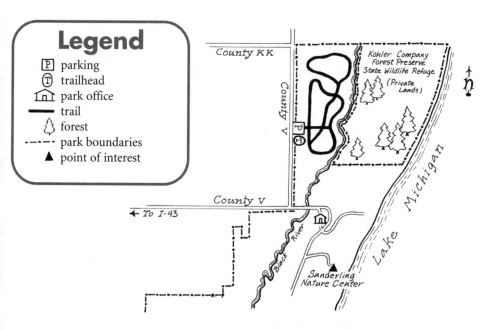

Legend
- P parking
- T trailhead
- 🏠 park office
- ▬ trail
- ⌂ forest
- ·—·—· park boundaries
- ▲ point of interest

County KK

County V

County V

Kohler Company Forest Preserve State Wildlife Refuge (Private Lands)

To I-43

Black River

Lake Michigan

Sanderling Nature Center

Location: Equestrian trails are in the northwestern section of Kohler-Andrae
State Park, on County Road V, south of County Road KK.

Contact(s): Kohler-Andrae State Park
1020 Beach Park Lane
Sheboygan, WI 53081

Phone: (920) 451-4080.

Web site: http://www.dnr.state.wi.us/org/land/parks/specific/ka

Trails: 2.5 miles of gently rolling trails. Horse trails go through
open prairie and woodlands.

Shared use: Shared with hikers and bicyclists.

Horse rentals: None.

Camping: Day use only.

Dates of use: Spring, summer, fall. Call for exact dates.

Passes: State park vehicle pass required.

Other: Please stay on marked trails. Horses are not allowed on the beach at any time.

High Cliff State Park
Calumet County

Located in east-central Wisconsin, High Cliff State Park offers miles of equestrian
trails along Lake Winnebago, Wisconsin's largest lake. High Cliff gets its name from
the limestone cliff of the Niagara Escarpment, which runs parallel to the eastern
shore of Lake Winnebago. (This ledge continues northeasterly to the Door County
peninsula and on to Niagara Falls, New York.)

The popular High Cliff Trail is a mix of grass and dirt, and is well-maintained.
The trail, although relatively flat, offers some beautiful vistas of the lake. The horse
trail is separate from hiking trails. It runs 8.5 miles from north to south, with loops
at each end.

Horse-trailer parking (see map) is midway along the trail, near the eastern park
boundary. There is a trailer dumping station between horse-trailer parking and
group camp (not available for horse camping). Trails are day use only.

Horse trail signs have arrows at High Cliff, and park personnel ask that you stay
on trails designated for horse use for everyone's safety and enjoyment. The trails are
shared with hikers and bicyclists.

Location: High Cliff State Park is 9 miles east of Menasha on Highway 114. In
Menasha, Highway 114 starts as U.S. Highway 10 and branches off to
the southeast. Turn south off Highway 114 at State Park Road and
drive about 2 miles to the park entrance. From Fond du Lac, take U.S.
Highway 151 north about 18 miles. Continue north on Wisconsin
Highway 55 to about 2 miles beyond Sherwood. Turn south on
Pigeon Road and drive 1.5 miles to the park entrance.

Contact(s): High Cliff State Park
 N7630 State Park Road
 Sherwood, WI 54169

Phone: (920) 989-1106.

E-mail: Joseph.Hennlich@dnr.state.wi.us

Web site: www.dnr.state.wi.us/org/land/parks/specific/highcliff

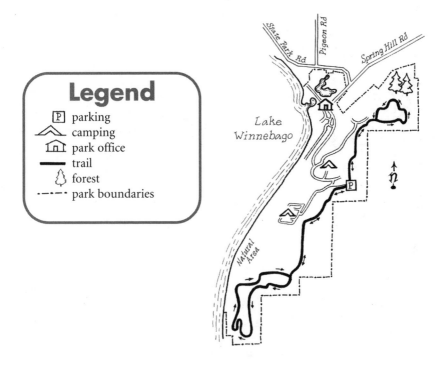

Legend

- P parking
- ⌂ camping
- 🏠 park office
- — trail
- 🌲 forest
- ·-·- park boundaries

Trails: 8.3 miles of grass and dirt trails that run along the ridge of Lake Winnebago.

Shared use: Shared with bikers and hikers.

Horse rentals: n/a.

Camping: Day use only.

Dates of use: Open May through mid-November.

Passes: Vehicle sticker required.

Kettle Moraine State Forest—Lapham Peak Unit
Waukesha County

The Lapham Peak Unit of the Kettle Moraine State Forest offers five miles of horseback-riding trails, which are shared with mountain bikers. The trails are only accessible from Evergreen Grove off County Road C, one mile south of Highway 94.

The horse trails, which are comprised of several loops, are ranked "intermediate" in terms of difficulty. The hills are rolling and there are several prairie restoration sites along the way, so wildlife is abundant.

The area is popular but not over-used. The trails are used by snowshoers, cross-country skiers, and dog-sledders in the winter, but can also be used by equestrians. There are two picnic shelters on the property, which can be reserved by calling the park office.

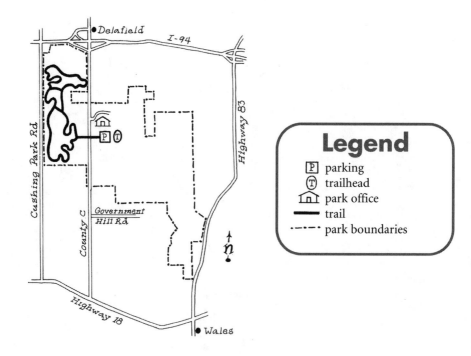

Location: Located 25 miles west of Milwaukee and 1 mile south of Interstate 94 near Delafield, on County Road C.

Contact(s): Kettle Moraine State Forest—Lapham Peak
W329 N846 County Road
Delafield, WI 53018

Phone: (262) 646-3025 or
(262) 646-4421 (trail conditions); (262) 646-4782 (fax)

E-mail: muzike@dnr.state.wi.us

Web site: http://www.dnr.state.wi.us/org/land/parks/specific/lapham

Trails: Five miles of rolling trails that are ranked "intermediate" in difficulty.

Shared use: Trails are shared with mountain bikers.

Horse rentals: Check the Yellow Pages for nearby stables.

Camping: Day use only.

Dates of use: Trails are open from 7:00–9:00 p.m. in the spring, summer, and fall. Call for exact dates.

Passes: Vehicle admission sticker required. Trail passes are required for all riders 16 and older.

Trailers lined up in the Kettle Moraine State Forest's Northern Unit, with 31 miles of trails.

Kettle Moraine State Forest—Northern Unit
Fond du Lac, Sheboygan, and Washington Counties

Kettle Moraine State Forest is known throughout Wisconsin as one of the most beautiful natural areas, and the fact that the forest is dedicated to serving horseback riders makes it all the more attractive.

The Northern Unit is made up of 30,000 acres, which are teeming with turkeys, Cooper's hawks, meadowlarks, and red-winged blackbirds. The dedicated horse trails, which comprise 39 miles of the park, are well-maintained and are rolling, with a few steep hills.

New Prospect Horseriders Campground offers 15 campsites; 12 for individuals and three for groups, and has separate shelters for people and horses, pit toilets,

133

and potable water. The campground and trails are open from April through mid-November. Riders can call for trail conditions and closures.

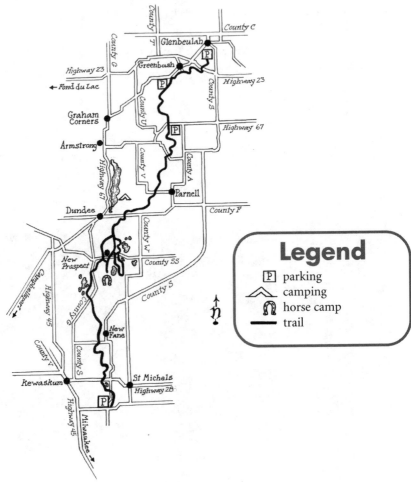

Location: From Madison, take U.S. Highway 151 to Highway 33 (Beaver Dam). Go east (right) to Highway 28 (Horicon). Take Highway 28 east to Highway 45, and go north (left) to Old Bridge Road. Turn right on Old Bridge Road to County Road G. From Milwaukee, take Highway 45 north to Highway 28 (Kewaskum). Go right (east) to County Road S. Take S north (left) to County Road G.

Contact(s): Kettle Moraine State Forest—Northern Unit
N1765 Highway G
Campbellsport, WI 53010

Phone: (262) 626-2116

E-mail: LeiteJ@dnr.state.wi.us

Web site: http://www.dnr.state.wi.us/org/land/parks/specific/kmn/index.html

Trails: Thirty-three linear miles from north to south, with two small loops near New Prospect that total six miles. Total riding distance is 39 miles. Terrain is rolling with some steep hills. There are rocks in some places, but the trails are well-maintained and generally kept clear of debris. Trails can get slippery when wet.

Shared use: Trails are designated for horseback riders. You may see some hikers.

Horse rentals: There are several stables nearby.

Camping: There are 15 sites available for horseback riders, with pit toilets, horse and human shelters, and water. Three of the sites are group sites; the rest are for individuals or smaller groups.

Reservations: Visit www.ReserveAmerica.com or call (888) 947-2757.

Dates of use: Trails are open late April through mid-November, depending on trail conditions. Call for exact dates.

Passes: Vehicle pass required. Trail passes are required for all riders 16 and older.

Other: Trails get muddy and slick when wet. Riders are urged to wait 4-6 hours after rain to ride.

Kettle Moraine State Forest—Southern Unit
Waukesha, Jefferson, and Walworth Counties

Horse trails in the Southern Unit of Kettle Moraine State Forest are some of the best maintained in the state. With trail associations like Glacial Drumlin and the Southern Kettle Moraine Horse Trails Association, this is one area that has plenty of support, and it shows.

Southern Kettle Moraine is also one of the most popular trail systems in Wisconsin. Granted, being based in Eagle helps. The forest is in the most populous area of the state, not far from Milwaukee, which makes having a natural getaway all the more important.

The Southern Unit encompasses 21,000 acres of glaciated hills. The horse trails, which encompass 54 acres of the park, are marked with orange diamonds. The terrain varies from sandy and flat to hilly with some rocks, but there is something for everyone at the Southern Unit. There are hardwood forests, pine plantations, oak savannas, and prairies. There are also several lakes and vistas overlooking wet kettles (small ponds caused by glacial drift). Trail Coordinator Ray Hajewski marvels at the burr oak trees, which he calls the wooly mammoths of the forest, and said the management is always diversifying plant life in the forest. There are several ongoing projects to prevent erosion on the equestrian trails.

The Southern Unit is unique for the number of campsites available. Horseback riders have 70 sites to choose from, including pull-through sites. Tying horses to trees is strictly forbidden.

Location: South of Palmyra. There is parking at the Horse Riders Camp and the Ottawa trailhead. The Eagle trailhead is east of the Horse Riders Camp and southwest of the Ottawa trailhead. From Palmyra, go south on 3rd street. Entrance will be on the left. The Ottawa trailhead can be accessed by taking Highway 59 to Piper Road (west), Waterville Road (north), and County Road ZZ (west).

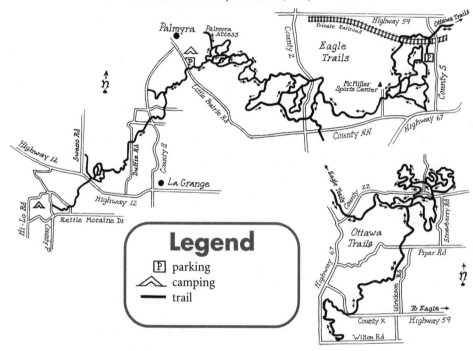

Contact(s): Kettle Moraine State Forest—Southern Unit
S91 W39091 Highway 59
Eagle, WI 53119-0070

Phone: (262) 594-6200, (262) 594-6201 (main office), or (262) 594-6221 (trail coordinator)

Web site: http://www.dnr.state.wi.us/org/land/parks/specific/kms

Trails: Contains 54 miles of trails, all marked with orange diamonds (trails are used for snowmobiles in the winter). Terrain ranges from sandy and flat to hilly with some rocks. Front shoes are recommended for soft-footed horses.

Shared use: Designated horse trails in spring, summer, and fall. Used by snowmobiles in the winter.

Horse rentals: Available nearby. Check the Yellow Pages.

Camping: Approximately 70 sites, including 35 back-in sites, 20 pull-through sites, and one group site accommodating up to 20 people. The campground has a picnic shelter, horse shower, manure deposit stations, drinking water, and pit toilets. Each site includes a tether post and a fire ring. Horse Riders Camp is open from mid-April through November.

Reservations: Reservations can be made by calling ReserveAmerica at (888) 947-2757 or visiting www.reserveamerica.com You can also register at the park office during regular office hours, space permitting. Reservations are strongly recommended during Memorial Day weekend.

Dates of use: Spring, summer, and fall. Trails are used by snowmobiles in the winter.

Passes: Vehicle and trail passes are required for all riders 16 and older.

Mascoutin Valley State Trail
Green Lake and Fond du Lac Counties

The horseback-riding section of the Mascoutin Valley State Trail, also known as the Rush Lake Trail, is one of two trail segments. The horse trail, which runs 12 miles from Berlin to Ripon, is a crushed-limestone trail that was formerly home to the Milwaukee Railroad.

The trailhead parking lot is on Locust Road north of Ripon. There is another parking site at Rush Lake Loop Road off County Road E by Rush Lake (hence the Rush Lake Trail moniker). The trail is mostly flat.

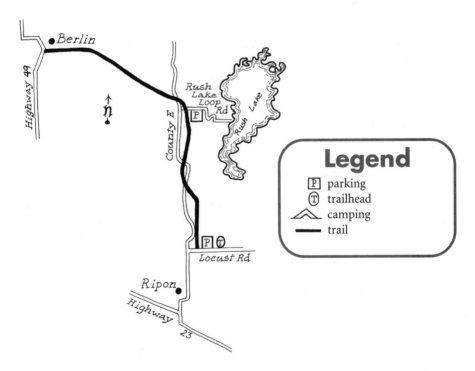

Legend

P parking
T trailhead
⌂ camping
▬ trail

Location: Between Berlin and Ripon. Parking is available at the intersection of Locust Road and the old Chicago & North Western line north of Ripon and at Rush Lake Loop Road off County Road E by Rush Lake.

Contact(s): Fond du Lac County Planning and Parks Department
160 South Macy Street
Fond du Lac, WI 54935

Green Lake County Courthouse
492 Hill Street
Green Lake, WI 54941

Phone: (920) 929-3135; (920) 929-7655 (fax).

Trails: Twelve miles of crushed-limestone trails running from Berlin in the north to Ripon in the south. The trail meanders through Fond du Lac, Winnebago, and Green Lake Counties, past wetlands and farms.

Shared use: Trail is shared with hikers and mountain bikers.

Horse rentals: n/a.

Camping: Day use only.

Dates of use: Open spring, summer, and fall. Trail is used for snowmobiling in the winter.

Passes: n/a.

Menomonee Park and Bugline Recreation Trails
Waukesha County

The Menomonee Park and Bugline Recreation Trails are two separate trail systems, but they intersect at Menomonee Park. While the equestrian portions of both trails are too short to merit individual descriptions, together they equal 5.5 miles. The Menomonee Park and Bugline Trails are day use only, but riders have access to water and bathrooms. The park office will allow overnight camping at the large campsite near the Menomonee Park trailhead, but riders should call to confirm this throughout the year. The site is not an official horse campground.

The 2.5-mile equestrian section of the Bugline Trail (the entire trail stretches for more than 12 miles) starts at the Ranch Riding Center in Menomonee Falls (see description in the Stables and Barns section of this chapter). The bridle trail, which is adjacent to the original recreational trail, is 4 feet wide and made of crushed limestone. Riders are not permitted to park at the riding center but may park a short distance away at the trailhead. Trails meander through the woods over relatively flat ground.

Once riders enter Menomonee Park, they hook up with a three-mile trail of crushed limestone, grass, and woodchips. The section of the trail in the park has some wetlands, but footing is relatively good, except after heavy rains, when the trails may be closed. The park also boasts of a number of nice wooded areas, dominated by maples and other hardwoods. There are also several picnic areas, two separate campgrounds, and Quarry Lake, which features a sandy beach and other amenities. All in all, it's a city park with lots of rustic touches.

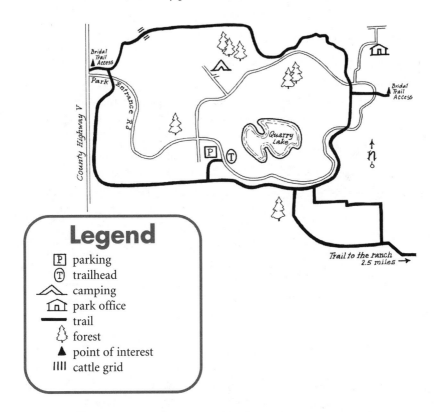

Legend

- P parking
- T trailhead
- camping
- park office
- trail
- forest
- ▲ point of interest
- IIII cattle grid

Location: Parking is available at Menomonee Park and in Menomonee Falls near the Ranch Riding Center. The park entrance is on County Road V, 1.5 miles north of Highway 74. The Bugline Trail starts near the riding center and connects with the Menomonee Park Trail.

Contact(s): Waukesha County Department of Parks and Land Use
Parks System Division, Room 230
1320 Pewaukee Road
Waukesha, WI 53188

Phone: (262) 548-7801(County Parks System Division office) or (262) 255-1310 (park); (262) 896-8071 (fax).

E-mail: rbaxter@waukeshacounty.gov

Web site: htpp://www.waukeshacounty.gov/parks/parks/men_main.asp

Trails: The Bugline Bridle Trail follows 2.5 miles of crushed limestone. Footing in the park includes grass, woodchips, and crushed limestone. Both trails are relatively flat and pass through woods. There are some wetlands in the park. Trails may be closed following bad weather. Call to confirm.

Shared use: Shared with hikers.

Horse rentals: n/a.

Camping: Day use only. There is one group camp.

Reservations: Call (262) 548-7801 to ask permission to camp with your horse. Permission may or may not be granted; this is not an official horse camp, but sometimes exceptions are made. Trails should be viewed as day use only.

Dates of use: Open spring, summer, and fall. Trails are used for cross-country skiing in the winter. Call office for exact dates.

Passes: Vehicle sticker required in the park. Trail use is free.

Did You Know?

Horses never forget, but they usually forgive. Mules never forget and never forgive.

Old Plank Road Trail
Sheboygan County

Running between Greenbush and Sheboygan, the Old Plank Road Trail is a place with two great beginnings—or two great ends. Running between the Northern Unit of the Kettle Moraine State Forest and Lake Michigan in Sheboygan, Old Plank Road offers 17 miles of scenic trail.

The equestrian trail, which runs alongside an asphalt multi-use trail, passes the towns of Sheboygan, Kohler, Sheboygan Falls, Plymouth, and Greenbush, where it dead-ends at the Ice Age Trail.

The trail runs along Highway 23, but is nevertheless a scenic ride. The trail is quieter once you get outside Sheboygan, and the second half of the trail, from Plymouth to Greenbush, is quite relaxing. The trail is open year-round, although it is used by snowmobilers in the winter. The asphalt portion of the trail is used by runners, hikers, rollerbladers, and bicyclists. The trail is equipped with benches, shelters, water, bathrooms, and emergency telephones.

The landscape is relatively flat, but the trail begins to undulate once you get past Plymouth, where you will find some rolling hills. There are intersections with roads approximately every mile, and riders can park their trailers on those roads or at any of the four designated trailheads (see map), which are large enough to accommodate snowmobile and horse trailers.

Location: There are four trailheads along the trail, all with parking lots big enough to accommodate horse trailers. You can also park on side

Legend
- P parking
- T trailhead
- — trail

streets along the trail. Trailheads are west of Sheboygan, near Sheboygan Falls, east of Plymouth, and in Greenbush.

Contact(s): Sheboygan County Planning Department
Administration Building
3rd Floor, Room 335
508 New York Avenue
Sheboygan, WI 53081

Phone: (920) 459-3060; (920) 459-1332 (fax).

Trails: Seventeen miles of trail from Sheboygan to Greenbush. Trail is relatively flat on the Sheboygan end, with rolling hills toward Greenbush. Trail has water, restroom facilities, shelters, rest benches, and emergency telephones. The trail runs along Highway 23, and the ride is more relaxing in the less-urban Greenbush area. The trail has won cycling awards for its ease of use.

Shared use: The trail is in fact two trails, one asphalt and one turf (they run side by side), and they are shared with rollerbladers, cyclists, walkers, and joggers. The trail is open year-round, and it is used by snowmobilers in the winter.

Horse rentals: n/a.

Camping: Day use only.

Dates of use: Open year-round.

Passes: n/a.

Great views from the trail at the Richard Bong State Recreation Area.

Richard Bong State Recreation Area
Kenosha County

The Richard Bong State Recreation Area is a popular and widely used area by horse people. The recreation area was originally slated to be a jet fighter base (Richard Bong was a WWII flying ace from Poplar, Wisconsin), but the state bought the land when those plans were scrapped in 1974. In addition to the equestrian trails, Bong is popular among hang gliders, hot-air balloonists, and those who fly ultra-lights and model airplanes. As you might imagine, the portion of the park used by such enthusiasts is kept separate from the horse trails. In fact, Bong has several "zones" that accommodate different activities.

Bong has more than 4,500 acres of recreation land, and the horse trails follow 13 miles through the recreation area. The trails loop around the southernmost portion of Bong and travel past Wolf Lake, the Sunrise Campground, and the Sunset Campground. There are 12 sites available at the Sunset Campground, which can by reserved through ReserveAmerica.com.

Bong is well-liked because of its gently rolling terrain. There are a few wet areas, but these can be avoided by riding on nearby roads. The area is popular among endurance athletes because of its varied terrain and scenery.

Location: The recreation area is 8 miles southeast of Burlington on Highway 142. The entrance is a little less than a mile west of Highway 75.

Contact(s): 26313 Burlington Road
Kansasville, WI 53139

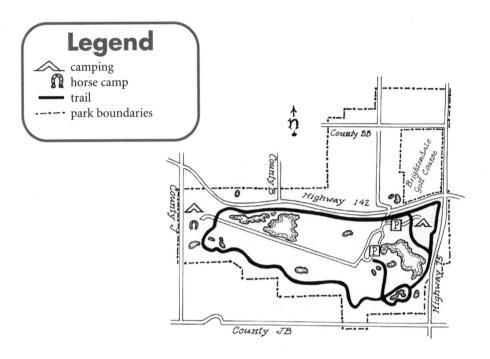

Legend
- ⌂ camping
- ♘ horse camp
- — trail
- ·—·—· park boundaries

Phone: (262) 878-5600 (office); (262) 878-5615 (fax).

E-mail: Patricia.Nelson@dnr.state.wi.us

Web site: http://www.dnr.state.wi.us/org/land/parks/specific/bong

Trails: 13 miles of well-maintained trails that loop around the southwestern end of the park. Riders are also allowed on service and paved roads that run throughout the recreation area.

Shared use: Trails are shared with hikers. No bikes or motorized vehicles are allowed.

Horse rentals: There are several nearby barns, some of which rent horses. Check the Yellow Pages.

Camping: The area has 12 sites that can be reserved for horse camping. Sites have solar showers.

Reservations: Log on to www.ReserveAmerica.com or call (888) 947-2757.

Dates of use: Open year-round.

Passes: Vehicle sticker required. All riders over the age of 16 must have a trail pass.

Other: If you do not feel like roughing it, see the listing for Brighton Acres Guest House in the Stables and Barns section of this chapter for human and horse lodging.

Wild Goose State Trail
Dodge County

The Wild Goose State Trail is a north-south multi-use trail that runs 15 miles between Highway 60 and Pautsch Road, just west of Horicon Marsh. This linear trail runs next to a limestone trail, and horses are required to stay on designated trails. The trail runs through some woodlands and some open areas. Wildlife is abundant, especially near the marsh. The trail can get soggy after rain, so use good judgment following storms.

Signage on the trail is good, and it is always clear where horses can and cannot traverse. There is a hitching rail at the trailhead on Highway 60 and at Minnesota Junction. Riders will encounter a shooting range about two miles north of the Highway 60 trailhead. This area is separated from the trail by a large berm, but riders often hear shots.

Terrain on the trail is generally easy. The footing is made up of grass, dirt, and wood chips. Caution is urged on side hills, and at highway and road intersections, especially after rain.

Parking and Porta-Potties are available at the Highway 60 trailhead and in the Minnesota Junction area, just north of Highway 33. There are also several other parking lots along the trail. The Friends of Dodge County Parks and the Dodge County Horsemen's Association have done a splendid job working with Dodge County to develop more horse trails in the county.

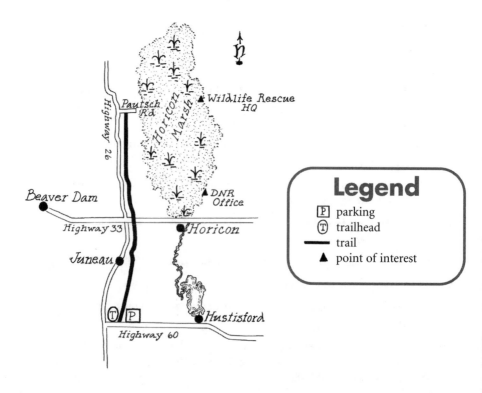

Legend
- P parking
- T trailhead
- —— trail
- ▲ point of interest

Location: The trail runs north from the southern trailhead at Highway 60, west of Hustisford, to Pautsch Road, west of Horicon Marsh.

Contact(s): Dodge County Planning and Development
127 East Oak Street
Juneau, WI 53039-1329

Phone: (920) 386-3700 or (920) 386-3705 (trail status); (920) 386-3979 (fax).

E-mail: dplanning@co.dodge.wi.us

Web site: http://www.co.dodge.wi.us/planning/recreation/map-horse.htm

Trails: Fifteen miles of trail running between Highway 60 and Pautsch Road in Dodge County. The horse trail is a pathway that runs alongside a limestone-surfaced trail, which is used by hikers and bikers. Horses are not allowed on the limestone trail except at designated horse trail crossings. The horse trail is relatively flat with some wet spots.

Shared use: The trail is shared with hikers, bikers, and cross-country skiers. The trail is open to snowmobiles and ATVs between December 1 and March 31, as conditions permit.

Horse rentals: n/a.

Camping: Day use only. Country Retreat bed, breakfast, and stable is next to the Wild Goose Trail. See listing.

Dates of use: Open year-round. Drivers of snowmobiles and ATVs use the trail in winter.

Passes: n/a. Donations accepted at donation boxes on Highways 60 and 33, and on County Road S.

More Riding Trails

Friendship Trail
Calumet County

The six-mile Friendship Trail, from Brillion to Forest Junction, is a new trail, open to horseback riders in the spring, summer, and fall. The trail, which is shared with hikers and bikers, was built on an abandoned railroad corridor and is relatively flat. It travels through woods, past a high school, and past agricultural areas. There is currently no fee for trail use.

Location: The trail (formerly known as the Brillion/Forest Junction Trail) runs along Highway 10 between Brillion and Forest about 12 miles southeast of Appleton. Parking is available at both ends of the trail.

Contact(s): Calumet County Parks
N6150 County Road EE
Hilbert, WI 54129
Phone: (920) 439-1008

Web site: http://www.co.calumet.wi.us

Did You Know?

All thoroughbred foals born after 1998 have microchips implanted in them for breed identification.

Gibbs Lake County Park
Rock County

Gibbs Lake is wildly popular, despite its small size. Still, the people who frequent Gibbs Lake do so for a number of reasons. The first is its proximity to Janesville (the park is about seven miles west of town), and the second is it is a nice alternative to the larger parks, especially when you are pressed for time.

The 3.8-mile loop in the park can be ridden in about an hour. The trail has a grass-and-gravel surface. The terrain is varied, and it receives high marks for beginning and experienced horses alike.

Location: Seven miles west of Janesville. Take Highway 14 to Eagle Road. Go north to Gibbs Lake Road, and turn west. The park is half a mile up Gibbs Lake Road.

Contact(s): Rock County Parks Director
3715 Newville Road
Janesville, WI 53545
Phone: (608) 757-5450

Harrington Beach State Park
Ozaukee County

There is only one horse trail at Harrington Beach State Park, and it is only a mile long. But despite its brevity, the trail is beautiful, running north to south, from County Road D to Cedar Beach Road, not far from the shores of Lake Michigan. Wild turkeys frequent the entrance to the park (not far from the horse trailhead), and luscious plants bloom in the park during the warmer months.

The horse trail, which is used for snowmobiling in the winter, is part of a 637-acre beachfront park that was once used for mining. The terrain is varied and can be challenging in some parts of the park. There are currently no plans for expansion of the horse trails.

All trails in the park are day use only, and riders are advised to clean up after their horses in the parking lot.

Location: Harrington Beach is approximately 10 miles north of Port Washington along the Lake Michigan shoreline. Take Highway D off Interstate 43 for one mile.

Contact(s): Harrington Beach State Park
531 County Road D
Belgium, WI 53004

Phone: (262) 285-3015

The end of a clean cross-country round.

E-mail: Andrew.Krueger@dnr.state.wi.us

Web site: http://www.dnr.state.wi.us/org/land/parks/

Kettle Moraine State Forest, Loew Lake Unit
Washington County

Located between the Northern and Southern Units of Kettle Moraine State Forest, Loew Lake offers 2.5 miles of designated horse trails. One of the shorter trails in the area, this area is lightly traveled and is used mostly by locals. If you're driving through, however, stop by. The looped trail is gently rolling and runs along the scenic Oconomowoc river valley. There are plans to add another two miles of trail in the near future. Keep an eye on this one.

Location: The parking lot is off of Emerald Drive. Take Highway 60 to County Road K south. Go approximately 8 miles to Emerald Drive.

Contact(s): Pike Lake Ranger Station
3544 Kettle Moraine Road
Hartland, WI 53027

Phone: (262) 670-3400

E-mail: John.Wald@dnr.state.wi.us

Magnolia Bluff County Park
Rock County

Magnolia Bluff is a small but well-visited park that offers 2.7 miles of trails over hilly, wooded terrain. The park, in western Rock County, has stunning beauty and is home to the largest limestone outcropping in the county. The area is used primarily by residents of Rock and Dane Counties because of its size, and it is certainly worth a stop if you are in the area. Magnolia Bluff has the only naturally occurring stand of white birch in Rock County, and the area is home to a wide variety of plants and animals.

There are bathrooms and a water pump in the picnic area (no horses allowed), which is about 1,000 feet up the hill from the parking area. The bridle path, which is shared with hikers, is a 2.7-mile one-way loop. The park is open from dawn to dusk. The bridle trails at Magnolia Bluff were made possible by the efforts of the Tri-County Riding Club.

Location: From Madison, take Highway 14 to Evansville. Exit on Highway 213 to Highway 59 West, then follow Highway 59 to Croak Road. The park is a half mile south of the intersection of Highway 59 and Croak Road, on Croak Road.

Contact(s): Rock County Parks Division
3715 Newville Road
Janesville, WI 53545

Phone: (608) 757-5450

Minooka Park
Waukesha County

Founded in 1870, Minooka Park has been a favorite among Waukesha County residents for more than a century. The park, which has 580 acres and a 2.5-mile horse trail (in addition to a few hiking and nature trails), is a day-use-only facility with restrooms and water readily available.

The horse trail is mostly flat with some rolling hills and runs mainly through wooded areas. The trail, which is open from May 1 through November 1, weather permitting, is lightly traveled.

Location: Minooka Park is 2 miles southeast of Waukesha at the corner of Racine Avenue and Sunset Drive.

Contact(s): Waukesha County Department of Parks and Land Use
Parks System Division, Room 230
1320 Pewaukee Road
Waukesha, WI 53188

Phone: (262) 548-7801 (Parks Department) or (262) 896-8006 (park); (262) 896-8071 (fax).

E-mail: rbaxter@waukeshacounty.gov

Web site: http://www.waukeshacounty.gov/parks/parks/minooka_main.as

Muskego Park
Waukesha County

Muskego Park offers one of the shortest trail rides (1 mile) in this book, but it goes through a beautiful section of hardwoods known as the park's State Scientific Area. The area is used to preserve plants, teach conservation, and study the area's natural history. The horse trails begin at the park entrance and wind through the woods over gently rolling land. There are some wetlands, but most of the trail is covered in woodchips, and the footing is good. Because it only takes about 15 minutes to ride, the trail is lightly used by equestrians. Note: The trail is open from May 1 through November 1, weather permitting.

Location: Muskego Park is in the southeast corner of Waukesha County on County Road L, approximately 1 mile west of Racine Avenue on County Road Y.

Contact(s): Waukesha County Department of Parks and Land Use
Parks System Division, Room 230
1320 Pewaukee Road
Waukesha, WI 53188

Phone: (262) 548-7801 (Parks Department)
(262) 679-0310 (park);
(262) 896-8071 (fax).

E-mail: rbaxter@waukeshacounty.gov

Web site: http://www.waukeshacounty.gov/parks/parks/muskego_main.asp

> "God forbid that I should go to any heaven in which there are no horses."
>
> —Robert Browning

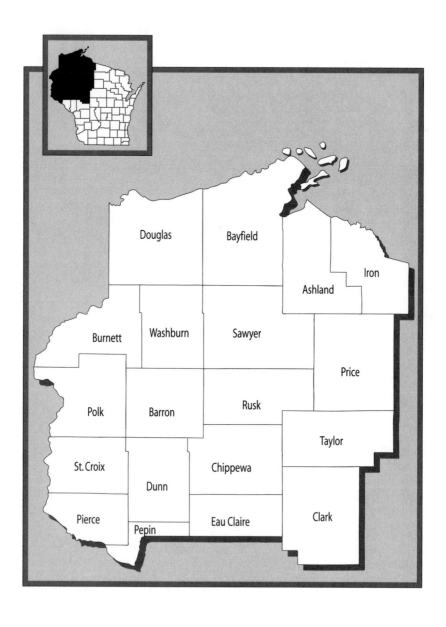

Northwest
Wisconsin

Stables and Barns

Amber Farm, Inc.
Chippewa Falls

Amber Farm is a hunter/jumper barn that caters to a wide variety of riders. While many of Kathy Jerome's students take jumping lessons and want to show, many choose to ride on the flat.

Amber Farm is a member of the Western Wisconsin Horse Show Association (WWHSA), an organization that hosts up to 10 hunter/jumper shows a year, in addition to dressage, western pleasure, and games shows. The group is a grassroots organization set up to expose riders to the world of showing.

Amber Farm is open year-round and offers lessons from 8:00 a.m. to 8:00 p.m., primarily to children but increasingly to adults and to the parents of kids who want to learn to ride. As a trainer, Jerome is a stickler for the basics, and believes in teaching students how to ride properly and effectively. "It doesn't matter if you're riding English or western, jumping or not, balance is balance," Jerome says. To reinforce her teaching, Jerome takes her students throughout the Midwest to audit from top-level clinicians, including George Morris. They bring much of what they learn home with them, applying it in their daily lessons.

Amber Farm is four miles from the Wissota State Park and Old Abe trail systems, for those who are interested in trail riding. The barn is within a fast-growing residential area, so Jerome recommends trailering, instead of riding, horses to the parks.

Location: 18798 70th Avenue, Chippewa Falls, WI 54729.

Phone: (715) 723-7050.

E-mail: Dhrsldy@aol.com

Year founded: 1996.

Owner(s): Kathy Jerome.

Hours: Tuesday through Sunday, 8:00 a.m.–8:00 p.m.; closed Mondays.

Specialization(s): Hunter/jumper; overnight stabling for travelers.

Facilities: Barn, 70 x 150-foot indoor arena, outdoor rings, small group turnout, indoor and outdoor wash racks.

Number of stalls: 12.

Board: $$$. Includes turnout, hay feedings three times per day, grain feedings twice a day, blanketing and unblanketing for horses in training (service available a la carte for those not in training).

Lessons: Private, group.

School horses: Number available varies; currently has four horses and ponies.

Requirements: Boots with heels, helmets.

Shows/clinics: Amber Farm offers two hunter/jumper shows annually and hosts clinics with Minneapolis- and Milwaukee-based trainers.

Transportation: Transportation is available to WWHSA shows and other hunter/jumper shows in the Minneapolis and Milwaukee areas.

Other: Horses for sale and lease.

Never too young (or too old) to wear a helmet.

Appa-Lolly Ranch and Riding Stables
Hayward

In 1989, Lolly Johnston founded Appa-Lolly Ranch in picturesque Hayward. The name of the ranch is a combination of the first four letters of "appaloosas," a nod to the many appaloosas she kept at the ranch, and her first name. When Johnson passed away, her sister Gina Benson purchased the facility, and she has continued to run Appa-Lolly in much the same way.

Well-known in the Hayward area, Appa-Lolly runs a safety-conscious program that regularly draws locals and tourists to its facility. Visitors to Appa-Lolly can take one-hour trail rides (kids under five ride double), two-hour picnic rides, overnight riding with campouts, sleigh excursions and hayrides with campfires, and games on horseback. Appa-Lolly also hosts horse-awareness seminars and barn dances.

If you are a local, Appa-Lolly offers boarding and training. Benson is quick to say "no offense" to those who train the "old cowboy way" (hobbling, tying up and throwing down), but stresses that they do things differently at their ranch. The facility has a 130 x 200-foot arena (which is available for special-event rental). There

155

is a round pen for free-lunging, a clubhouse, viewing area, cross-country course, miles of trails, and campfire sites. The boarding philosophy at Appa-Lolly is an outdoor one, so if you like your horse pampered indoors, you might be better off looking elsewhere. Call for information on memberships.

Location: W501 East River Road, Hayward, WI 54843.

Phone: (715) 634-5059.

E-mail: appalolly@centurytel.net

Year founded: 1989.

Owner(s): Gina Benson.

Hours: Summer, 9:00 a.m.–6:00 p.m.; can take riders out until dark by appointment. Rides are by reservation only in the winter.

Specialization(s): Western pleasure, performance, driving, eventing, jumping, trail riding, rental/livery horses, horse-awareness seminars, barn dances.

Facilities: Barn, outdoor arena, pasture, turnout paddocks, clubhouse, viewing area, tack room, cross-country course, trails.

Number of stalls: 6–8.

Board: $$. Full service or pasture. Appa-Lolly believes that horses prefer to be outside, and stresses that if you do not want your horse rained or snowed on, Appa-Lolly is not the place for you. Some stalls are available for those desiring them.

Lessons: Private, semiprivate, group, adult. Minimum age is 7.

School horses: 30

Requirements: Boots or paddock shoes.

Clinics/Shows: On-site shows and clinics.

Transportation: Boarders provide their own transportation to shows.

Other: Horses for sale, memberships available.

Artesian Farm at Lighthouse Stable
Ashland

Northern Wisconsin is known for numerous outdoor opportunities: kayaking, hiking, mountain biking, and trail riding among them. Still, you would not necessarily expect to find an FEI-level dressage instructor in the North Woods.

Head out to Artesian Farm at Lighthouse Stable, and you will find just that and more. Cari Chellstorp (owner of Artesian Farm, while Jackie and Art Carpenter own Lighthouse Stable), is a Grand Prix-level rider who teaches dressage, jumping, and Pony Club riders the finer points of riding. She rode at Temple Farms in Illinois for many years and has been an equine professional for more than three decades.

Lighthouse Stable is at the southeastern end of Chequamegon Bay, right in the heart of Wisconsin's vacationland. The barn caters to locals but is seeing an increasing number of summer vacationers who either bring their horses with them, lease a horse for the summer, or stop by for lessons. Chellstorp welcomes all of the above, and the owners work hard to make everyone feel welcome.

On a clear day, you can see the Apostle Islands offshore, and the fall offers a particularly beautiful view of this unique area. The farm is half a mile inland from Chequamegon Bay. Only 45 minutes from the major ski areas of the Upper Peninsula, Chellstorp is starting to draw people in the winter as well.

This is a first-class operation that provides top-quality English instruction in the North Woods.

Location: 2900 Knight Road, Ashland, WI 54806.

Phone: (715) 372-4060.

E-mail: Myfenrir@baysat.net or lhs@ncis.net

Year founded: 1995.

Owner(s): Jackie and Art Carpenter own Lighthouse Stable. Carrie Chellstorp owns Artesian Farm (the training arm of Lighthouse Stable).

Hours: No set hours but open daily.

Specialization(s): Dressage, eventing, Pony Club.

Facilities: Barn, 72 x 154-foot indoor arena, heated tack room, indoor wash rack, large outdoor dressage arena, jump field, small cross-country course on 60 acres, Porta-Potty.

Number of stalls: 20.

Board: $$. Includes turnout, feedings, daily stall cleaning.

Lessons: Private, semiprivate, group jumping lessons. Minimum age is 8. Pony Clubbers receive 20 percent discount on all lessons.

School horses: 1–2.

Requirements: Helmet and hard-soled shoes with a heel are required.

Shows/clinics: Hosts clinics and one schooling show a year.

Transportation: Can transport students to shows.

Other: Lighthouse Stable always has horses for sale and/or lease.

Coventry Cove Farm
Menomonie

The owners of Coventry Cove Farm are dedicated dressage people and run their facility accordingly. Owner and trainer Karen Lee-Veith is a bronze and silver medallist with the United States Dressage Federation (USDF) and is currently riding at the intermediate level.

157

All of Veith's boarders are in a training program or, at a minimum, taking lessons. Coventry Cove is set up with indoor and outdoor arenas, as well as all the other amenities of a quality barn. Outside riders haul in to take lessons with Veith, who travels with her students to shows in Wisconsin and beyond.

Coventry Cove is a complete dressage facility, and is located just one hour from Minnesota's Twin Cities.

Location: E3472 770th Avenue, Menomonie, WI 54751.

Phone: (715) 235-6260.

E-mail: coventry@pressenter.com

Year founded: 1989.

Owner(s): Steven Veith and Karen Lee-Veith.

Hours: Call for appointment.

Specialization(s): Dressage.

Facilities: Barn, 60 x 120-foot indoor arena with crushed-rubber-and-sand footing, viewing area, tack room, 70 x 200-foot outdoor arena with dressage letters, turnout paddocks, pasture.

Number of stalls: 15.

Board: $$. Includes daily feeding, turnout, and stall cleaning. All boarders must be in training or taking lessons.

Lessons: Private and haul-in lessons available. All horses at Coventry Cove are in training. Minimum age for students is 7, but trainer prefers 12 and above.

School Horses: None.

Requirements: Boots or paddock shoes and hunt cap.

Shows/clinics: Clinician comes in from Florida.

Transportation: Travels with students to dressage shows.

Other: Horses for sale and lease.

Otter Creek Farm
Wheeler

Otter Creek Farm came late to the world of USEA eventing, but made a fast bid to become one of the most popular eventing venues in Wisconsin. The owners, Lena and Mark Warner, have been hosting schooling shows since 1993, but held their first USEA- and USA-Equestrian-recognized horse trials in 1999. Their first event had beginner novice, novice, and training courses. They have since added a preliminary-level course and are in the process of building a intermediate course, which, when launched, will be a first for a public barn in Wisconsin.

Otter Creek employs two trainers who teach everything from dressage to stadium to cross-country jumping. In addition to its annual horse trials, Otter Creek hosts dressage shows, Pony Club rallies, clinics, and schooling shows. It hosts the Midwest Pony Cup, a popular event for young riders 21 years of age and under, and the facility hosted the 2003 Western DeBroke Championship.

Otter Creek holds a Rider and Horse Development Program (RHDP) several times a year, which offers between 2 and 3.5 hours of riding instruction per day. The horse-and-rider teams work on everything from dressage to trail riding to learning to anticipate the unexpected. The land in Wheeler is hilly, so Otter Creek draws a lot of riders from surrounding areas, including many from the Twin Cities, who come to condition their horses.

Otter Creek sits on 225 acres in the beautiful hills of west-central Wisconsin about 25 miles northwest of Eau Claire—ideal country for eventing. Their horse trials have drawn competitors from Wisconsin, Minnesota, Michigan, Iowa, South Dakota, and North Dakota. Most of Otter Creek's boarders show, although "it's not a requirement by any means," says co-owner Mark Warner.

Location: E5847 1170th Avenue, Wheeler, WI 54772-9459.

Phone: (715) 658-1105.

E-mail: scan@chibardun.net

Web site: http://www.ottercreekfarm.com

Year founded: 1993.

Owner(s): Lena and Mark Warner.

Hours: No set hours but open daily. Owners live on-site.

Specialization(s): Eventing, dressage.

Facilities: Barn, 20 x 60-meter indoor arena, viewing area with heated restrooms, tack room, 20 x 60-meter outdoor arena, and two 20 x 40-meter outdoor arenas, pastures, wash rack.

Number of stalls: 15 permanent stalls for boarders, 30 permanent stalls for shows. Otter Creek owns 80 temporary stalls for shows and rents more as needed.

Board: $$$. Includes turnout, two feedings per day, constant access to pasture outside or hay inside.

Lessons: Private, semiprivate, group.

School horses: None. Boarders own their own horses. Riders are welcome to trailer in for lessons. Cross-country schooling and conditioning sessions are available.

Requirements: Hard hats required at all times. Owners strongly encourage the use of safety vests for jumping.

Shows/clinics: Hosts dressage and jumping clinics/shows.

Transportation: Transportation available to some shows.

Other: Horses for sale and lease. The owners stand two stallions on-site and sell Swedish and American Warmbloods.

**Splashing through a creek at Kinni Valley Riding Academy.
Photo courtesy of Carolyn Lowe.**

Kinni Valley Stables and Riding Academy
River Falls

Kinni Valley Riding Academy, owned by Carolyn Lowe, is one of northwestern Wisconsin's favorite stables. Voted a "Family Favorite" by *Minnesota Parent Magazine* (Kinni Valley is just 30 minutes from Saint Paul), the place is popular because it responds so well to its customers' goals, be they to increase confidence, learn more about horse-keeping, or perfect that imperfect seat. Kinni Valley does all this while taking excellent care of its horses and the facility.

The riding academy, which operates in conjunction with Kinni Valley Stables (owned by Loew's father, Tom), offers lessons, training, and camps for children and adults. Comments from students are glowing. They range from statements such as Carolyn "makes me feel like a friend, not a client," to "My daughter's riding lesson is the highlight of her week."

Carolyn has more than 20 years of experience as a riding instructor and runs Kinni Valley like a business, not a hobby. The lessons are not cheap, but neither are they unreasonably expensive. Lowe understands what it takes to make a business run, and handles hers accordingly. On top of that, Lowe has a way with children and horses, and has been able to combine these gifts with her business.

Lessons at Kinni Valley are offered in packages, with anywhere from six to seven lessons per session. Make-up sessions are available, and procedures are outlined on the Web site. For the kids, summer day camp is offered each week from June through August. Children between the ages of 8 and 18 come and get instruction in riding and horsemanship, spending up to three hours per day in the saddle.

Beginning and more advanced adult camps are available various weeks throughout the year. Beginners learn equitation through riding, lectures, and demonstrations, while intermediate and advanced riders focus on the discipline of their choice, including dressage, western pleasure, driving, colt training, and jumping. Those wishing to join can register in person or online.

Location: 1171 30th Avenue, River Falls, WI 54022.

Phone: (715) 426-1321; (715) 426-1485 (fax).

E-mail: kvriding@pressenter.com

Web site: http://www.pressenter.com/~kvriding

Year founded: 1995.

Owner(s): Carolyn Lowe. Father Tom Lowe owns the adjoining Kinni Valley Stables, which offers one-hour guided trail rides along the Kinnickinnic River.

Hours: 9:00 a.m.–7:00 p.m. daily. Lessons by appointment. Lesson hours change throughout the year—call for details.

Specialization(s): Dressage, show jumping, driving, colt breaking, western pleasure.

Facilities: Barn, full-size heated indoor arena, heated viewing room, two full-sized outdoor dressage arenas, show-jumping pasture, 150 acres of trails along the Kinnickinnic River.

Number of stalls: 20.

Board: $$$–$$$$. Includes turnout and two feedings per day. The 10 x 12-foot and 12 x 14-foot box stalls are cleaned daily.

Lessons: Private, semiprivate, group, bought in packages of six or seven. Minimum age is 4.

School horses: More than 20.

Requirements: Long pants and boots or shoes with a hard sole and heel. Helmets are provided. There is a tack shop on-site at Kinni Valley for those who want to purchase their own helmets.

Shows/clinics: There are shows at the end of each kids-camp session during the summer. Parents and family are encouraged to attend.

Transportation: Transportation provided to shows.

Other: Horses for sale and lease. At Kinni Valley, those who want to ride can start out with guided trail rides, move on to lessons, and graduate to ownership.

Wilderness Pursuit
Neillsville

Wilderness Pursuit, located in Neillsville southeast of Eau Claire, is a getaway for those who want to experience nature to the fullest. The facility caters to groups and individuals looking for outdoor adventure.

In business since 1981, Wilderness Pursuit takes adults and children on rides that last anywhere from two hours to six days. Rides take place in the Clark County Forest, which boasts more than 130,000 acres and 40 miles of horse trails.

In addition to its daily trips, Wilderness Pursuit offers summer camps (both day and overnight) for youth. During their weeklong stay, the kids learn to groom and tack up, then ride for a few hours. They come back to the base camp for lunch, head out for another ride, and then return to camp for dinner. All children get a one-hour private lesson during the week. There is a gaming day toward the end of the week, where groups have egg-and-spoon races and ride mini barrels.

Wilderness Pursuit emphasizes Native American horsemanship, the history of horses in America, and crafts. The kids do horse painting, a favorite activity, and bead their horses' manes.

Although it caters to city folks and cowboys alike, Wilderness Pursuit trips are not for those looking to be pampered. The facility is not a resort or a lodge. (Currently, all sleeping is in tents, but bunkhouses for overnight stays are being built.) The preferred customer is one who is not afraid to roll up his or her sleeves and help with camp, dishes, meals, tearing down tents, and horses. People should think of their stay here as a fun working vacation.

Location: N5773 Resewood Avenue, Neillsville, WI 54456.

Phone: (715) 743-4484.

E-mail: wpwpw@tds.net

Web site: http://www.wildernesspursuit.com

Year founded: 1981.

Owner(s): Larry and Lynette Engevold.

Hours: By appointment.

Specialization(s): Western pleasure, trail rides, overnight trips for youth and adults, summer camp.

Facilities: None.

Number of stalls: None.

Board: $. Pasture board available, including water, pasture, good fences, and supervision.

School horses: 12.

Lessons: Private, semiprivate, group, adult. Minimum age is 6.

Requirements: Boots with a heel, hard hat.

Shows/clinics: n/a.

Transportation: None to shows. All horses are transported to Clark County Forest to ride the trails.

Other: Horses occasionally for sale.

More Stables and Barns

The Farm Bed and Breakfast
718 South Main Street
Birchwood, WI 54817
(715) 354-3367
E-mail: gloriaj@chibardun.net
Specialization(s): Bed-and-breakfast that can accommodate 14 guests.
Facility has six stalls and two 2-acre pastures for horses. Prices are
reasonable. Tuscobia State Trail is accessible from the farm.

Frontier Trails
11124 Whispering Pines Road
Frederic, WI 54837
(715) 327-8572
Specialization(s): Guided trail rides in the spring, summer, and fall.

Galloping Hills Equestrian Center
1178 290th Street
Glenwood City, WI 54013
(715) 265-7754
E-mail: Brian@gallopinghills.com
Web site: http://www.gallopinghills.com
Specialization(s): Dressage, jumping, and eventing for beginning and inter-
mediate riders. Also works with Pony Club riders.

Hay Lake Ranch
Hay Lake Road
Springbrook, WI 54875
(715) 766-2305
Specialization(s): Guided trail rides spring to fall. Minimum age of 8 for
one- and two-hour rides, minimum age of 12 for all-day rides. Horses are
ridden in Arizona during the winter. Call for reservations.

Heartland Equestrian Center
1175 County Road H
New Richmond, WI 54017
(715) 248-3011
E-mail: Horselady@superiorwi.com
Specialization(s): Resistance-free training in hunt seat, dressage, western
pleasure, and driving. Located just minutes from Stillwater, Minnesota.

Kinni Valley Riding Stables, Inc.
1181 30th Avenue
River Falls, WI 54022
(715) 425-6184
Specialization(s): Guided trail rides in the spring, summer, and fall; call for

appointment in the winter. See the description of Kinni Valley Stables and Riding Academy in the Stables and Barns section of this chapter for lessons and boarding.

Rising Star Stables

2309 Panorama Road
Menomonie, WI 54751
(715) 233-6200
E-mail: risingstar-amy@sbcglobal.net
Specialization(s): English pleasure, western pleasure, summer day and half-day camps for children and adults (minimum age of 6). Rising Star also hosts birthday parties. Call for details. Owner travels to breed shows with students and offers clinics on horsemanship, showmanship, groundwork, and other educational classes. Inquire about overnight stabling.

**Taking a moment to maintain the bond between horse and rider.
Photo courtesy of Creative Equine Photography.**

Silvermine Farm

309 Pavelski Road
Eau Claire, WI 54703
(715) 874-6170
E-mail: Silvermine@bis-net.net
Specialization(s): Dressage lessons and training.

Spider Lake Ranch Riding Stable

10881 West State Highway 77
Hayward, WI 54843
(715) 462-3386

E-mail: spiderlakeranch@jrec.net
Specialization(s): Half-hour and one-hour guided trail rides. Open spring, summer, and fall. Call for appointment.

SummerVale Farm, LLC
11939 MacArthur Drive
Chili, WI 54420
(715) 676-2169
Specialization(s): Dressage, English pleasure, western pleasure. Owner is an FEI-level instructor and trainer. Clinics international dressage trainers are scheduled throughout the year. Call for more information. SummerVale Farm is 15 miles southwest of Marshfield in west-central Wisconsin.

Trinity Equestrian Center
S5300 Highway 37
Eau Claire, WI 54703
(715) 835-4530
E-mail: info@trinity-ec.com
Web site: http://www.trinity-ec.com
Specialization(s): western pleasure, English pleasure, kids horse camp, guided trail rides.

What's Left Ranch
W10462 County Road MM
Thorp, WI 54771
(715) 669-7332
E-mail: whtslft@discover-net.net
Web site: http://www.geocities.com/diablo292002/index.html
Specialization(s): Local riding club (Wild Mares Riding Club) hosts trail rides in the Clark County Forest a few times each year. Riders leave from What's Left Ranch, which is located on the northern side of the forest.

Riding Trails

Brule River State Forest
Douglas County

Brule River State Forest might be best known for trout fishing, but riders love the miles of horseback riding offered on more than 50,000 acres of forest. There are two areas for horseback riding: 26 miles of snowmobile trail from Brule to Saint Croix Lake, and 38 miles on the Hunter Walking Trails, running between Brule and Solon Springs.

The Brule River State Forest horse trails, which double as snowmobile and ATV trails in the winter, are sandy and hilly, traveling through woods and into the river valley. Because of its varied terrain, the forest supports a wide variety of wildlife. Riders are likely to see plenty of deer and birds, including geese, ruffed grouse, bald eagles, osprey, and songbirds.

There is no camping in the state forest, but a nearby fly-and-bait shop, Brule River Classics, has rustic lodging available and allows horse camping.

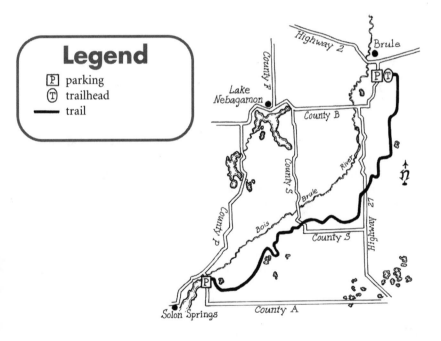

Location: Off Highway 27 in Brule, northeast of Solon Springs. Parking is in the snowmobile trail parking lot, just south of Highway 2.

Contact(s): Brule River State Forest
6250 South Ranger Road
P.O. Box 125
Brule, WI 54820

167

Phone: (715) 372-4866 or (715) 372-8539; (715) 372-4836 (fax).

E-mail: petersp@dnr.state.wi.us

Web site: http://www.dnr.state.wi.us/org/land/Forestry/StateForests/
meet.htm#BruleRiver

Trails: Brule to Saint Croix Lake: 26 miles open in the spring, summer, and
fall. Hunter walking trails: 38 miles.

Shared use: Shared with mountain bikers in the spring, summer, and fall. (The
trail is open to snowmobilers and ATV drivers only in the winter.)

Horse rentals: n/a.

Camping: Day use only. Lodging and camping is available at Brule
River Classics.

Reservations: Call (715) 372-8153 for information about camping and
lodging at Brule River Classics.

Dates of use: Spring, summer, and fall.

Passes: State park vehicle sticker required.

Douglas County Wildlife Area (Bird Sanctuary)
Douglas County

The Douglas County Wildlife Area, often referred to as the Bird Sanctuary, offers
more than 4,000 acres for riding. The trails, which are currently undesignated, are best
known for field trials and occasional dogsledding. The trails total 13 miles and travel
over rolling hills, through brush and some woods. The land is preserved as a brush
prairie habitat, and it is a wonderful place for viewing wildflowers and wildlife. The
entire area lies in the drainage basin of the Saint Croix River, and it is relatively flat.

A clubhouse and stable are available for rent (these are very popular, so make your
reservations early). The stable area has pipe corrals that can be used for a few dollars
a day. The clubhouse, which has a large stone fireplace, is available for day or overnight
gatherings (users are billed for two days when they reserve the cabin overnight).

The path that riders currently use makes a large loop, with a smaller loop on the
western side of the wildlife area. The log clubhouse and stables are in the center of
the large loop. The wildlife area is popular with hunting dog trainers, but harness
groups, sleigh groups, and individual riders have all utilized the facility and given it
high marks.

Note: The state is currently designating horse trails at the Bird Sanctuary. These
trails may change in the future. Please be flexible and show respect for other wildlife-
area users at all times.

Location: Near Solon Springs on County Road M, just west of Highway 53.

Contact(s): Douglas County Forestry Department
P.O. Box 211
Solon Springs, WI 54873

Legend

P parking
—— trail
🌲 forest
·—·—· park boundaries

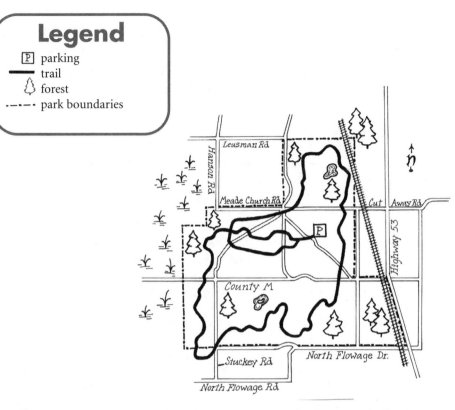

Phone: (715) 378-2219 or (715) 378-4528 (recreational information hotline); (715) 378-2807 (fax).

E-mail: forestry@douglascountywi.org

Web site: http://www.douglascountywi.org/countydepartments/forrestry/ recreationareas.htm

Trails: Horses can follow 13 miles of trail year-round. Snowmobiles are not currently allowed in the Bird Sanctuary (there is a snowmobile/ATV area on the eastern side of the property outside of the sanctuary), but riders may encounter these in the winter, as snowmobilers sometimes enter the sanctuary even though they're prohibited. Riding is best in the spring and summer. Trails are used extensively for field trials in the fall.

Shared use: Trails are shared with dogs, hikers, and bicyclists. Local schools sometimes use the trails for cross-country practice.

Horse rentals: n/a.

Camping: The Douglas County Wildlife Area has a popular clubhouse and stabling, both available for rent. Reserve early! Overnight guests will be charged for two days of clubhouse use.

Reservations: The clubhouse can be rented for a nominal fee. Call for prices and reservations.

Dates of use: Open year-round. Trails are used by sled dogs in the winter.

Passes: Nominal per-horse fee to ride in the wildlife area. A fee is required for clubhouse use. Reservations are necessary.

Eau Galle Lake Recreation Area
Saint Croix County

Eau Galle Lake Recreation Area is about six miles south of Interstate 94, not far from the Wisconsin/Minnesota border. The Eau Galle Lake trails, which stretch seven miles through the recreation area, are popular among Twin Cities and west-central Wisconsin trail riders.

The terrain is rugged: The Army Corps of Engineers is quick to point out that most of the trails are cut into side hills, making for scenic but sometimes difficult riding. The trails primarily roll through hardwood forests and fields. There are several water crossings, but they are narrow and relatively easy to navigate.

Horse-trailer parking is available at Lousy Creek Landing, on the northeastern side of Eau Galle Lake, and at the northwestern day-use area on the Ox Trail. Horse trails on the Ox Trail are located between Eau Galle Lake and the Eau Galle River, and these are particularly scenic.

The trails at Eau Galle Lake Recreation Area are not particularly well-marked, but this is an issue the Army Corps of Engineers is addressing. The ground is clay-like, and it can get slick after rain and snow; footing can be treacherous especially if you do not know the trails well. Riders are permitted to ride the roads on the northern side of the park.

Trails are currently open year-round, but the recreation area is experimenting with allowing hunters in the area. This may result in the closure of riding trails during the deer gun season.

Location: Just north of the town of Spring Valley, 40 miles west of Eau Claire and 50 miles east of Minneapolis/St. Paul. From I-94, take Exit 28 (Highway 128) south. Go right (west) on 10th Avenue, then left (south) on County Road NN to the Lousy Creek Landing.

Contact(s): Eau Galle Lake Recreation Area
P.O. Box 190
Spring Valley, WI 54767-0190

Phone: (715) 778-5562 (office); (715) 778-4678 (fax).

E-mail: Eau.galle.lake@mvp02.usace.army.mil

Web site: http://www.mvp.usace.army.mil/recreation/default.asp?pageid=153

Trails: Seven miles of equestrian trails, cut through steep side hills and narrow creeks. Plans for expansion have been on the books since 1999, so look for an additional five miles of trails and a horse campground in the nearfuture.

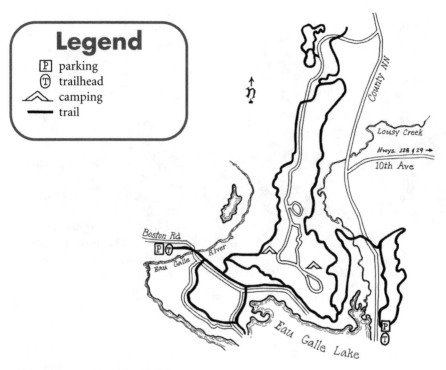

Shared use: Shared with hikers.

Horse rentals: n/a.

Camping: Not currently available, but a horse campground is planned.

Reservations: n/a.

Dates of use: Open year-round. May be closed during deer gun
season in the future.

Passes: n/a.

Governor Knowles State Forest, Trade River Horse Trails
Polk County

The horse trails in Governor Knowles State Forest are some of the more popular in the state—and with good reason. The forest, which is more than 50 miles long and two miles wide, runs along the eastern bank of the Saint Croix River. Wildlife frequents the area, and the trails offer beautiful vistas.

The state forest has more than 40 miles of horse trails. The trails etch across a slightly rolling landscape, often through woods. There are some swampy areas, so it is important that you stay on marked horse trails.

Advanced riders may find the trails a bit easy for their liking, but the loops are good for green riders and horses. The area can get buggy in the summer, so spring

Taking a break at Governor Knowles State Park.
Photo courtesy of Laura Kampfer and Raven Flores.

and fall riding are the best times to head out, with fall particularly striking.

The trails can be accessed from one of two trailheads: the Trade River Campground trailhead and a trailhead along the Saint Croix River (see directions under Location in the following listings). Detailed maps of all the trails are provided at the trailheads.

The horse trails are at the southern end of the forest. Riders may encounter deer, woodcock, grouse, and eagles. The observant eye may even find a mink or muskrat. Bring your bug spray if you ride in the summer.

Location: The campground trailhead is on Evergreen Avenue, five miles west of Highway 87. Riders can also access another trailhead by parking four miles south of County Road O along the Saint Croix River, on 340th Street near 290th Avenue.

Contact(s): Governor Knowles State Forest
P.O. Box 367
325 State Highway 70
Grantsburg, WI 54840

Phone: (715) 463-2898; (715) 463-5806 (fax)

Web site: http://www.dnr.state.wi.us/org/land/Forestry/StateForests/
meet.htm#GovernorKnowles

Trails: More than 40 miles of relatively flat and well-maintained trails. Loops include Barrens Loop Horse Trail, 4.5 miles; Barrens/Sunrise Horse Trail, 2 miles; a horse, snowmobile, and ATV trail, 30.5 miles; Sunrise Cutoff Horse Trail, 4 miles; and Wolf Creek Horse Trail, 2.5 miles. All

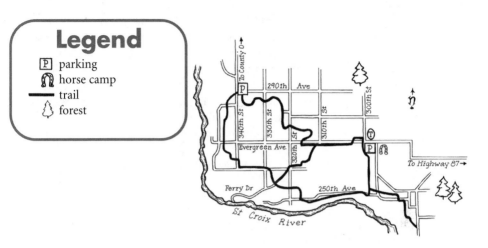

Legend
- P parking
- 🐴 horse camp
- — trail
- 🌲 forest

are quite scenic. Note: There are some swampy areas in the forest, so it is important that all riders stay on designated trails, which are generally well-marked. There are some wooden bridges along the trails.

Shared use: Trails are multi-use. Other users, including ATV riders, are generally courteous.

Horse rentals: n/a. Check Yellow Pages for local stables.

Camping: The Trade River Campground has 40 undeveloped, free campsites. The sites have fire rings and primitive toilet facilities. There are no refuse-removal services available. If you pack it in, pack it out.

Reservations: Call the state forest office at (715) 463-2898 for reservations. All campsites are free.

Dates of use: Trails are open year-round, but they are used by snowmobilers in the winter. It is not advised to use the trails in snowy conditions.

Passes: Trail passes required for all riders over 16 years of age. There are self-pay boxes at the trailheads. Remember, these funds are used for improvements, so it is important that everyone pays for use.

Other: Stay on designated horse trails. Some swampy conditions exist off the trails.

Hay Meadow Horse Trail
Chippewa County
The Hay Meadow Horse Trail is in the southwestern corner of the Chippewa County Forest northeast of Bloomer. This trail starts one mile north of Bob Lake Road and travels in two loops for a total of 8.75 miles. The terrain is rolling but moderate; the trail is easy enough for beginning riders. The scenery changes constantly, and riders can expect to see woodlands, wetlands, and streams.

There are a few boggy areas off the trail, so riders are encouraged to stick to the

173

designated trails. There are several lakes along the horse trail, and riders will pass by several ponds and woodland streams, in addition to riding through hardwood forests. The glacial moraine in this area has created a landscape that changes constantly.

Like many trails in the state, a trail riders association is largely responsible for the amenities you will find along the Hay Meadow Horse Trail, including pit toilets at the trailhead parking area, signing, and trail maintenance. The Chippewa Valley Trail Riders Association continues to work in conjunction with the Chippewa County Forest and Parks Department to improve the trails. Give them your thanks if you see them out on the trail.

Location: One mile north of Bob Lake Road, north of County Road E.

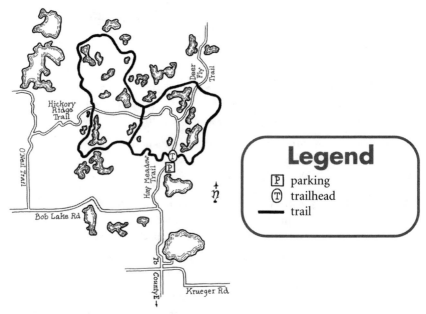

Contact(s): Chippewa County Forest and Parks Department
P.O. Box 482
711 North Bridge Street, Room 104
Chippewa Falls, WI 54729

Phone: (715) 726-7880.

E-mail: DRichards@co.chippewa.wi.us

Web site: http://www.co.chippewa.wi.us

Trails: 8.75 miles of rolling trail through hardwoods, wetlands, and streams.

Shared use: Shared with hikers, berry pickers, and hunters. Trails are used by snowmobilers and cross-country skiers in the winter.

Horse rentals: n/a.

Camping: Camping is allowed. Call the Forest and Parks division for more information. There is a lake less than a quarter-mile from the parking lot where horses can drink. Bring your own water for human consumption.

Reservations: Call the Forest and Parks division at (715) 726-7880 for more information.

Dates of use: Spring, summer, and fall. Trails are used by snowmobiles and skiers in the winter.

Passes: n/a.

Horseshoe Lake Saddle Trail
Bayfield County

Horseshoe Lake, found in the heart of the Chequamegon National Forest about 15 miles west of Ashland, offers two loops of horse trails totaling 12 miles. These loops are easy for anyone to navigate and can be ridden in one day.

Horseshoe Lake Saddle Trail is moderately difficult, with sandy footing. Bugs are kept at a minimum on this trail due to the clay, silt, and sand surface. The trail is closed to ATVs, but it is easy to get confused and venture off on the wrong trail (carry a trail map and look closely at signs at the trail intersections). ATVs may be encountered on other trails, including forest and logging roads. The horse trails are shared with mountain bikes, so use caution and courtesy when encountering other trail users.

Horseshoe Lake is scenic and gently rolling. One of the most popular Chequamegon riding areas, the trail passes through hardwoods and pine forests, and has some open areas with beautiful vistas.

There are three parking areas: one off of Forest Road 245 in the west, one along Forest Road 691 in the northeast, and one near Horseshoe Lake in the south. Horseshoe Lake recently opened a horse campground with 11 sites, which includes drinking water and horse shelter. As always, if you pack it in, pack it out.

Location: To reach the trailhead at the Horseshoe Lake Saddle Campground, go west from Ashland on State Road 2 for about 13 miles to Forest Road 236. Turn north and take that to Forest Road 237. Continue on that for about 5.5 miles to Forest Road 245, then turn west and drive 1 mile to the campground on the left.

Contact(s): Washburn Ranger District
Chequamegon National Forest
113 East Bayfield Street
Washburn, WI 54891

Bayfield County Tourism
P.O. Box 832F
Washburn, WI 54891

Phone: (715) 373-2668, (715) 373-2878 (both Washburn Ranger District), or (800) 472-6338 (Bayfield County Tourism).

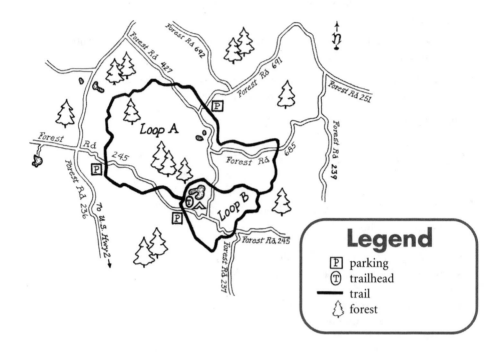

E-mail: dmklein@fs.fed.us

Web site: http://www.fs.fed.us/r9/cnnf

Trails: Twelve miles in two loops. The larger "A" loop is 9.25 miles. The smaller "B" loop is 3.7 miles. The outside of both loops measures 10.25 miles and can be ridden in under three hours. Terrain on all trails is moderately difficult, and the routes pass through pine forests and hardwoods. Horseshoe Lake is on the northwestern side of loop "B." Horses are not allowed in swimming, picnicking, and boating areas, as well as in non-horse-designated campsites.

Shared use: Twelve miles of nonmotorized horse trails that see light mountain bike and hiking use. Forest roads and logging roads are shared with ATVs. Use caution.

Horse rentals: Local rentals available. Please see yellow pages.

Camping: There is a relatively new horse campground at Horseshoe Lake with 11 individual sites. Sites have drinking water and shelter for horses.

Reservations: Call for information.

Dates of use: Campground is open May 1 through October 25.

Passes: n/a.

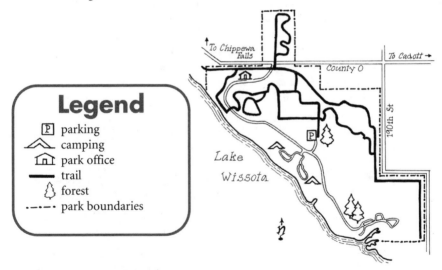
Lake Wissota State Park
Chippewa County

There are 6.5 miles of equestrian trails at Lake Wissota State Park. The trails are day use only (no camping), and they are open from April 15 until snowmobile season, which is the first snowfall that is heavy enough to allow snowmobiling. Riders make their way through hardwoods and pines over a relatively flat, sandy trail. Riders are treated to a view of Lake Wissota, which was created in 1918 when the Wisconsin-Minnesota Power and Light Company created a dam on the Chippewa River just northeast of Chippewa Falls. The area has since been home to many species of waterfowl.

The horse trail is shared with hikers and mountain bikers, but is not overly used. (Note: Hikers are allowed on portions of the horse trail, but horses are not allowed on the hiking and biking trails. Please observe trail signs.) The state park sees several mounted individuals and horseback-riding groups per year, but is by no means over-loaded. The terrain is pleasant and undemanding, a place where you can gather your thoughts and enjoy a one- to two-hour ride, depending on your pace.

The wildlife at Lake Wissota is abundant, including deer, rabbits, songbirds, and the occasional eagle or fox.

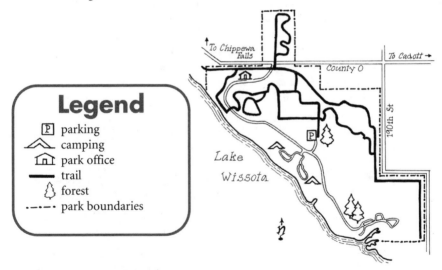

Legend
- P parking
- camping
- park office
- trail
- forest
- park boundaries

Location: 18127 County Road O, Chippewa Falls.

Contact(s): Chippewa County Forest and Parks Department
711 North Bridge Street, Room 104
Chippewa Falls, WI 54729

Phone: (715) 726-7880 (Forest and Parks Department) or (715) 382-4574 (state park office); (715) 382-5187 (fax).

E-mail: DRichards@co.chippewa.wi.us

Web sites: http://www.co.chippewa.wi.us orwww.dnr.state.wi.us/org/ land/parks/specific/lakewissota

Trails: 6.5 miles of relatively flat, scenic trails. Footing is mostly sand. Trails travel in several loops.

Shared use: Trails are shared with hikers and bikers.

Horse rentals: n/a.

Camping: Day use only.

Dates of use: April 15 to snowmobile season. Snowmobilers use some trails in the winter.

Passes: State park vehicle sticker required. Trail pass required for all riders 16 years and older.

Old Abe State Trail
Chippewa County

The Old Abe State Trail runs from Chippewa Falls in the south to Cornell in the north, but the equestrian portion runs from Lake Wissota to Jim Falls, a 5.8-mile section of the 19.5-mile trail. The abandoned railroad grade is paved and makes for relatively easy riding. The equestrian section, which runs alongside the paved trail, passes through agricultural land along the Chippewa River, until you enter Jim Falls. No motorized vehicles are allowed on the trail in the spring, summer, and fall.

There are parking lots for equestrians at the beginning and end of the trail, one at the three-way junction of County Road S, County Road O, and 97th Avenue, and one in Jim Falls on County Road K at Anson Town Hall. A Wisconsin State Trail pass is required for riders 16 and older and can be purchased on the trail from the Friends of Old Abe State Trail or at local merchants.

The Chippewa Valley Trail Riders were instrumental in getting access for horses on the Old Abe Trail.

Location: Just south of County Road O on the northeastern shore of Lake Wissota. Trailhead parking is at the junction of County Road S, County Road O, and 97th Avenue. Parking is also available on Highway K in Jim Falls.

Contact(s): Friends of the Old Abe Trail
615 Grant Court
Chippewa Falls, WI 54729

Chippewa County Forest and Parks Department
711 North Bridge Street
Chippewa Falls, WI 54729

Phone: (715) 726-7880.

E-mail: DRichards@co.chippewa.wi.us

Web site: http://www.co.chippewa.wi.us/Departments/Forest-parks/Old_Abe.htm

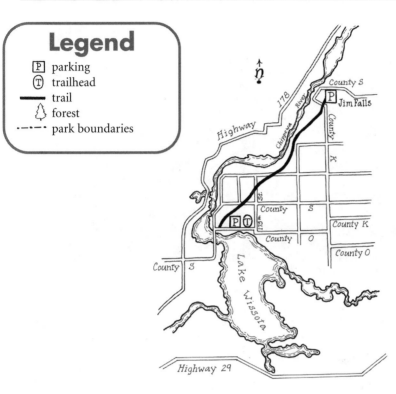

Trails: 5.8 miles that are flat for the most part. The trail winds through agricultural lands.

Shared use: The equestrian trail is a mowed-grass trail that runs alongside a blacktopped trail used by walkers, cyclists, and inline skaters. The trail is used by snowmobilers in the winter.

Camping: Day use only.

Dates of use: Spring, summer, and fall. Call for exact dates.

Passes: State trail pass required for all riders 16 and older.

Other: There are plans to extend the trail south toward Chippewa Falls as funding becomes available. This extension may or may not be open to horseback riders.

Pine Line Trail
Price and Taylor Counties

The Pine Line Trail runs 26 miles north to south between Prentice and Medford. The trail, which is named for the massive quantities of white pine lumber shipped along the former railroad corridor that makes up the trail, runs through groves of white pine, meanders past dairy farms, and slogs through swampy land in northwestern Wisconsin.

179

Enjoying a fog-shrouded morning ride.

The route was home to the Wisconsin Central Railroad from 1876 until 1988, but today the trail is home to hikers, bikers, joggers, and equestrians in the spring summer, and fall, as well as snowmobilers and ATV riders in the winter.

The terrain is relatively flat, and the southernmost portion of the trail in Taylor County is surfaced with limestone screenings. The rest of the trail is covered in crushed gravel, and it is generally well-maintained. The southern portion of the trail runs past numerous dairy farms, while the northern section, in Price County, runs through a moraine left by the most recent Wisconsin glacier, some 12,000 years ago. There are several cedar swamps along the trail (bring your bug spray!) and numerous types of vegetation and wildlife. Riders can see beaver dams near the trail, so bring a camera if you have a patient horse.

You can park at the trailheads in Medford and Prentice. Well water is available during the summertime at Medford City Park, Chelsea Lake County Park, Rib Lake Village Park, and Buccaneer Park in Prentice.

Location: Parking is available at the Buccaneer Park trailhead in Prentice; the Allman Street trailhead in Medford; on municipal streets in Ogema, Westboro, and Chelsea; and at the Whittlesey parking lot.

Contact(s): Price County Tourism Department
Price County Courthouse
126 Cherry Street
Phillips, WI 54555

Taylor County Forestry and Recreation
Taylor County Courthouse
224 South 2nd Street
Medford, WI 54451

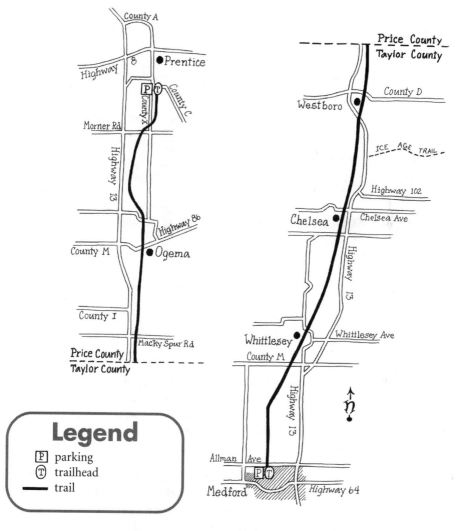

Legend

- P parking
- T trailhead
- ▬ trail

Phone: (800) 269-4505 or (715) 339-4505 (both for Price County); (715) 339-3089 (Price County fax). (888) 682-9567 and (715) 748-4729 (both for Taylor County).

E-mail: Price County: tourism@co.price.wi.us
Taylor County: chamber@dwave.net

Web site: http://www.pricecountywi.net/trails/pineline.html

Trails: Twenty-six miles of former railroad grade from Prentice to Medford. Well-maintained with agricultural and hardwood scenery, some swampland, and a terminal moraine dating from the last ice age. Horses are restricted to one side of the path. Footing is limestone and crushed gravel.

Shared use: Shared with hikers and bikers. Riders must stay on half of the trail and should ride single file, not abreast.

Horse rentals: n/a.

Camping: Day use only. Call the Price County Tourism Department if you plan to head out with a large group.

Dates of use: April 1 through November 30, depending on conditions. Trail is used by snowmobiles and ATVs in the winter.

Passes: n/a.

Other: The Price-Taylor Rail Trail Association performs trail maintenance.

Smith Rapids Saddle Trail
Price County

The Smith Rapids Saddle Trail is in the heart of the Chequamegon-Nicolet National Forest. The trail, which runs along the Flambeau River and through a beautiful stretch of northern woodlands, takes you 18.5 miles through woods, near wetlands, and over flat to gently rolling terrain. There are several vistas that provide views of the South Fork of the Flambeau River.

The trail connects with the Round Lake semiprimitive nonmotorized trails to the east, and with the Flambeau multi-use trail (which is lightly used by equestrians because of heavier use by ATV riders) to the southwest.

The Chequamegon-Nicolet National Forest gets buggy in the summer, so the best times to ride are spring and fall. The trails are lightly traveled, so the Smith Rapids Saddle Trail is a great place for solitude and one-on-one time with your horse.

At the trailhead, the Smith Rapids Campground offers 11 campsites, so gather up some of your friends and come enjoy the Chequamegon-Nicolet National Forest.

Location: About 2 miles north of Highway 70, 25 miles west of Minocqua, and 12.5 miles east of Fifield. Travel along Highway 70 to Forest Road 148. Turn left (north) and drive 1.8 miles to the campground road. Turn left (west) and continue to the trailhead.

Contact(s): Park Falls Ranger District
Chequamegon-Nicolet National Forest
1170 South 4th Avenue
Park Falls, WI 54552

Phone: (715) 762-2461; (715) 762-5179 (fax).

Web site: http://www.fs.fed.us/r9/cnnf

Trails: 18.5 miles of trail running east and west along the Flambeau River. There is one loop in the middle of the trail. The trail passes through some wetlands, and riding in these areas requires caution. The trail has a lot of mosquitoes in the summer (dependent on spring rains), so the best time to ride is the fall. Trail connects to the Flambeau multi-use trail (not recommended because of ATV use) and the lightly traveled Round Lake Trail (nonmotorized) to the east.

Shared use: Shared with hikers, especially near the Smith Rapids covered bridge. You will also encounter people fishing along the river.

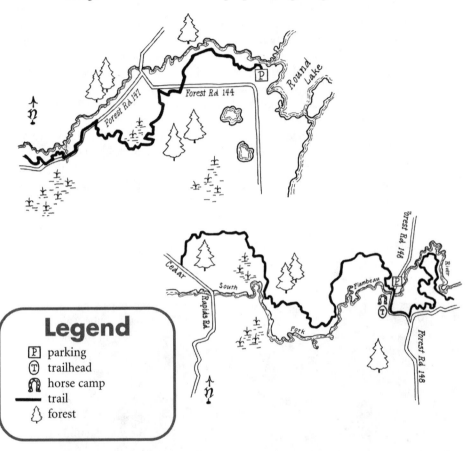

Legend

P parking
T trailhead
🐎 horse camp
— trail
🌲 forest

Horse rentals: n/a.

Camping: There are 11 sites at Smith Rapids Campground, with direct access to the equestrian trails. There is a pump and river water available. The ranger's office asks that you bring water to your horse instead of letting him drink out of the river. Do not tie horses to trees. Leave no trace.

Reservations: Reservations can be made by calling (888) 947-2757 or visiting www.reserveamerica.com

Dates of use: Trails are open year-round. Campground is open May through October.

Passes: Parking fee required.

Wild Rock Park
Clark County

Wild Rock Park is part of the Clark County Forest, a 133,000-acre parcel of wilderness northwest of Neillsville. The horse trails follow more than 40 miles through forests and fields, and the difficulty of the routes ranges from easy to extreme. The new Seven Sisters Trail is the most difficult section, but only takes up two of the park's 40 miles of trails. This section is almost straight up and down, and it is recommended for horses and riders with a solid conditioning base.

Some of the Wild Rock trails are shared with ATVs, but they are patrolled by the sheriff's department, and drivers have historically been respectful of horseback riders. Most pull off to the side of the trail and cut their engines, or drive by slowly.

Keep your eyes open for deer, fox, coyote, grouse, turkeys, and maybe, just maybe, a gray wolf. Those who ride the Wild Rock Park trails regularly give them high marks in almost every regard. Because the trails have widely varying levels of difficulty, it is advisable to connect with someone who has ridden them before (both Saddle Tramps and the Old Ladies Riding Club go there regularly; see their listings in Appendix A: Wisconsin-Based Horse Associations). The campground at Wild Rock is easily accessible and offers 25 sites, some with electricity.

If you do not have a horse of your own and want to ride in the forest, check out Wilderness Pursuit in Neillsville (see the listing under Stables and Barns earlier in this chapter). Wilderness Pursuit offers guided rides from a few hours to several days, all on rental horses.

The Saddle Tramps at Wild Rock Park. Photo courtesy of Brenda Schnabel.

Location: Wild Rock Park is part of the Clark County Forest, 16 miles west of Neillsville. To get to the campground and parking area, take Highway 73 to County Road H at Christie. Go west on H, then west on County Road G, and west again on County Road I. Wild Rock Park is just south of the intersection of County Roads M and I.

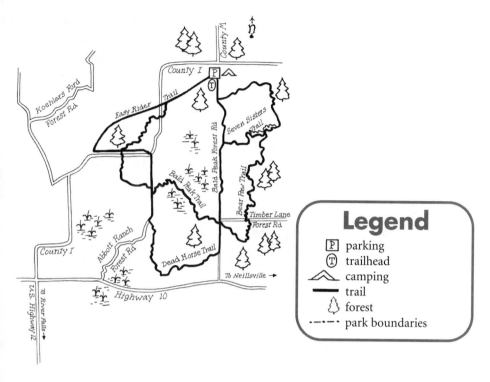

Contact(s): Clark County Forestry and Parks Department.
517 Court Street
Neillsville, WI 54456

Phone: (715) 743-5140;
(888) CLARK-WI;
(715) 743-5154 (fax).

Web site: http://www.clark-cty-wi.org/horse.htm

Trails: More than 41 miles of trails, suitable for beginning to advanced riders. Some trails are wide enough for buggies. Trails are marked. Terrain is varied, with some stream crossings. Seven Sisters Trail is particularly difficult.

Shared use: Some trails are shared with ATVs. It is advisable to wear reflective clothing when riding toward dusk.

Horse rentals: Contact Wilderness Pursuit in Neillsville for guided trail rides.

Camping: 25 sites, some with electricity. Shelter, playground, grills, water, and sanitary dump station available. Hitching posts and a corral were recently installed.

Reservations: Call the Forestry and Parks Department.

Dates of use: Open year-round. Use caution during deer-hunting season.

Passes: Trail passes can be purchased at the self-registration station in Wild Rock Park. Season passes available at the Clark County Forestry and Parks Department.

Wildwood Trail
Saint Croix County

The Wildwood Trail is a seven-mile path owned by Saint Croix County that runs from Woodville to the Saint Croix/Pierce County line. Four miles of the trail, from 50th Avenue, just south of I-94, to 10th Avenue near Spring Valley, are open to horseback riders.

The trail is an abandoned railroad corridor and runs past farms, wood lots, and rural homes. It is mostly shady, and wildlife and plant life are abundant. The path is mowed to a width of 15 feet by the Saint Croix County Parks Department, and the trail is well-maintained with crushed limestone. Motorized vehicles are prohibited on the Wildwood Trail in the spring, summer, and fall.

Plans for the future include an extension to the Eau Galle Lake Recreation Area (see description earlier in this section), potentially linking to the horse trails there.

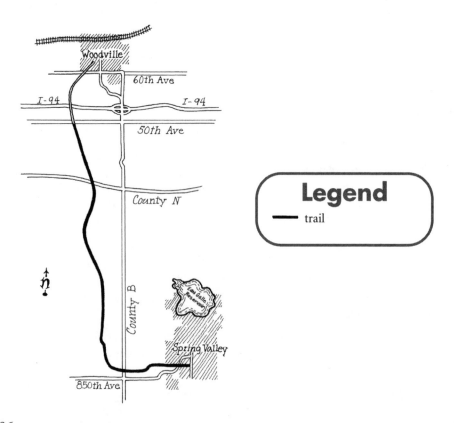

Location: The horse section of Wildwood Trail starts at 50th Avenue, south of Woodville (just south of I-94), and continues for four miles to 10th Avenue (west of Spring Valley).

Contact(s): Saint Croix County Parks Department
1960 8th Avenue, Suite 130
Baldwin, WI 54002

Phone: (715) 684-2874 (extension 4).

E-mail: davel@co.saint-croix.wi.us

Web site: http://www.co.saint-croix.wi.us

Trails: Four miles of trail with a gravel-and-limestone base. The trail is mowed to a width of 15 feet, and it is mostly flat and shaded.

Shared use: Shared with bikers and hikers.

Camping: Day use only.

Dates of use: Spring, summer, and fall. Trails are used by snowmobilers in the winter.

Passes: n/a.

More Riding Trails

Backwater Trail
Eau Claire County

The Backwater Trail meanders nine miles through the Eau Claire County Forest, just north of Augusta. The gently rolling trails follow two loops: one that is shared with vehicles and one that is shared with mountain bikes.

Riders are likely to see birds and deer along the trail, in addition to rabbits and other small animals. The footing is sandy with rolling topography, and riders will travel through woods and open fields.

The Backwater Trail is day use only. There are no trail fees. There is a parking lot, but no bathrooms or water. Please clean up after your horses in the parking lot.

Location: Drive 4 miles north of Augusta on Highway 27. Turn right on County Road GG/G, and drive approximately 6 miles to the parking area on County Road G.

Contact(s): Eau Claire County
Parks and Forest Department
227 1st Street West
Altoona, WI 54720

Phone: (715) 839-4738.

E-mail: parks-forest@co.eau-claire.wi.us

Buffalo River State Trail
Eau Claire, Jackson, and Trempealeau Counties

The Buffalo River State Trail is south of Eau Claire and runs along the Buffalo River, from Mondovi to Fairchild. Passing through Eleva, Strum, and Osseo, the trail runs for approximately 36.5 miles over an abandoned railroad right-of-way. The Buffalo River State Trail runs through farmland, woods, and marshland. The terrain and footing are varied.

The trail is used by ATVs year-round, by hikers and bikers in the summer, by snow-mobiles in the winter, and by hunters. Equestrians are free to ride when there is not enough snow for snowmobiling. All riders should use caution when riding around ATVs.

Note: State trail passes are required for all riders 16 and older.

Location: Between Mondovi and Fairchild. Parking lots are at each end of the trail.

Contact(s): Perrot State Park
Buffalo River Trail
W26247 Sullivan Road
P.O. Box 407
Trempealeau, WI 54661-0407

Phone: (608) 534-6409.

Web site: http://www.dnr.state.wi.us/org/land/parks/specific/findatrail.html

Taking a break in the Nicolet National Forest near Eagle River. Photo courtesy of Marsha Cooper.

Flambeau River State Forest
Sawyer County

There are no established horse trails in the Flambeau River State Forest, but equestrians are permitted on more than 55 miles of ATV and snowmobile trails in the spring, summer, and fall. Riders are permitted on ATV/snowmobile trails, as well as forest and logging roads, and are prohibited from riding in high-use areas, including established hiking, biking, and ski trails. Horses are also restricted from campgrounds and beaches. Please use caution when riding around ATVs.

The area is beautiful, and it is home to stands of white pine that are nearly 300 years old. The terrain is largely wooded, and trails run up and down over maintained trails.

One of the trails connects with the Tuscobia State Trail at the northern edge of the park, which borders the Chequamegon-Nicolet National Forest.

Location: The state forest is 22 miles northwest of Phillips and 22 miles southwest of Park Falls. Take County Road W west from Phillips to the main parking lot. State Highway 70 also runs through the forest's northern edge.

Contact(s): Flambeau River State Forest
W 1613 County Road W
Winter, WI 54896

Phone: (715) 332-5271; (715) 332-5279 (fax).

Web site: http://www.dnr.state.wi.us/org/land/Forestry/StateForests/
meet.htm#FlambeauRiver

Flambeau Trail System
Price County

Located in the Chequamegon-Nicolet National Forest, the 60-mile long
Flambeau Trail System has numerous facilities and five access points/parking lots.
Trails are shared with bikes, ATVs, and motorcycles, and the tree-lined paths pass
over bridges and through wooded, rolling terrain. The system connects with and sur-
rounds the Smith Rapids Saddle Trail (see the listing in the Riding Trails section of
this chapter), which is 14 miles long and does not allow motorized vehicles. Use caution when riding near ATVs.

Location: The westernmost access point/parking lot is 5 miles east of Park
Falls, and the easternmost is about 16 miles west of Minocqua.

Contact(s): Park Falls Ranger District Chequamegon-Nicolet National Forest
1170 South Fourth Avenue
Park Falls, WI 54552

Phone: (715) 762-2461 or (800) 372-2737.

E-mail: dmklein@fs.fed.us

Web site: http://www.fs.fed.us/r9/cnnf

Tom Lawin Wildlife Area
Chippewa County

Northeast of Chippewa Falls, the Tom Lawin Wildlife Area offers three miles of
equestrian trails, with a large parking lot located off County Road K midway along
the trail. Trails are mowed grass and well-maintained by members of the Chippewa
Valley Trail Riders saddle club.

There are two easy water crossings on the trail, both with good footing. The
equestrian trails are stand-alone trails, meaning they are not connected with any
other trails in the wildlife area; they dead-end at both ends.

This area is particularly good for starting green horses and introducing riders and
horses to water.

Location: A parking area, large enough for horse trailers, is off County Road
K, southeast of Jim Falls. Another lot is on 115th Street, east of
County Road S.

Contact(s): John Dunn, wildlife biologist
(715) 839-3771
Tower Ridge Recreation Area

Eau Claire County: Tower Ridge Recreation Area is part of the Eau Claire County Forest and offers approximately six miles of equestrian trails in the spring, summer, and fall. There are two parking lots: one at the trailhead on the western side of the trail (this site is also the disc golf parking lot) and one in the southwestern area of the trail. The trail itself is winding and makes six loops through woods over sandy, gently rolling terrain. The trails are day use only.

Location: Take Highway 53 north from Eau Claire to County Road Q. Go east on Q to County Road L. Turn right and proceed a half mile to the main parking lot.

Contact(s): Eau Claire County Parks and Forestry Department
Agriculture and Resource Center
227 1st Street West
Altoona, WI 54720

Phone: (715) 839-4738.

E-mail: parks-forest@co.eau-claire.wi.us

Web site: http://www.co.eau-claire.wi.us/Parks_Forest/Recreation.htm

Tri-County Recreational Corridor
Ashland, Bayfield, and Douglas Counties

The name of the Tri-County Recreational Corridor speaks for itself. The 62-mile trail traverses three large counties in the uppermost corner of northwestern Wisconsin, between Ashland and Superior. A former railroad grade, the trail runs through the heart of the rugged Chequamegon National Forest, paralleling Highway 2 for most of the way. The Tri-County Recreational Corridor is a multiuse trail for ATV riders, hikers, bikers, and equestrians, so use caution when riding on the trail.

Location: Connects Ashland to Superior, via Ashland, Bayfield, and
Douglas Counties.

Contact(s): Tri-County Corridor Commission
P.O. Box 663
Iron River, WI 54847
Phone: (715) 372-5959.

Bayfield County Tourism and Recreation Department
County Courthouse
Washburn, WI 54891

Phone: (800) 472-6338 or (715) 373-6114; (715) 373-6310 (fax).
E-mail: forestry@bayfieldcounty.org

Ashland Chamber of Commerce
P.O. Box 746
Ashland, WI 54806

Phone: (800) 284-9484

Email: ashchamb@centurytel.net

Website: (For both Ashland and Bayfield counties):
http://www.travelashlandcounty.com/

Keep your eyes up!

Tuscobia State Trail
Barron, Washburn, Sawyer, and Price Counties

Tuscobia State Trail is a former railroad grade trail that runs 74 miles from Rice Lake to Park Falls. The beautiful trail, which is shared use with motorized vehicles, is the longest state trail in Wisconsin. Use caution when traveling with ATVs, especially along corridor trails. Footing may be rough in some places.

Camping and lodging are available nearby. For example, check out the listings for the Farm Bed and Breakfast in the More Stables and Barns section of this chapter and Smith Rapids Campground in the Riding Trails section of the Northeast Wisconsin chapter.

Location: The Tuscobia State Trail is north of Rice Lake on County Road SS. Trail travels through the Flambeau River State Forest and Chequamegon National Forest to Park Falls. There may be occasional detours on the trail.

Contact(s): Tuscobia State Trail
c/o Department of Natural Resources
Highway 27 South
Route 2
P.O. Box 2003
Hayward, WI 54843

Phone: (715) 634-6513 or (800) 269-4505.

E-mail: tourism@co.price.wi.us

Web site: http://www.tuscobiatrail.com

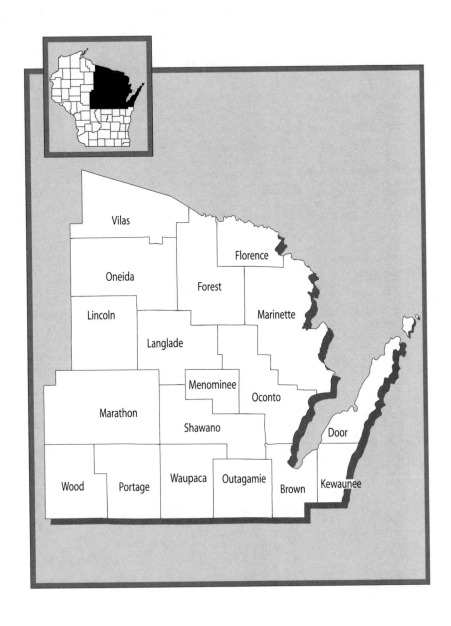

Northeast
Wisconsin

Stables and Barns

Ahnapee Ranch
Brussels

Ahnapee Ranch, formerly located off the Ahnapee Trail, offers beginner lessons, intermediate lessons, and guided trail rides for more experienced riders. Owner Maureen Olsen has a firm belief that people should be started out gently and correctly. Keeping riders safe while they are having fun, she says, is her main objective.

The bulk of Ahnapee's business deals with lessons. It offers the Cowkid's Program for children ages 5–8 (or older if kids are nervous or inexperienced), which teaches kids how to groom, tack up, and handle their horses. Time is spent on the ground before the children mount their horses, and they get a good feeling for what it is like to handle a 1,200-pound animal.

Adults and older kids can sign up for the Wrangler Adventure, which includes ground instruction, riding, and games on horseback (women tend to like the egg-and-spoon game, Olson says, and men prefer cowboys and Indians. When is the last time you got to play these games as an adult?)

For families, Ahnapee offers a Rodeo Ride, which includes barrel racing, roping, and poles. All activities are based on rider experience, and Olsen is careful not to overface anyone. For that reason, she attracts a lot of riders who have been scared or hurt around horses and want to overcome their fears.

Ahnapee offers day camps for children and adults during the summer and over school breaks. The minimum age is 8. The facility offers trail riding and sunset trail riding, with a minimum age of 12. They begin all trail rides with a "getting to know you" warm-up in the arena. Nobody leaves the arena until riders feel comfortable starting, turning, and stopping their horse, and if riders want to trot and canter, they are encouraged to do so.

One of Ahnapee's strengths is its personalized approach to lessons. The staff strives to make its customers better, safer riders, whether they ride recreationally or competitively.

Location: 990 Shoemaker Road, Brussels, WI 54204.

Phone: (920) 825-7804.

Web site: http://www.innline.com/doorweb/property.asp?propertyId= IL5200&areaId=0

Year founded: 1995.

Owner(s): Maureen Olsen.

Hours: 7:00 a.m.–7:00 p.m.

Specialization(s): Recreational riding, western pleasure, English pleasure, barrels and poles, public trail rides.

Facilities: Barn, indoor arena, outdoor arena, indoor and outdoor round pens, heated lounge with full bathroom facilities, outdoor wash rack.

Number of stalls: 20 indoor box stalls, three outdoor loafing barns.

Board: $. Includes full turnout, three feedings a day, personalized care and service.

Lessons: Private, semiprivate. Guided trail rides are taken in groups.

School horses: 12.

Requirements: Helmets required for everyone under 18. Long pants required. Prefers boot with a heel.

Shows/clinics: Hosts natural horsemanship clinics on-site.

Transportation: Can provide transportation to clinics and shows.

Other: Leases and half-leases horses regularly. Horses occasionally for sale.

Bjorkman's Horse Outings
Niagara

Do you know any romantic souls? You know the type. They are the ones who get engaged on sleigh rides and have weddings on stagecoaches. If so, you have probably wondered where these events take place. Weddings and proposals, not to mention family reunions, are commonplace at Dick and Angie Bjorkman's Rocky Top Ranch, home of Bjorkman's Horse Outings in Niagara.

The Bjorkmans have been offering guided trail rides, stagecoach jaunts, and sleigh rides for years. Located just a few miles south of Iron Mountain and Norway, Michigan, Bjorkman's is the place to go for something as familiar as a guided trail ride or as unusual as a covered wagon or sleigh ride. The Bjorkmans plan customers' outings according to their clients' needs. Often, mixed groups will come to Bjorkmans, where some folks like to ride and others do not, so the Bjorkmans will saddle up some trail horses and hitch up the wagon, letting riders ride and nonriders ride along.

Bjorkman's offers catered meals, including pig roasts, and allows groups to enjoy the woods for as little as an hour or as long as a few days. The scenery is beautiful regardless of the season, so this is an ideal place for a reunion, company picnic, or just a good time with friends.

Location: W5994 Chapman Road, Niagara, WI 54151.

Phone: (715) 251-4408 or (888) 467-7367.

E-mail: horsefun@netnet.net

Web site: http://www.horsefun.net

Owner(s): Dick and Angie Bjorkman.

Specialization(s): Guided trail rides, covered wagon and stagecoach rides, sleigh rides ranging from one hour to overnight.

Events: Bjorkman's hosts weddings, family reunions, birthday parties, company picnics, and other kinds of get-togethers. Bjorkman's can arrange catering and entertainment for any occasion.

Other: Bjorkman's uses only its own horses. It is not a boarding facility and does not have overnight stabling.

Kids love riding in the great outdoors.

Dunroven Farm
Rhinelander

Northern Wisconsin may be known as trail-riding heaven, but that is not to say serious dressage riders cannot find a place to hang their hats—or their hard hats.

Dressage trainer Kathy Kopp and her husband own Dunroven Farm, a place they have shared since 1985. They started boarding in 1986, and the rest, as they say, is history. Kopp regularly gives dressage and light-jumping lessons to her barnfull of students. Dunroven hosts two dressage shows a year (both are recognized by the Wisconsin Dressage and Combined Training Association, or WDCTA). Kathy serves on WDCTA's board.

People like Dunroven for its quality instruction, its cleanliness, and its organization. The barn sits on 80 acres with access to miles of trails. This, of course, is part of the beauty of living and riding up north. Open land is not as much an issue as it is in the southern part of the state, and friends and neighbors seem to open their gates and say, "come on through."

In addition to its shows, Dunroven is home to several clinics and WDCTA events. Kathy travels to dressage shows throughout the summer and can trailer students with her for a fee.

Location: 2219 County Road G, Rhinelander, WI 54501.

Phone: (715) 362-5318.

E-mail: sfc@newnorth.net

Year Founded: 1986.

Owner(s): Kathleen and Chuck Kopp.

Hours: 9:00 a.m.–8:00 p.m.

Specialization(s): Dressage, basic jumping.

Facilities: Barn, 70 x 150-foot indoor arena, 60 x 180-foot outdoor arena, matted 12 x 12-foot stalls, heated viewing room, tack room, jump field, trails.

Number of stalls: 25.

Board: $$$. Includes daily turnout, blanketing, two feedings per day, stalls cleaned daily. Dunroven has several large pastures. Horses are turned out during the day in the winter and are turned out in the night during the hottest part of the summer.

Lessons: Private.

School horses: 3.

Requirements: Hard-hat and boots with a heel required.

Shows/clinics: Two WDCTA-recognized dressage shows per year, plus clinics and special events. Kopp also travels to shows.

Transportation: Can transport students to some clinics and shows.

Other: Dressage horses for sale and lease.

Heartland Stables and Show Arena
Custer

Heartland Stables and Show Arena is one of central Wisconsin's largest show facilities. Situated on 40 acres, Heartland has indoor and outdoor arenas, a lot of stabling space, wash racks, and the popular Heartland Café, which serves a full menu of items. Heartland is home to dozens of shows and clinics per year, including dressage shows, barrel racing, foundation Quarter Horse shows, Pony of America (POA) shows, and a winter barrel series. All this is run by Bill and Betty Foss, who have been working around horses for decades, and their daughter Alysa, who rides English and western, and rides in barrel and roping events. The Fosses added an eventing course with 12 jumps in the summer of 2003 and plan to expand that the course in the future.

For those who own horses but do not want to show, Heartland offers an extensive array of lesson and boarding services. The Fosses can teach students everything from dressage to trail riding. The secret to the success of the Foss's operation is their acceptance of all levels of riders, and their steadfastness in hiring the high-quality trainers necessary to teach both the rider and the horse.

The Fosses are involved with youth, and they host several 4-H shows per year. Their facility is clean, safe, and friendly, all must-haves for a successful show facility.

Location: 7510 Deer Road, Custer, WI 54423.

Phone: (715) 592-4171.

Web site: http://www.heartlandstables.com

Year founded: 1996.

Owner(s): Bill and Betty Foss.

Hours: 6:00 a.m.–10:00 p.m. daily.

Specialization(s): Dressage, English pleasure, hunt seat, western pleasure, barrel racing and speed events, basic horsemanship, trail riding.

Facilities: Large facility consists of heated barn, two indoor arenas (80 x 200 feet and 60 x 110 feet), three outdoor show arenas (one with underground sprinklers), individual turnout paddocks, pasture, indoor and outdoor wash racks, two heated tack rooms, trails, cafeteria, campground, trailer parking, and 24-hour security. Heartland Stables is a few miles from the Tomorrow River State Horse Trail and a half-hour drive from Hartman Creek State Park.

Number of stalls: 32 in the main barn and 80 covered, portable stalls in domes (used for shows).

Board: $$$. Includes daily turnout, personalized feeding programs. 10 x 10-foot box stalls with rubber mats and pine sawdust bedding are cleaned daily. Blanketing and unblanketing services can be provided for an additional fee. Heartland has a regular farrier, worming, and vaccination program.

Lessons: Private.

School horses: 5.

Requirements: Protective headgear.

Shows/clinics: Heartland Stables is home to the Heartland Stables Dressage Show, WDHA Dressage show, Heartland Stables Silver Classic, Heartland Winter Barrel Series, Donkey and Mule show, Great Lakes Morab Horse Show, Foundation Quarter Horse Show, and others. The stable also offers a variety of clinics throughout the year.

Transportation: Boarders are responsible for their own transportation to and from shows.

Other: Horses for sale and lease.

Tina Judge of Judgement Farms.

Judgement Farms
Boulder Junction

As one of the few "A" circuit hunter/jumper barns in northern Wisconsin, Judgement Farms is one of the area's top facilities, a reputation that Tina and George Judge, who started Judgement Farms in 1990, strive to maintain.

The barn provides them with a nice respite from their travels around the country to show, train, and look at new horses. In fact, the Judges, who also own Fairlane Farm in Naperville, Illinois, travel the world looking for prospects, both for themselves and for their clients. They always have an excellent selection of sale horses available.

Tina, who calls herself a "typical hunter/jumper," has a clean, top-notch facility. While she accepts all kinds of riders, her facility is set up for the serious show rider. Tina is a Grand Prix-level jumper, and she travels regularly to shows, offering transportation to the students who want to travel with her.

Judgement Farms offers excellent horse care. The horses are treated to 15 quiet acres with a lake on one side. "It's very private out here, very quiet," she says. The stalls are 12 x 12 feet, rubber matted, and extremely clean.

Location: 10550 Campo Fiesta Lane, Boulder Junction, WI 54512.

Phone: (715) 385-9369.

E-mail: judgementfarms@hotmail.com

Year founded: 1990.

Owner(s): George and Tina Judge.

Hours: 9:00 a.m.–6:00 p.m., Tuesday through Sunday; closed Monday.

Specialization(s): Hunter/jumper.

Facilities: Barn, indoor arena, outdoor arena, turnout paddocks, pasture, indoor and outdoor wash racks, and tack room. Judgement Farms is surrounded by state land, which offers unlimited hours of trail riding.

Number of stalls: 24.

Board: $$$. Includes daily turnout and two feedings per day. Stalls are cleaned daily.

Lessons: Private.

School horses: None. Boarders ride their own horses.

Requirements: Proper riding attire, including boot with a heel and helmet.

Shows/clinics: Travels to shows.

Transportation: Can provide transportation to clinics and shows.

Other: Quality horses for sale and lease.

Kurtz Corral
Sturgeon Bay

Over the last 30 years, Kurtz Corral has billed itself as Door County's premier stable. Open year-round, the facility offers trail rides for people from a wide range of age groups.

With 15 miles of trails spread over 500 acres (which have been in the Kurtz family since 1871), the Kurtz Corral offers excellent opportunities for everyone in the family, especially the young ones. Kids can start out in the arena and ride a horse without ever having to leave the barn. More-adventurous adults can venture out on walk/trot trail rides, and experienced riders (more than 40 hours in the saddle) can enjoy the "end of day journey," which offers a walk, trot, and canter ride through wooded farmlands and a stop at Simon Creek Winery. Riders 14 years and older can join an understudy ride, where riders can learn from and assist the trail guide—an excellent way for anyone to learn the ropes.

But Kurtz Corral is not just a trail-riding facility. It also hosts birthday parties, weddings, company picnics, and other special events. In addition, the facility offers western pleasure lessons (sold in packets of 10–15), which include grooming, saddling, and basic horsemanship, in addition to riding.

Location: 5712 Howard Lane, Sturgeon Bay, WI 54325.

Phone: (800) 444-0469 or (920) 743-6742.

E-mail: riding@kurtzcorral.com

Web site: http://www.kurtzcorral.com

Year founded: 1958.

Owner(s): Jim Kurtz and Paul Connor.

Hours: 9:00 a.m.–3:00 p.m., Memorial Day to Labor Day (roughly); call for winter hours.

Specialization(s): Guided trail rides for all levels of riders, lesson programs (western pleasure), birthday parties, New Years' Eve celebrations, corporate outings, and weddings.

Facilities: Barn, outdoor arena, turnout paddocks, pasture, clubhouse, viewing area, tack room, cross-country course.

Board: n/a.

Lessons: Offers lessons privately and in groups. Lessons can be tailored to beginning, intermediate, or advanced riders. All lessons are one hour long, and they are by reservation only. Kurtz Corral uses its own horses for all lessons.

School horses: 20.

Requirements: Boots with a heel, helmet (provided).

Shows/clinics: n/a.

Thornberry Stables
Oneida

 Thornberry Stables is proof that good things come in small packages. Situated on seven acres just outside Green Bay, Thornberry is a small facility that caters to hunter/jumper riders and their horses in a clean, homey environment. Indeed, most of co-owner Cheryl LaPlante's clients enjoy the oasis. "It's a really friendly atmosphere," she says. "We're small, and it's a quiet wooded area. There are ponds out back and you see ducks and deer all the time."

 The indoor facility at Thornberry is big enough to offer a variety of needs. There are two outdoor arenas, one with lights, both with plenty of room to ride. A short trail on the site will be of interest to those who want to get out of the ring. There is a heated lounge (the whole barn is heated to 45 degrees in the winter) with a TV and VCR for kids who come to the barn with their parents, and a washer and dryer, so you can clean your saddle pads on-site.

 Thornberry currently employs two trainers, one from the Brazilian Olympic team. They can handle everyone from beginning to advanced riders, and their six school horses are qualified to show beginning and intermediate riders the ropes. Although they have mainly hunter/jumpers, LaPlante says they welcome all styles of riding.

203

The well-maintained grounds at Thornberry Stables.

Location: 820 Brookwood West, Oneida, WI 54155.

Phone: (920) 497-0925.

E-mail: owners@thornberrystables.com

Web site: http://www.thornberrystables.com

Year founded: 2000.

Owner(s): Cheryl and Maurice LaPlante.

Hours: 9:00 a.m.–9:00 p.m. daily.

Specialization(s): Hunter/jumper, English pleasure for beginning to advanced riders.

Facilities: Heated barn, indoor arena with viewing area, tack room with individual tack lockers, wash rack with warm/cold water, outdoor arena.

Number of stalls: 25.

Board: $$. Includes turnout, three feedings per day, stalls cleaned daily.

School horses: 6.

Lessons: Private, semiprivate, group, adult.

Requirements: Helmet required, boot with a heel recommended.

Shows/clinics: None on-site.

Transportation: Can transport students to clinics and shows.

Other: Horses for sale and lease.

Wisconsin Equestrian Center
De Pere

The Wisconsin Equestrian Center (WEC) is one of the premier riding and showing facilities in eastern Wisconsin. Home to dressage enthusiasts who show to the FEI level, WEC is a place for dedicated horse people to further their education and showing abilities. True to its origins, WEC also caters to "a lot of women who have wanted to ride all their lives," says co-owner Bobbie Wier, who strives to make everyone feel welcome. While some are intimidated at first sight of the well-manicured facility, they feel right at home once they walk in and start talking to people.

WEC features more than 100 acres, an indoor riding arena, four outdoor rings, 10 paddocks for individual turnout, a hunt field with cross-country jumps, and trails. The board is extremely reasonable, given the amenities.

WEC hosts a handful of shows each year, including two USDF-recognized dressage shows and a WHJA hunter/jumper show. The facility also hosts Pony Club and associated rallies. While the dressage and hunter/jumper shows are rated, there are classes for beginners who want a show experience without all the pressure, an indication of WEC's commitment to providing opportunities for riders at all levels.

Beyond treating boarders' well, WEC is renowned for pampering horses. Mares and geldings are separated into all-day pastures, or horses can be turned out in a private or semiprivate paddock for part of each day. Feeding programs are personalized as needed, and the care is first rate.

Location: 2486 Old Martin Road, De Pere, WI 54115.

Phone: (920) 336-8005.

E-mail: wiwec@aol.com

Year founded: 1986.

Owner(s): Bobbie and Mike Wier.

Hours: 7:00 a.m.–9:00 p.m. daily.

Specialization(s): Dressage, hunt seat, jumping, English pleasure.

Facilities: Heated barn with excellent ventilation, 225 x 80-foot indoor arena, observation/viewing area, two indoor hot/cold wash stalls, four tack rooms, four outdoor arenas, individual turnout paddocks, pasture, hunt course, cross-country course, trails. The indoor and three of the outdoor arenas have Permaflex footing.

Number of stalls: 41.

Board: $$$. Stall sizes and turnout options are personalized to each horse and rider.

Lessons: Private, semiprivate, adult. No minimum age.

School horses: 3 all-purpose horses.

Requirements: Boots with a heel. Protective headgear recommended. Helmets required for those under 18 years of age.

Shows/clinics: WEC hosts USDF-recognized dressage shows, one hunter/jumper "B" show, and Pony Club rallies each year. Clinics are held at the center throughout the year.

Transportation: n/a, although students with trailers help each other get to clinics and shows.

Other: Quality horses occasionally for sale or lease.

More Stables and Barns

Blue Haven Stables

4853 West Business Highway
Merrill, WI 54452
(715) 536-4210
Specialization(s): English and western pleasure for kids and adults. Owners have run a successful business for nearly 20 years. Recently had 10 blind students out for trail rides. Versatile horses and staff.

Blue Meadow Stables

4760 Townline Road
Green Bay, WI 54311
(920) 863-6660
Specialization(s): English pleasure, western pleasure, most disciplines.

Campbell's Training Center

810 Highway 8 East
Monico, WI 54501
(715) 487-5542
Specialization(s): western pleasure, English pleasure, hunt seat, jumping, barrel racing and most speed events.

Cedar Springs Stables

N1975 Municipal Drive
Greenville, WI 54942
(920) 757-5371
Specialization(s): Western, open year-round.

Copperview Farm

N5274 County Road O
Manawa, WI 54949
(920) 538-1761
E-mail: copperviewfarm@hotmail.com
Web site: http://www.copperviewfarm.org
Specialization(s): halter, western pleasure, hunt seat.

Desperado Ranch

13419 Highway 32/64
Mountain, WI 54149
(715) 276-1764
Specialization(s): beginner western, basic horsemanship, English pleasure, saddle seat, hunt seat.

Green Acres Stable

1378 Lime Kiln Road
Green Bay, WI 54311

(920) 468-8114
E-mail: rfnrfn@aol.com
Specialization(s): English pleasure, western pleasure, jumping, dressage, guided trail rides; will trailer riders to state parks.

Greenview Valley Farm
5847 Old Highway 8 Road
Crandon, WI 54520
(715) 478-5380
E-mail: greenviewvalleyfarm@yahoo.com
Specialization(s): English pleasure, hunt seat, dressage, and western pleasure for children and adults. Owners can provide transportation to shows and events.

Holiday Acres Riding Academy
Highway 51 South
Minocqua, WI 54548
(715) 356-4400
Specialization(s): Guided trail rides from May through mid-October.

Holiday Stables
Old Farm Road
Rhinelander, WI 54501
(715) 362-1881
Specialization(s): Guided trail rides. Open Memorial Day through Labor Day.

Lakedrive Stables
W5684 Lake Drive
Shawano, WI 54166
(715) 524-2829
E-mail: tmrogo@charter.net
Specialization(s): English pleasure, western pleasure, basic dressage, beginning jumping for children and adults. Open year-round.

Mountain Meadows Ranch
13807 Whiffen Lane
Mountain, WI 54149
(715) 276-3860
Specialization(s): English pleasure, western pleasure, guided trail rides in the Nicolet National Forest. Open May through October.

New Heights Hunter and Jumper
1481 Liberty Street
Green Bay, WI 54304
(920) 490-9519
Specialization(s): Hunter/jumper.

Open Heart Ranch
6847 Pleasant Drive
Almond, WI 54909
(715) 824-2319
Specialization(s): Resistance-free riding. Trainer Becky Bauknecht will travel to a customer's facility to give lessons or clinics in natural horsemanship. She is especially effective with those who have fear issues. Call for an appointment.

Palo Verde Training Stable
4121 Washington Street
Wisconsin Rapids, WI 54494
(715) 424-4060
E-mail: palovrde@wctc.net
Specialization(s): reining, western pleasure, English pleasure on your horse.

Paradise Acres
2604 River Drive
Aurora, WI 54151
(715) 589-4252
E-mail: Weber589@hotmail.com
Specialization(s): hunter/jumper, hunt seat equitation in spring, summer, and fall; schooling horses available.

Pratt Riding Academy
8434 Central Sands Road
Bancroft, WI 54921
(715) 335-4130
E-mail: prattfarm@hotmail.com or paula@prattfarm.com
Web site: http://www.prattfarm.com
Specialization(s): dressage, hunter/jumper, English pleasure, western pleasure for kids and adults; hosts shows at its facility.

Red River Riders
Therapeutic Horseback Riding for the Disabled, Inc.
N6669 Cherry Road
Shawano, WI 54116
(715) 526-6400 (barn); (715) 524-2228 (fax)
E-mail: Info@redriverriders.com
Web site: http://www.redriverriders.com
Specialization(s): Offers therapeutic riding lessons for the disabled in the summer and fall. Organization is currently raising funds for an indoor arena, so that they can offer lessons year-round. The therapeutic instructor has been certified by North American Riding for the Handicapped (NARHA) and is a member of the Certified Horsemanship Association. Red River Riders also offers lessons to able-bodied children in English pleasure, western pleasure, dressage, and saddle seat.

Seeing the sights along one of Kewaunee County's recreational trails.

Rentmeester's Ranch
909 South Grandview Road
Green Bay, WI 54311
(920) 465-9561
E-mail: Ann@rentmeestersranch.com
Web site: http://www.rentmeestersranch.com
Specialization(s): western pleasure, English Pleasure, hunt seat, trails;
owner travels to local shows.

Rocking W Stables
Pleasure Island Road
Eagle River, WI 54521
(715) 617-6779
Specialization(s): guided trail rides from Memorial Day to Labor Day;
wagon and sleigh rides by appointment.

Rocky Valley Stable
W6183 Rock Road
Hortonville, WI 54944
(920) 733-9026
E-mail: keddells@aol.com
Specialization(s): dressage, English pleasure, western pleasure, hunt seat;
has a 24-stall barn with a full-sized indoor arena.

RR'S Southern Comfort Stables
199 Cherneyville Road
Luxemburg, WI 54217
(920) 845-5103
Specialization(s): saddle seat, hunt seat, and western pleasure.
Teaches trail riding safety on 50 acres of trails. Open year-round.
Facility also offers summer day camp for children from
May through August.

Sandy Creek Stables
W180 Highway 96
Kaukauna, WI 54130
(920) 532-6187
Specialization(s): English pleasure, western pleasure.

SMJ Arabians, Inc.
650 Macco Road
Luxemburg, WI 54217
(920) 866-2685
Specialization(s): boarding and training facility for Arabians
and half-Arabians. Lessons in dressage, western pleasure,
saddle seat, and hunt seat.

Sunny Meadows Farm, Inc.
M426 County Road East
Marshfield, WI 54449
(715) 387-0565
Specialization(s): dressage, English pleasure, western pleasure.

Triangle B Stables
5630 Old 29 Drive
Green Bay, WI 54313
(920) 865-7849
E-mail: mrgburk@aol.com
Specialization(s): hunter/jumper, saddle seat, western pleasure.
Facility is 15 minutes from the Brown County Reforestation
Camp, which offers 7 miles of horseback-riding trails. Facility
hosts open horse shows in the summertime.

Wild West Kampground and Korral
9495 Highway 54
Amherst, WI 54406
(715) 824-5112
E-mail: Lynvo2@bellsouth.net
Specialization(s): western pleasure, five miles of trails,
camping (water and electric available).

Riding Trails

Ahnapee State Trail
Kewaunee and Door Counties

Door County is a beautiful place, and some say it is even more beautiful when viewed from the back of a horse. Enter the Ahnapee State Trail, which covers nearly 30 miles between Casco Junction in Kewaunee County and Sturgeon Bay in Door County.

Part of the Ice Age Trail (see www.iceagetrail.org), the multi-use Ahnapee follows an abandoned railroad right-of-way. The trail was whipped into shape by Rails to Trails, which then turned it over to the Friends of the Ahnapee, a nonprofit organization that has done a wonderful job of trail development and maintenance.

The Friends of the Ahnapee have worked with Kewaunee and Door counties and the Wisconsin Department of Natural Resources to keep the Ahnapee rider-friendly and available for a variety of needs. The trail is 8 to 10 feet wide along its entire length and can accommodate wagons, carriages, and carts. It is used by hikers, horseback riders, bicyclists, and horse-drawn vehicles. Motorized vehicles are not allowed. Trail users peacefully coexist because respect is maintained by and for all groups—something the grassroots founders couldn't be happier about.

Each year since 2000, the group has hosted an Ahnapee Family Trail Day, which supports development and maintenance of the Ahnapee State Trail. The organizers offer free wagon and pony rides, among dozens of other events.

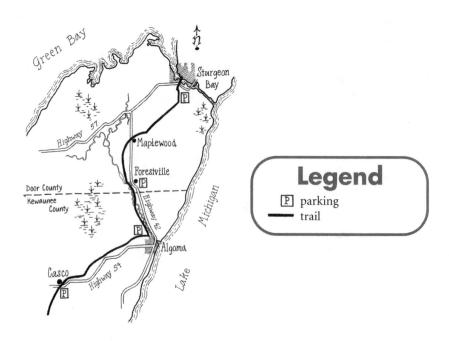

Legend

P   parking
—   trail

Location: Between Casco Junction and Sturgeon Bay. Parking is available in Algoma, Forestville, and south of Sturgeon Bay.

Contact(s): Kewaunee County Promotion and Recreation Department
613 Dodge Street
Kewaunee, WI 54216

Phone: (920) 388-0444.

E-mail: KewauneeCounty@hotmail.com

Web site: http://www.ahnapeetrail.org

Trails: Views range from the rocky shoreline of Lake Michigan to pasture and the Ahnapee River. Wildlife is abundant but not intrusive.

Shared use: Shared with hikers, bikers, and carriage drivers.

Horse rentals: n/a.

Camping: Day use only.

Reservations: n/a.

Dates of use: Currently open year-round, although this may change to spring, summer, and fall. The trail requires extensive maintenance when riders use it during the thaw, so please ride responsibly.

Passes: n/a. Donations are accepted.

Other: The Friends of the Ahnapee State Trail have established the following right-of-way guidelines: "Wagon, buggy, and cart drivers are asked to yield to horseback riders, who are asked to yield to bikers, who are asked to yield to walkers and runners."

Bailey Lake Equestrian Trail
Forest County

Bailey Lake Equestrian Trail stretches 15 miles in the Chequamegon-Nicolet National Forest. Located near Eagle River, the trail meanders over abandoned logging roads and a former railroad corridor.

The equestrian trail was developed in the 1970s. Trails were reworked in the early 1990s, including the installation of a bridge across Four-Mile Creek. Riders share a road with motor vehicles along some sections in the western part of the loop; caution is urged on that part of the trail. The terrain is relatively flat and easy. Wildlife abounds, so bring your camera and your friends.

Location: From the town of Three Lakes, take State Highway 32 east for 4 miles to Military Road. Turn left and go north 2 miles to Sheltered Valley Road. Turn right and go east 2 miles to the parking area, which has room for about a dozen trucks with trailers.

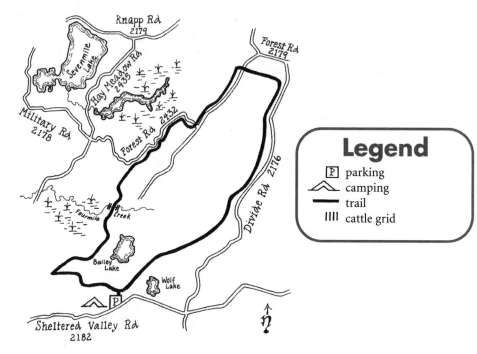

Contact(s): Nicolet National Forest
Eagle River Ranger Station
4364 Wall Street
Eagle River, WI 54521

Phone: (715) 479-2827.

E-mail: pswanson@fs.fed.us

Web site: http://www.fs.fed.us/r9/cnnf/rec/trailsntours/nic_11.html

Trails: The terrain is generally flat, with some rolling hills. The trail runs
through scenic forestland, and the route is especially beautiful in the
summer and fall. Trail ratings are "easy." This is a good trail for beginners and green horses.

Shared use: Shared with hikers.

Horse rentals: n/a.

Camping: Camping is available at the parking area and at campgrounds
throughout the forest. The parking area campground has no water or
toilets. "If you pack it in, pack it out."

Dates of use: The trail is open until it snows. Snowmobilers use the trail in
the winter.

Passes: n/a.

Evergreen Horseback Riding Trails
Langlade County

The 10.5-mile loop of the Evergreen Horseback Riding Trails circles amidst 126,000 acres of the Langlade County Forest in northeastern Wisconsin, just 8 miles east of Antigo. The land in this part of the state is beautiful, with hills (some are steep), valleys, and huge stands of hardwoods. The forest is managed for timber, recreation, and wildlife, so it is possible that loggers will be present when riders are on the trail. The horse trails themselves are on county lands and private property.

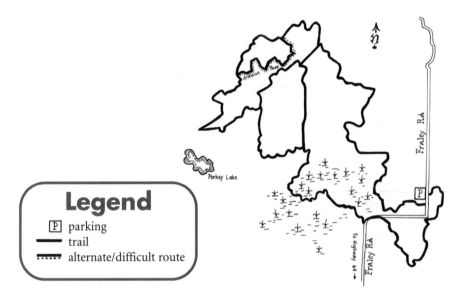

Legend

P parking
— trail
····· alternate/difficult route

Location: Between Langlade and Antigo. Take State Highway 64 to Fraley Road; turn north and follow it as it jogs east, then north once again. The trailhead is just west of Fraley Road.

Contact(s): Langlade County Forestry and Recreation Department
1633 Neva Road
Antigo, WI 54409

Phone: (715) 627-6300.

Web site: http://www.co.langlade.wi.us/forestandparksinformation.htm

Trails: The trail is very scenic, with hardwoods, steep hills, and valleys. There is an optional, difficult passage at the northwestern corner of the loop that runs for less than a mile, but you can ride north of that area for an easier ride.

Shared use: During spring, summer, and fall, hikers and bicyclists share the trail. Riding is not allowed during winter, when dogsledders use the trail.

Camping: Day use only.

Reservations: n/a.

Dates of use: Trails can only be used when they are free of snow.

Passes: Passes are not necessary, but donations are appreciated. The trails are funded in part by a local horse club and the Langlade County Forestry Department in Antigo.

Fox River Trail
Brown County

The 7.7-mile equestrian portion of the Fox River Trail runs from Heritage Road in De Pere to the trail's end in Greenleaf. This former railroad corridor was recently turned into a trail, and it is used by hikers, bikers, and horseback riders. The equestrian portion is cut along the main trail and runs largely through rural areas. The trail is relatively flat and very scenic, especially in the fall. Dogs are allowed on the trail, but must be kept on a five-foot leash. Maintenance crews ask that you tread lightly or choose not to ride when conditions are wet, as the trail can become quite soft.

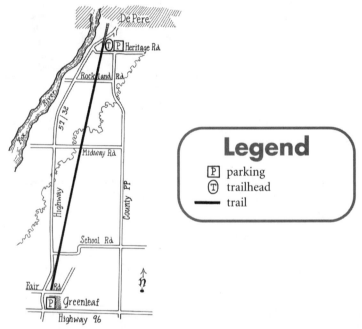

Location: The trailhead for equestrians is on Heritage Road approximately 1-1/2 miles south of De Pere. Trailer parking is limited. There is also parking at Fireman's Park in Greenleaf.

Contact(s): Brown County Park Office
305 East Walnut Street, Third Floor
Green Bay, WI 54301

Phone: (920) 448-4466; (920) 448-4290 (fax).

Web sites: http://www.co.brown.wi.us/parks/parks/fox-rivertrail/index.shtml or http://www.foxrivertrail.org

Trails: The 7.7 miles of the equestrian trail follow the Fox River Valley Corridor from just south of De Pere to Greenleaf. The bridle trail, designated for equestrian use only, is set off to the side of the main trail. The trail is open from sunrise to sunset.

Shared use: A trail that runs parallel to the equestrian trails is used by hikers and bikers.

Camping: Day use only.

Reservations: n/a.

Dates of use: Open year-round, but the trail is not plowed in the winter.

Passes: An annual state trail pass or a daily pass is required for horseback riders over 16 years old.

Hoofing it at Hartman Creek State Park.

Hartman Creek State Park
Waupaca County

Sitting on nearly 1,500 acres, Hartman Creek State Park offers a variety of equestrian trails. Located just five miles west of Waupaca, Hartman Creek is a quiet park, with four lakes (no motorized watercraft allowed) and seven miles of equestrian trails. The equestrian trails are new and are still fairly quiet, making for a peaceful ride. Not surprisingly, they are quickly being discovered by riders in the Fox River Valley area.

Like many horse trails throughout the state, one horse club has played an important role in the development of Hartman Creek. The Rodeo City Riders, who were responsible for the construction of the equestrian trails and who help maintain them, host up to three trail rides per year. The club recently established a rest stop

217

near the dam, complete with a picnic table and hitching post. For more information on the Rodeo City Riders, visit http://www.geocities.com/rodeocityriders.

The trails at Hartman Creek run through gently rolling prairie lands, pine plantations, and hardwood forests. All trails are shared with hikers.

Parking for horse trailers is on the south side of East Windfeldt Lane at the trailhead. Trailering in and out is easy, and the parking lot, which was designed for riders, is scheduled to double in size in the near future.

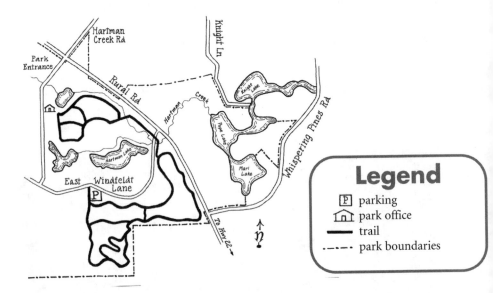

Location: The state park is on Hartman Creek Road, south of Highway 54 and north of Wisconsin Highway 22, five miles west of Waupaca.

Contact(s): Hartman Creek State Park
N2840 Hartman Creek Road
Waupaca, WI 54981-9727

Phone: (715) 258-2372; (715) 258-9613 (fax).

E-mail: Brian.Hefty@dnr.state.wi.us

Web site: http://www.dnr.state.wi.us/org/land/parks/specific/hartman

Trails: Seven miles of new trails over slightly rolling terrain. Trails are sandy and travel through fields and pine forests. There are bathrooms and fresh water at the equestrian parking area.

Shared use: Trails are shared with hikers.

Horse rentals: n/a.

Camping: Day use only.

Reservations: n/a.

Dates of use: Open year-round, weather permitting (trails are usually closed during the spring thaw, so call ahead).

Passes: State park vehicle pass necessary to enter the park. All riders 16 and over must also have a trail pass.

Mountain-Bay State Trail
Shawano County

The entire Mountain-Bay State Trail runs 83 miles, and horses are allowed on more than 50 miles of the trail across Shawano County from Eland to Pulaski. Along the way, riders can enjoy varied scenery, including marshes, woodlands, and farms, all populated by an abundance of songbirds. The trail is also dotted by several small communities and, about midway, the larger town of Shawano.

The Mountain-Bay State Trail is on a former Chicago & North Western Railroad right-of-way. The trail has a smooth limestone surface that is wide enough for carriages, but is also open to ATVs, so caution is urged. Bicyclists and hikers also use the trail.

The trail travels past fields, woods, and Shawano Lake. Parking is available at four spots along the way. Trail passes are required for bicyclists but not for equestrians.

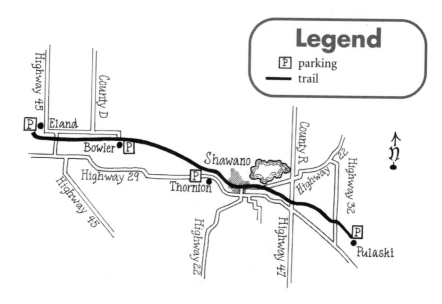

Location: Spans the entire width of Shawano County and, on the way, passes through the town of Shawano. Parking for the trail can be found in Eland, Bowler, Gresham, and Pulaski.

Contact(s): Shawano County Park Department
311 North Main Street
Shawano, WI 54166

Phone: (715) 524-4349.

Web site: http://www.mountain-baytrail.org

Trails: Smooth limestone that runs 51 miles along former railroad corridor. Scenes include wetlands, pastures, and woods. Starting in Pulaski, the trail runs past Zachow, Bonduel, Shawano Lake, Thornton, Lyndhurst, and Bowler, before ending in Eland.

Shared use: Shared with ATVs, hikers, and bicyclists.

Camping: Day use only.

Reservations: n/a.

Dates of use: Spring, summer and fall. Call for exact dates.

Passes: n/a. Passes only required of bicyclists.

Northern Highland–American Legion State Forest
Oneida and Vilas Counties

The Northern Highland–American Legion State Forest encompasses 225,000 acres, much of which is available for horseback riding, in parts of Vilas, Oneida, and Iron Counties. The forest does not have a marked horseback riding trail, but riders can go anywhere they like, with the exception of designated hiking, biking, ski, or nature trails. Campgrounds and the beach are also off-limits.

The basic trail stretches for about 20 miles between Boulder Junction and Lake Tomahawk, but in between, hundreds of miles of eminently rideable old logging roads and forest roads stretch out in all directions. Lakes of all shapes and sizes dot the forest.

The American Legion State Forest is the largest of Wisconsin's state forests. Riding here is beautiful—the forest offers an abundance of woods and water. It can get buggy in the summer, especially June, so be sure to bring your bug spray.

The area is teeming with wildlife, including endangered species like the wood turtle, Cooper's hawk, and bald eagle. The area sees more than two million visitors per year, but the forest is so large that you can ride along for hours in solitude. Because there are no marked trails, it is best to ride with a buddy.

Location: Between Lake Tomahawk at the southern end of the forest and Boulder Junction at the northern boundary. Trailheads can be found in Boulder Junction, Sayner, and Lake Tomahawk.

Contact(s): American Legion State Forest Superintendent
Wisconsin Department of Natural Resources
8770 County Road J
Woodruff, WI 54568

Phone: (715) 358-2400.

E-mail: dennis.leith@dnr.state.wi.us

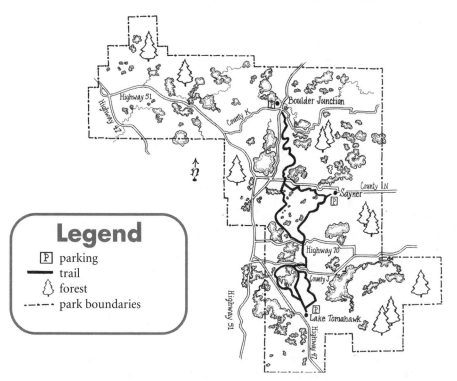

Legend

☐ parking
— trail
🌲 forest
·—·—· park boundaries

Web site: http://www.dnr.state.wi.us/master_planning/nhal/index.htm

Trails: Hundreds of miles of old logging roads. Wooded with lakes.

Shared use: Shared with snowmobiles in the winter.

Horse rentals: n/a.

Camping: Day use only.

Reservations: n/a.

Dates of use: Spring, summer, fall and winter. In winter trails are used for snowmobiling.

Passes: Vehicle sticker is required to enter the forest.

Oconto County Machickanee Forest
Oconto County

The equestrian trails in the Oconto County Machickanee Forest were largely established by the Outback Riders, a local riding club, and the Oconto County Forestry division.

With approximately 13 miles of trails, the Machickanee Forest offers riders relatively flat logging roads and other roads that are closed to vehicular traffic. Riders are likely to encounter deer, coyotes, rabbits, and fox on their rides.

Horses must stay on the designated trails at Machickanee, but the equestrian trails are well-marked and easy to follow. Parking is available near the northern portion of the forest and is easily accessible. There is no electricity or water, but there are bathrooms east of the parking area off Timberline Road.

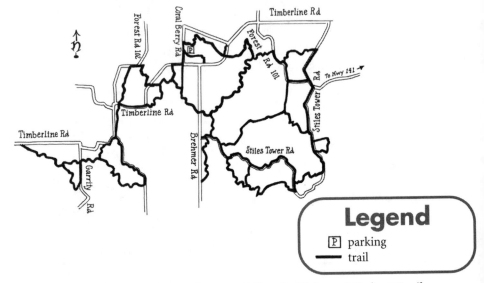

Legend

P parking

—— trail

Location: Four miles east of Oconto Falls, take Highway 141 about 2 miles south to Timberline Road. Go west for 3 miles to Brehmer Road, then south for 1 mile.

Contact(s): Oconto County Forest and Park Administrator
301 Washington Street
Oconto, WI 54153 or
The Outback Riders

Phone: (920) 834-6995 (Oconto County);
(920) 834-6805 (fax)
(920) 434-1911(Outback Riders)

E-mail: robert.skalitzky@co.oconto.wi.us

Web site: http://www.ocontocounty.net

Trails: Approximately 13 miles of trails along roads and logging roads that are closed to motor vehicles. Terrain is relatively flat. Wildlife is abundant.

Shared use: Shared with hikers and bicyclists.

Horse rentals: n/a.

Camping: There are a few primitive campsites, but no running water or electricity.

Reservations: Contact the Oconto County Forestry Department at (920) 834-6995.

Dates of use: The trail is open from April 15 to November 10.

Passes: n/a.

Showing riders the way around Otter Springs Trail. Photo courtesy of Ken Carpenter.

Otter Springs Trail
Forest County

The Otter Springs Trail is best known as a winter cross-country ski trail, but in the summer, it is home to hikers, hunters, equestrians, and mountain bike riders. Popular because of its length (the trail totals eight miles, making for a nice two-hour ride), the area offers beautiful scenery and access to wildlife.

The Otter Springs Trail is relatively flat with a few small hills. The trail leads through hardwood forests past Otter Springs and Bug Lake. On a good day, riders might see deer, grouse, and turkey. There are bobcats and coyote in the area, but their nocturnal habits make sightings by humans unlikely.

The Otter Springs Trail is well-maintained by the Forest County Forestry Department, and signage is ample. There is no fee for riding the trail, so pack up your food and water (horses can drink from the streams), head out, and enjoy the day.

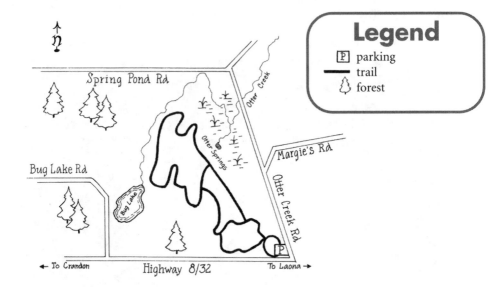

Location: Four miles east of Crandon off Highway 8, or 6 miles east of Laona on Forest Road 2378.

Contact(s): Forest County Forestry Department
Courthouse
Crandon, WI 54520

Phone: (715) 478-3475.

E-mail: information@forestcountywi.com

Web site: http://www.forestcountywi.com

Trails: Eight miles of hiking and cross-country ski trails that are shared with equestrians in the spring, summer, and fall. Trails range from flat to rolling and winding. There is a shelter between the two intermediate trails. Otter Springs Trail runs through a vast hardwood forest with views of Otter Springs and Bug Lake, and the route is very scenic.

Shared use: Trails are shared with hikers and cross-country skiers. Motorized vehicles are not permitted on the trails.

Horse rentals: n/a.

Camping: Day use only.

Reservations: n/a.

Dates of use: Spring, summer, and fall. Call for exact dates.

Passes: n/a.

Other: A map, available from the Forestry Department, indicates that trails are open to hikers, mountain bikers, picnickers, hunters, and cross-country skiers, but does not list horseback riders. Equestrians were accidentally omitted from this list. Riding is permitted on the entire eight miles of trail.

Popple Ridge Horse Trail
Oconto County

The Popple Ridge Horse Trail, which has been growing in popularity, sits in the Lakewood/Laona district of the Chequamegon-Nicolet National Forest. The equestrian trail runs 24 miles through hilly, wooded areas, passing Rose Lake and weaving among several other lakes. Some areas of the trail are hilly, some with steep sections. The trail circles through several loops, and the horse camp is located in the west central portion of the trail. Additional logging roads are available for equestrian use in the immediate area.

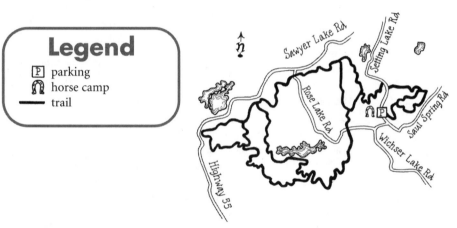

Location: From the town of Mountain, take Highway 64 west. Drive 5 to 6 miles to County Road T. Go north to Saul Springs Road. The road will turn into gravel, and you will have to turn left (west). Follow the dirt road to the first stop sign and turn right. Travel half a mile until you see signs for the horse camp on Setting Lake Road.

Contact(s): USDA Forest Service.
Lakewood Ranger Station
15085 State Highway 32
Lakewood, WI 54138

Phone: (715) 276-6333; (715) 276-3594 (fax).

Trails: Twenty-four miles of trail with some challenging areas. Bring bug spray in the summer.

Shared use: Trails are shared with hikers and bikers. ATVs are not allowed on the Nicolet portion of the trail in the Chequamegon-Nicolet National Forest.

Horse rentals: There are several places nearby that rent horses. Check yellow pages. Many have their own trail systems.

Camping: Camping is allowed anywhere along the trail. The Popple Ridge Horse Camp is popular and has plenty of room for parking. Pack it in, pack it out. Water and bathroom facilities are not available.

Reservations: n/a.

Dates of use: Trails open spring, summer, and fall. Skiers use the Jones Spring area during winter.

Passes: Vehicle pass required.

Reforestation Camp
Brown County

The Reforestation Camp north of Green Bay in Brown County offers eight miles of equestrian trails that run along the eastern, northern, and western boundaries of the 1,600-acre natural area.

The Reforestation Camp, which is home to the Northeastern Wisconsin (NEW) Zoo, has mostly flat terrain, with soft, sandy trails. There is a nice loop at the beginning of the trail and a larger loop at the end. The trail forms a peninsula around the NEW Zoo, which is open March through December.

There is a large "pull-in, pull-out" parking lot at the trailhead on Sunrise Road. Riders are encouraged to park their rigs on either side of the lot and exit through the middle. The Forest Department asks that you remove all manure from the parking lot.

The Northeastern Wisconsin Zoo occasionally hosts horse-drawn carriage rides along candlelit trails at night, which are open to the public; the proceeds benefit the zoo. The trails are open to individual riders from 8:00 a.m. to sunset each day. Walking, trotting, and cantering are permitted on the trails, but the management does not permit racing. Keep it under control, and enjoy your day on the trails.

Location: 4418 Reforestation Road. Take Highway 41/141 north from Green Bay to County Road B at Suamico. Turn left on B and go about 4 miles to County Road IR (Reforestation Road). Turn right and proceed straight ahead to the Reforestation Camp (and Northeastern Wisconsin Zoo). Trailer parking is available on Sunrise Road.

Contact(s): Brown County Park Office
305 East Walnut Street, Third Floor
Green Bay, WI 54301

Phone: (920) 448-4466; (920) 448-4290 (fax).

E-mail: Nthals_KM@co.brown.wi.us

Web site: http://www.co.brown.wi.us/parks/rates/index.shtml

Trails: Eight miles of trails, which run around the perimeter of the 1,600-acre Reforestation Camp. Trails are marked and vary in width from 5 to 25

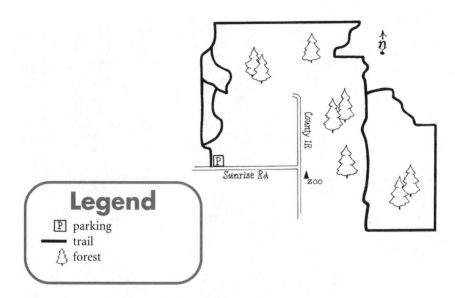

Legend

P parking
— trail
🌲 forest

feet. There is a small loop at the beginning of the trail and a large loop at the end. Trails are open 8:00 a.m. to sunset. The parking lot is off Sunrise Road, and has drive-through parking. Riders should park their rigs on either side and exit down the middle.

Shared use: Short sections of the trail are shared with mountain bikers.

Horse rentals: n/a.

Camping: Day use only.

Reservations: n/a.

Dates of use: Trails open mid-May through early November, depending on weather. Call for specific dates.

Passes: Trail passes are required for all riders 16 and older. Trail passes must be worn on the outside of your clothing or on your horse's tack.

Tomorrow River State Trail
Portage County

The Tomorrow River State Trail runs east-west for nine miles between Plover (located just south of Stevens Point) and Amherst Junction. Opened in the spring of 2001, the Tomorrow River State Trail is regularly traveled and well-liked. The six-foot-wide mowed horse trail runs alongside the limestone trail, which is used by hikers, bikers, and hunters. The trail undulates between ravines and ridge tops. The parks department has leveled off the trail so riders are not riding on side hills.

There are plans to open an additional eight miles of trail, four in Portage County and four in neighboring Waupaca County. Note that when this guide was being compiled, there was no bridge over Highway 10, but one was in the works.

Along the Tomorrow River State Trail.

Location: Between Plover, just south of Stevens Point, and Amherst Junction. There are several parking lots, including those on the east side of Plover, off Twin Towers Drive, and off County Road B. There is another lot, which accommodates horse trailers, at Lake Emily Park in Amherst Junction.

Contact(s): Gary Speckmann
1462 Strongs Avenue
Stevens Point, WI 54481

Phone: (715) 346-1433; (715) 343-6226 (fax).

E-mail: parks@co.portage.wi.us

Web site: For trail map: www.co.portage.wi.us/Parks%20Department/tomorrow.htm

Trails: Nine miles accessible to horses. Eight miles will be added on the other side of Highway 10 in the near future. Trail is on grass, cut six feet wide. Trails are open 6:00 a.m.–11:00 p.m. daily. Trails are closed during the nine-day deer gun season.

Shared use: Hikers and bikers use the adjacent limestone path. No motorized vehicles are allowed on the trail.

Horse rentals: n/a.

Camping: Day use only.

Reservations: n/a.

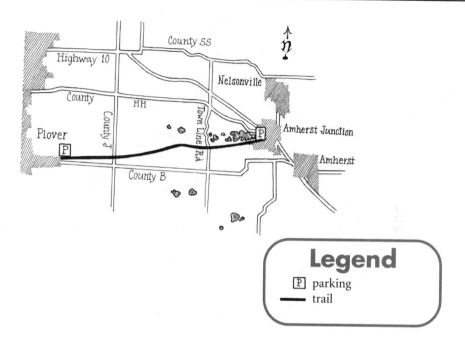

Legend

P parking

— trail

Dates of use: Open year-round. Limestone trails are used by snowmobiles in the winter. Riders generally stay off the trails during that time.

Passes: State trail pass required for anyone over 16 years of age. Self-registration boxes are available at the trailhead.

Underdown Recreation Area
Lincoln County

Underdown is one of the more popular horse areas in the state and is home to the Underdown Horse Club, which hosts fund raisers and competitive rides on a regular basis. The club is solely responsible for maintenance of the horse trails in the recreation area. The club also organizes relaxing and fun trail rides open to the public.

The Underdown Recreation Area, between Merrill and Tomahawk, consists of 4,600 acres. The recreation area is named for a bootlegger who hid his stills in the forests during prohibition, and it is easy to see why this would be an ideal place for moonshining: The park is densely wooded, which, in addition to providing cover for illicit stills, makes for some beautiful riding. Filled with pine, aspen, and northern hardwoods, the forest creates a great habitat for wildlife. There are more than 10 small lakes in the recreation area, and riders will see plenty of waterfowl.

Primitive camping is available on 11 sites, which have water and toilets. Reservations are not necessary. For all its beauty (Lincoln County is referred to as the gateway to the great North Woods), it is a generally quiet trail. While the trails are shared with bikers and hikers, it is a serene and relaxing place where you can gather your thoughts and enjoy the scenery.

Location: From Merrill, take Highway 51 north for about 8 miles to County Road H. Follow H east, then north to Copper Lake Avenue. Proceed on Copper Lake Avenue for about 3.5 miles to the trailhead.

Contact(s): Lincoln County Forestry
Department of Land and Parks
1106 East Eight Street
Merrill, WI 54452

Underdown Horse Club
N6334 County Road H
Irma, WI 54442

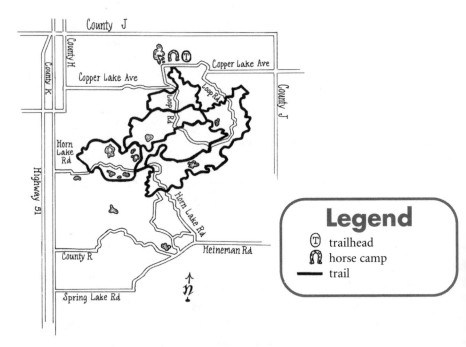

Legend
Ⓣ trailhead
🎠 horse camp
— trail

Phone: (715) 536-0327 (Lincoln County Forestry).
(715) 536-7612 (Underdown Horse Club).

Web sites: http://co.limcoln.wi.us/html/underdown_recreation_area.html or http://www.discoverlincolncounty.com/underdownmap.htm

Trails: The recreation area features four trail loops, five, 10, 15, and 21 miles in length. The terrain is hilly, with thick woods and plenty of lakes. Wildlife is abundant. Carry bug spray, as it gets buggy in the summer months. Maps are available at the trailhead and at the Lincoln County Web site.

Shared use: Hikers and mountain bikers also use the trails.

Horse rentals: n/a.

Camping: Eleven campsites big enough for horse trailers. Toilets and a well-pump are available at the site.

Reservations: No reservations necessary. Call Underdown Horse Club or Lincoln County for information.

Dates of use: May 1 through the first snowfall. Call for exact dates.

Passes: No passes necessary. Donations are accepted at the trailhead off Copper Lake Avenue.

A typical multi-use trail sign.

Wiouwash Trail
Winnebago and Outagamie Counties

The Wiouwash Trail is a point-to-point trail (running 20 miles between Oshkosh and Hortonville), but there are six access parking lots that allow riders to start at one site one day and another the next. There is a bathroom facility (with playground equipment and a picnic area) in Larsen, which is about midway along the trail.

Situated on an abandoned railroad corridor, the Wiouwash Trail was named by taking the first two letters of each county the trail runs through: Winnebago,

231

Outagamie, Waukesha, and Shawano. Horseback riding is only permitted on the Winnebago County and Outagamie County sections. The entire stretch of trail is shared with hikers and bikers, and the trail is popular with joggers.

The Winnebago County section of the trail starts near the intersection of Highways 41 and 110 on Westwind Road in Oshkosh and travels 14 miles to the Outagamie County line. It is an additional six miles to Hortonville; there is a picnic area just north of Highway 10 in Medina.

The first stretch of the trail passes near Lake Butte des Mortes and then meanders through several wetlands, and it is a popular trail for birding. The people who use it are generally respectful of each other and its multi-use status. No motorized vehicles are allowed on the trail.

Location: Between Oshkosh and Hortonville. There are no fewer than six parking lots along its 20-mile stretch.

Contact(s): Winnebago County Parks Department
625 East County Road Y, Suite 500
Oshkosh, WI 54901

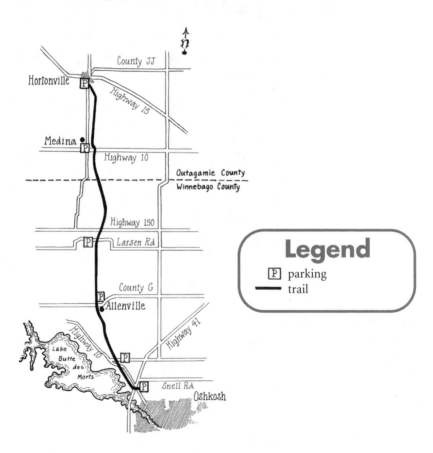

Outagamie County Parks
1375 East Broadway Drive
Appleton, WI 54913

Phone: (920) 232-1960 (Winnebago County).
(920) 832-4791 (Outagamie County).

E-mail: cbrandt48@aol.com (Outagamie County)

Web site: http://www.focol.org/greenways/trailpages/newwiouwash.html

Trails: Twenty miles of trail that run through woods, marshes, farm fields, and prairies. The surface is crushed limestone. Wildlife is abundant.

Shared use: Trail is shared with hikers and bikers. No motorized vehicles are allowed on the trail.

Camping: Day use only.

Reservations: n/a.

Dates of use: Spring, summer, and fall. Trail is closed to horseback riders during gun deer season in the fall. Trail is used by skiers and snowmobilers in the winter.

Passes: n/a.

Wood County Forest
Wood County

Wood County, in central Wisconsin, has set aside 36,000 acres of forestland for sporting and recreational use by the public, and most of it is open to horseback riders. There are no specific and clearly defined horseback-riding areas here, and there are few restricted areas. The area's many logging roads afford the best opportunities for pleasant riding. Because some of the forested land is used for logging, riders may encounter heavy equipment from time to time, but these areas are well-marked and easy to avoid. Currently, there are no accurate maps showing logging roads through the forest, but the county administration is developing one.

The terrain is generally flat with sandy trails, and riders can cut through light brush if necessary. Numerous lakes and streams dot the area. No permit is necessary for individual riders, but organizers of group rides and events must get permits from the forest administrator at the Wood County Parks and Forestry Department in Wisconsin Rapids.

Camping is permitted in designated areas within the forest. The parks also restrict horseback riding, except for permitted special events.

Location: West of Wisconsin Rapids. The various segments of Wood County forestland are scattered in an area between Highway 73 and the Adams County line to the south. Highway 80 runs north and south through the area. County Forest maps are available from the Wood County Parks and Forestry Department.

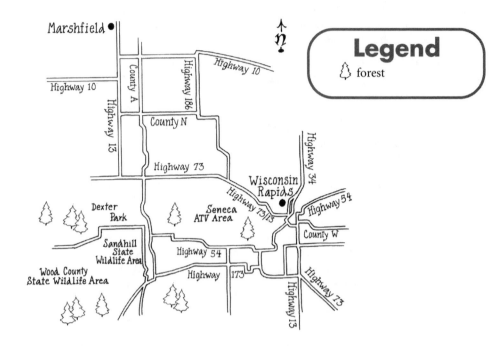

Contact(s): Wood County Parks and Forestry Department
400 Market Street
Wisconsin Rapids, WI 54494
Phone: (715) 421-8422.

E-mail: parks@co.wood.wi.us

Web site: http://www.co.wood.wi.us/parks

Trails: About 36,000 acres of flat, sandy trails with some hills. The forest has large wooded, marsh, and upland areas. There are several stream crossings.

Shared use: Forestlands are shared with hunters, hikers, and bicyclists. There are separate designated trails for snowmobilers and ATV riders. No motorized vehicles are allowed in the principal forest.

Horse rentals: n/a.

Camping: Camping is allowed in the county forest for up to two weeks at a time. There is no camping in areas that are designated as formal areas, such as parks.

Reservations: n/a.

Dates of use: Open year-round. Snowmobiles and ATVs stay on designated trails.

Passes: n/a.

More Riding Trails

Florence County Forest
Florence County

The Florence County Forest is in the far northeastern corner of the state. The forest encompasses more than 36,000 acres, and it is open to riding over forest and logging roads. Two rivers, the Pine and Popple, flow through the forest, so wildlife and waterfowl are abundant.

Location: The forest is located in central and eastern Florence County, just east of the Chequamegon-Nicolet National Forest.

Contact(s): Florence Natural Resource and
Wild Rivers Interpretive Center
State Highway 70/101 and
U.S. Highway 2
Florence, WI 54121

Phone: (888) 889-0049 or (715) 528-5377.

E-mail: info@florencewisconsin.com

Web site: http://www.explorewisconsin.com/countypages/florence.html

Kronenwetter and Leather Camp Forest Units
Marathon County

The Kronenwetter and Leather Camp Forest Units, about 10 miles east of Mosinee, offer more than 9,000 acres of forest. Within them, you'll find 10 miles of horse trails on wide graded and seeded paths. The terrain is flat and easy; it is good for first-time riders and horses, but may not be challenging enough for advanced riders.

Both of these forest units have a mix of upland and marshy terrain. Riders may encounter deer, ruffed grouse, black bear, coyote, and woodcock.

Location: Nine miles east of Highway 39/151 on Highway 153.
Parking is available at the start of the horse trail and at another point along the way. Call the Marathon County Forestry Department for specific directions.

Contact(s): Marathon County Forestry Department
212 River Drive, #2
Wausau, WI 54403

Phone: (715) 261-1580 or (715) 847-5267.

E-mail: forestry@mail.co.marathon.wi.us

Web site: http://www.co.marathon.wi.us/infosite.asp?dep=25

Neshota Park
Brown County

Located southeast of Green Bay, Neshota Park features 2.5 miles of trail over rugged hills and wooded areas. It is a scenic setting, where King Creek and the Neshota River meet. Horses are permitted only on designated sections of the trail, and those areas are well-marked. Nearby, you can ride the southern portion of the Fox River Trail and 8 miles in the Reforestation Camp (see descriptions of both in the Riding Trails section of this chapter). Neshota Park, a county facility, is made up of 260 acres of riverbed, valleys, and wooded hills.

Location: From Green Bay, take Highway 141 to Highway 29 at Bellevue and turn east. Proceed to County Road T and turn south, then east on Park Road. Neshota Park is at 5757 Park Road, about 10 miles from Green Bay.

Contact(s): Brown County Park Office
305 East Walnut Street, Third Floor
Green Bay, WI 54301

Phone: (920) 448-4466; (920) 448-4290 (fax).

E-mail: Nuthals_KM@co.brown.wi.us

Web site: http://www.co.brown.wi.us/parks/

Nine Mile County Forest
Marathon County

The horse and snowmobile trail in Nine Mile County Forest southwest of Wausau travels in a large loop over nearly 10 miles of varied terrain. Horses are only allowed on the snowmobile trails, which travel the perimeter of the forest, and not on designated mountain bike trails. Use is heavy on these trails, so the county forestry department has started setting seasons for different uses. Horses are currently allowed on the trails May 15–October 15, depending on trail conditions.

Location: From Wausau, take Interstate 39 south a short distance to County Road N. Go west 3.5 miles to Red Bud Road. Go south on Red Bud 1.5 miles to the trailhead.

Contact(s): Marathon County Forestry Department
212 River Drive, #2
Wausau, WI 54403

Phone: (715) 261-1580.

E-mail: forestry@mail.co.marathon.wi.us

Web site: http://www.co.marathon.wi.us/infosite.asp?dep=25

Successfully navigating a water jump.

Spur of the Moment Ranch
Mountain

Spur of the Moment Ranch offers overnight lodging for those wishing to ride on the Oconto County Recreation Trail and in the Nicolet National Forest. Located off the trail and next to the forest, Spur of the Moment is one of those rare places with an abundance of trail access.

Spur of the Moment offers four cabins that can sleep up to 20 people. Lodging here is rustic, so bring your own sheets and towels. However, all cabins come with microwaves, coffee pots, and refrigerators. You can see photos of the cabins and bathhouses (which offer toilets and hot showers) on the ranch's Web site.

For the horses, Spur of the Moment offers box stalls and a large turnout area. The 20-stall barn is open-style. Riders feed and clean up after their own horses, and can enjoy hours of riding on trails over thousands of acres.

Ranch owners Skip and Ann Maletzke are members of the Dairyland Driving Club and own hackney, saddlebred, and Percheron horses and miniature donkeys, which they use for pleasure and competition carriage driving.

Location: From Highway 141, drive to State Highway 64, turn west, and drive for less than 20 miles to Kingston Road. Turn west and travel about 1 mile to the ranch.

Contact(s): 14211 Helen Lane, Mountain, WI 54149.

Phone: (800) 644-8783 or (715) 276-3726.

237

E-mail: skipm@spurofthemomentranch.org or
annm@spurofthemomentranch.org

Web site: http://www.spurofthemomentranch.org

Waupaca County Forest
Waupaca County

Just a few miles south of Weyauwega and east of Waupaca, you can find three miles of horse trails over the rolling hills of the Waupaca County Forest. The trails are shared with hikers and bikers. If you prefer a longer ride, Hartman Creek State Park west of Waupaca is a good bet.

Location: Horse trailer parking is on Desert Road between Highway 49 and County Road U.

Contact(s): Waupaca County Park and Recreation Department
811 Harding Street
Waupaca, WI 54981

Phone: (715) 258-6243.

E-mail: parks@co.waupaca.wi.us

Wisconsin-Based Horse Associations

Castlerock Trails Club

Horseback riding group in central Wisconsin. This group sponsors trail rides and helps maintain the equestrian trails at Castle Rock in Adams County.
E-mail: castlerocktrails@yahoo.com
Web site: http://www.castlerocktrails.homestead.com

Chequamegon EZ Riders Saddle Club

Established saddle club that sponsors trail rides, horse shows, and educational activities in the Chequamegon Bay area. In existence for more than 25 years.
E-mail: Infor@ezriders.net
Web site: http://www.ezriders.net

Dairyland Driving Club, Inc

Web site: http://www.dairylanddriving.org

Distance Riders Association of Wisconsin (DRAW)

Promotes distance riding in Wisconsin.
E-mail: jjmlfeller@powerweb.net
Web site: http://www.powerweb.net/draw

Friends of Wisconsin State Parks

See Web site for information on joining a "Friends" group.
Web site: http://www.wistateparkfriends.org/chapter.asp

Glacial Drumlin Horse Trail Association (GDHTA)

Promotes public horse trail advocacy in Wisconsin, serves as a conduit between park management and horse riders, and sponsors work days and fun events.
E-mail: nails21@charter.net
Yahoo group: http://groups.yahoo.com/group/gdhta

Little Britches of Wisconsin Rodeo

A nonprofit organization that promotes rodeo for kids ages 6–18.
E-mail: lbwrodeo@mhtc.net
Web site: http://lbwrodeo.com

Madison Polo Club

Matches are free and open to the public. Student memberships available.
(608) 829-1929
E-mail: info@madisonpolo.com
Web site: http://www.madisonpolo.com

Madison Area Recreational Equestrian Sisters (MARES)
A Madison-based equestrian club for adult women.
Web site: http://www.geocities.com/maresclub/

Milwaukee Polo Club
Plays 11 matches between June and September. The club also travels to play other teams. See Web site for schedule.
(262) 367-8227
Web site: http://milwaukeepolo.com

Neillsville Saddle Tramps
Riding club that offers 4-H fun shows, educational clinics, and a spring and fall trail ride. Members also advocate for horse trails in the Clark County Forest.
Web site: http://www.homestead.com/smagacz/saddle.html

Oregon Horse Association
Nonprofit organization promoting horsemanship in southcentral Wisconsin.
Web site: http://danenet.danenet.org/oha

Richland Saddle Club
Based in Richland Center, club participates in group trail rides and parade rides. Plans to expand activities in the future.
Web site: http://groups.msn.com/RichlandRidersSaddleClub

Rodeo City Riders
The Group sponsors trail rides each year and sponsors the Rodeo City Riders drill team, which opens rodeos in the area. See Web site for more information. The organization is responsible for the development of the Hartman Creek State Park equestrian trails near Waupaca.
E-mail: bacady@netnet.net
Web site: http://www.geocities.com/rodeocityriders/index.htm

Southern Kettle Moraine Horse Trail Association (SKMHTA)
Horse club with emphasis on social activities, including trail rides, camping, and potlucks. Members also assist the DNR with projects in the Southern Kettle Moraine Forest.
Web site: http://www.eaglewi.org/SKMHTA/SKMHTAhome.htm

Tomah Saddle Club
Family-oriented saddle club based in Tomah. Sponsors trail rides and other events for horse lovers throughout the year.
E-mail: tomahsaddleclub@hotmail.com
Web site: http://groups.msn.com/TomahSaddleClub

Tri-City Riding Club

Horse club with members that meet once a month and sponsor trail rides, gymkhana fun shows, and speed shows in the Wisconsin Rapids area. Tri-City also helps with the Little Britches Rodeo.
E-mail: tricityridingclub@horsemail.com

Underdown Horse Club

Riding club dedicated to maintaining and sustaining horse trails in the Underdown Recreation Area. Hosts fund raisers, competitive rides, and public trail rides several times a year. Dedicated horse group that has been working for the trails for more than 20 years.
(715) 536-6320 or (715) 536-7612

Upper Midwest Endurance and Competitive Ride Association (UMECRA)

Organization that sanctions up to 50 endurance and competitive rides per year in the upper Midwest, including a 100-mile ride over three days at Castle Rock Horse Trails (see description in section III). All endurance rides are sanctioned by the American Endurance Ride Conference (AERC). See Web site for more information. Web site: http://www.umecra.com

UW–Madison Hoofers Riding Club

Open to everyone. Based near the University of Wisconsin–Madison.
Web site: http://www.hoofers.org

Wazee Riders Horse Club

Located in Black River Falls, the group sponsors gymkhanas during the year and a pleasure horse show once a year.

Western Wisconsin Horse Show Association

Established to promote horse shows in western Wisconsin.
Web site: http://www.wwhsa.org/clubs.html

Wisconsin Arabian Horse Association

Provides programs and events for Arabians and half-Arabians.
E-mail: gayjbower@yahoo.com

Wisconsin Dressage and Combined Training Association (WDCTA)

A charter member of the United States Dressage Federation (USDF), the WDCTA offers support to eventing and dressage enthusiasts throughout Wisconsin.
Web site: http://www.wdcta.org

Wisconsin Horsemen's News

A publication that lists upcoming horse-related events in Wisconsin.
E-mail: Contact@wishorse.com
Web site: http://www.wishorse.com

Wisconsin Horses
Web site dedicated to those interested in horseback riding in Wisconsin.
Includes message board and chat groups.
Web site: http://communities.msn.com/wisconsinhorses

Wisconsin Hunter/Jumper Association (WHJA)
Established to promote competition of juniors and amateurs in Wisconsin.
Web site: www.equinebiz.com/whja

Wisconsin Mustang Club
A club for mustang owners and lovers in Wisconsin. Group hosts trail
rides, horse camping, picnics, and shows.
E-mail: PDSpanishMustangs@msn.com
Web site: http://www.wisconsinmustangclub.com

Wisconsin State Horse Council, Inc.
An organization that takes a proactive role in the growth and development
of the equine industry in Wisconsin. Each spring, it puts on the very pop-
ular Midwest Horse Fair in Madison.
E-mail: info@wisconsinstatehorsecouncil.org
Web site: http://www.wisconsinstatehorsecouncil.org

Wisconsin Quarter Horse Association
A group that promotes Wisconsin quarter horses.
Web site: http://www.wqha.com

Wisconsin Walking Horse Association
Created to share information and promote events regarding the Tennessee
walking horse in Wisconsin.
E-mail: wwha@execpc.com
Web site: http://my.execpc.com/~wwha

Wolf River Trail Blazers
Hosts spring and fall trail rides in Waupaca County. Based in New London.
(715) 982-4185

Selected Tack Shops
Wisconsin

Ace's Cayuse Shop
500 Water Street
Sauk City, WI 53583
(608) 643-2433
Web site: http://www.cayuseshop.com

A Storybook Farm
W10521 Tritz Road
Portage, WI 53901
(608) 742-1006
Web site: http://www.astorybookfarm.com

Bea's Saddle Shop
W6250 State Hwy 54
Black Creek, WI 54106
(920) 984-3497

Blue Haven Stables & Tack Shop
W4853 County Road Q
Merrill, WI 54452
(715) 536-4210

Caine's Saddle Shop
5076 Byrne Road
Oregon, WI 53575
(608) 255-4577
Web site: http://www.horsemouth.com/Caine.htm

Coyotes
W6916 Wisconsin Avenue
Greenville, WI 54942
(920) 757-8819

Crane Echo Tack
5600 Woodland Street
Suite # 4
Stevens Point WI 54481
(715) 343-6111
Web site: http://www.craneechotack.com
E-mail: ivanho@CraneEchoTack.com

Critter's Cuisine
4838 County Road Y
Milton, WI 53563
(608) 754-4251; (800) 867-5708

Deadwood Saddlery
244 North Main Street
Richland Center, WI 53581
(608) 647-6661
Web site: http://www.deadwoodsaddlery.com

Equine Source
W5140 County Road O
Plymouth, WI 53073
(920) 893-4455;
(877) 920-TACK(8225)
Web site: http://www.equinesource.com/findus.html
E-mail: EquineSrce@aol.com

Fleet Farm
3110 County Road C
Plymouth, WI 53073
(920) 893-5115

Goman's Tack Shop
N625 Byington Road
Wonewoc, WI 53968
(608) 464-5542

Hall's Saddlery
19255 West Bluemound Road
Brookfield, WI 53045
(262) 782-4499
http://www.hallsaddlery.com

Hill Top Saddle & Tack
(608) 968-3303
Web site: http://hilltoptack.com

Hoofinit
W8419 Badger Drive
Wautoma, WI 54982
(920) 787-1878
E-mail: hoofinit@centurytel.net

Horse & Hound Tack Shop
301 Sky Harbour Drive
La Crosse, WI 54603
(608) 783-7504
Web site: http://www.horse-and-hound.com
E-mail: shop@horse-and-hound.com

Horse Emporium
280 West Main Street
Waukesha, WI 53186
(262) 549-5422; (800) 236-5507
Web site: http://www.horseemporium.com

JB Tack Shop, LLC
W6563 Kiesling Road
Jefferson, WI 53549
(920) 674-5020
Web site: http://www.polocenter.com/tack/tackuswi.htm

McDaniels Tack
11140 West State Road 81
Beloit, WI 53511
(608) 879-9476

McFarlanes'
1259 Water Street
Sauk City, WI 53583
(608) 643-2309
Web site: http://www.polocenter.com/tack/tackuswi.htm

Mounds Pet Food Warehouse
5350 King James Way
Fitchburg, WI 53719
(608) 271-1800
Web site: http://www.moundspet.com

Painted Pony
320 Superior Avenue
Tomah, WI 54660
(608) 374-3883

Palmyra True Value Hardware
229 West Main Street
Palmyra, WI 53156
(262) 495-2161

RM Tack
1671 County Road I
Somerset, WI 54025
(715) 247-5517

Spirit of the West
111 North Second Street
Palmyra, Wisconsin 53156
(262) 495-8515
Web site: http://www.spiritofthewest.biz

Shamrock Embroidery and Tack
N3720 Old F Road
Rio, WI 53960
(920) 992-6153

Sunset Saddle Shop
N5635 Willow Road
Plymouth, WI 53073
(920) 893-5634

Tack Barn & Stuff
N4693 County Road East
Waupaca, WI 54981
(715) 258-9120

Tomah Tack & Trailer
804 Superior Avenue
Tomah, WI 54660
(608) 372-5537

Walmer's Tack Shop
16379 West Milbrandt Road
Evansville, WI 53536
(608) 882-5725

Out-of-State
These shops carry a full range of apparel, tack, and supplies that are available by mail order. Check their Web sites for more information, including how to obtain a catalog.

Barrington Saddlery
760 West Northwest Highway
Barrington, IL 60010
(800) 560-8008

Web Site: http://www.barringtonsaddlery.com
Carries high-quality English tack, apparel, and supplies. Located northwest of Chicago. Barrington Saddlery has a mobile tack shop that appears at many area shows.

Dover Saddlery

P.O. Box 1100
525 Great Road
Littleton, MA 01460
(800) 989-1500
Web site: http://www.statelinetack.com
English tack and apparel for all riding needs.

Liberty Saddle Shop

306 Peterson Road, Highway 137
Libertyville, IL 60048
(800) 872-3353
Web site: http://www.saddleshop.com
Tack, apparel, and barn supplies for all types of riding. Located north of Chicago, about 15 miles south of the Wisconsin border.

Mary's Tack and Feed

3675 Via De La Valle
San Diego, CA 92014-4245
(800) 551-MARY (6279)
Web site: http://www.marystack.com/contact.asp
Riding, barn and ranch supplies for all riding disciplines. Mary's has a large selection of apparel, gifts, books, and videos, in addition to its tack and supplies.

Stateline Tack

16 Atkinson Depot Road
Plaistow, NH 03865
(888) 839-9640
Web site: http://www.statelinetack.com
English and western tack, riding clothes, and supplies.

Glossary

above the bit. Term used to describe the activity of a horse when raising its head to avoid contact with a bit.

aged. Word sometimes used to describe a horse older than 15.

American saddlebred. A breed developed in Kentucky that can be three- or five-gaited. Used mainly as a saddleseat show horse.

Appaloosa. Breed of hearty saddle horse, usually spotted and standing 14.2 to 15.2 hands high.

appendix. A quarter horse-thoroughbred cross.

Arabian. Type of horse that originated in the Middle East. Arabians have had a strong influence on many other breeds and are used extensively in endurance riding, dressage, western pleasure, and several other disciplines.

arthritis. Inflammation or stiffing of the joints.

bale. Unit of hay consisting of 10 flakes.

barn sour. A horse that causes problems when leaving the barn or stable.

barrel racing. A rodeo event in which a horse and rider must go around three barrels in a cloverleaf pattern as fast as possible.

bar shoes. Horseshoes with no opening between the heels, thus forming a continuous circle.

behind the bit. Term used to describe the activity of a horse when inverting its head to avoid contact with a bit.

bit. A metal piece of the bridle placed in a horse's mouth as a means of control.

brand. A way to identify horses.

breaking. Training or teaching a horse to adapt to human commands.

breeder. Person who breeds horses.

bridle. The piece of tack that goes over the horse's head.

broodmare. A mare used for breeding.

broken to ride. Term used to describe a horse that can be ridden under saddle but still additional training (also known as "green-broke").

canter. A three-beat gait, also known as a lope or a slow gallop.

cinch. Device to secure a western saddle around a horse's stomach.

Clydesdale. A large draft horse originating in Scotland often used to pull large loads.

cob. Horse with a heavy and stocky appearance. Well-adapted to carrying large riders.

Coggins test. A blood test for equine infectious anemia (EIA). If a horse tests positive for EIA, it will most likely have to be put down.

collection. The shortening of a horse's stride. It's the opposite of extension.

colic. General term for abdominal pain in a horse. Warning signs are sweating, pawing at the ground, lack of intestinal movement or sound, and lying down. A vet should be called if you think your horse has colic.

combined training. Equestrian competition lasting one to three days that includes dressage, cross-country jumping, and stadium jumping. Also known as eventing.

conformation. The overall appearance of a horse.

Connemara. One of the nine breeds of ponies native to the British Isles. Originating in Western Ireland.

cribbing. Term used to describe the activity of a horse when it hooks its teeth onto something solid, such as a stable door, and sucks air through its mouth.

crop. Device used to encourage horses to move forward or faster; also known as a short whip or bat.

cross tie. Two ropes that attach to either side of the halter; used to secure a horse in a stall or barn aisle.

dam. The mother of a horse.

dock. The bony part of the tail.

double bridle. An English bridle with two reins on each side of the bit; it aids in maintaining a collected gait and control.

dressage. Competitive sport that tests a horse's natural movement and level of training.

endurance riding. Competitive riding with one horse and rider that covers distances of 50–100 miles within a specified amount of time. Limited endurance rides cover 25–35 miles.

English pleasure. A class judged on attitude, manners, and quality of a horse while being ridden under an English saddle.

EIA. Equine infectious anemia. Horses with EIA usually have to be put down. (See also Coggins test.)

EPM. Equine protozoal myleoencephalitis, a degenerative nerve condition.

equitation. A class in which the rider, not the horse, is judged.

eventing. A competitive event held over one to three days that includes dressage, cross-country jumping, and stadium jumping. Also known as combined training.

extension. Lengthening of a horse's stride. Extension is the opposite of collection.

farrier. A blacksmith that trims and shoes horse's hooves.

filly. Female horse under the age of four.

five-gaited horses. In addition to the walk, trot, and canter, five-gaited horses also have two gaits called the slow gait and rack. The most common five-gaited horse is the American saddlebred.

flake. One-tenth of a bale of hay.

floating. The filing or rasping of a horse's teeth.

flying change. A change of canter lead. A flying change is considered "clean" when a horse makes the change, both front and back, in one movement.

foal. A young horse or pony under one year old.

forelock. Tuft of hair that hangs over a horse's forehead.

founder. Occurs when the bond between the hoof wall and the coffin bone is weakened, leading the bone to tip downward. In severe cases, the bone can rotate through the sole of the foot.

four-in-hand. A team of four harness horses.

frog. A V-shaped area on the sole of a horse's foot that acts as a shock absorber.

gait. The paces at which horses move—usually the walk, trot, and canter.

gaited horse. A horse that moves at paces other than the walk, trot, and canter.

gallop. A fast three-beat gait. Racehorses gallop.

gelding. A castrated male horse.

green. An inexperienced horse or rider.

gray. The color of a coat that can range from pure white to dark gray.

groom. A person who looks after horses (also called a stable hand). Also, the act of brushing or cleaning a horse.

ground manners. The behavior of a horse while being handled from the ground, not from the saddle.

gymkhana. A series of games played on horseback.

gymnastic. A series of fences, placed at relative distances to each other, used in jumping training.

habit. Traditional riding attire for sidesaddle riders.

hack. To ride a horse at a normal pace.

hackney. Light harness horse known for its high-stepping gaits; also a type of carriage.

Haflinger. A compact, chestnut-colored horse with a light-colored mane and tail. Originally from the southern Austrian Tyrol, Haflingers are especially good for riding and light draft work.

half-halt. Exercise used to improve communication between horse and rider.

half-pass. A maneuver, most often used in dressage, in which the horse moves sideways and forward at the same time.

hand. A measurement, equal to four inches, used to measure the height of horses.

harness. The tack or equipment needed to drive a horse rather than ride it.

heaves. Excessive wheezing or coughing in horses.

hoof. A horse's "foot."

hoof pick. A pick that helps remove dirt and rocks from a horse's hooves.

hoof wall. The outer layer of the foot of a horse.

horn. Part of a western saddle around which is twisted a lariat when roping animals; also known as a saddle horn.

horsemanship. The art of dealing with horses.

hunter. In England, a type of horse used for foxhunting.

hunter/jumper. A horse with the ability not only to negotiate jumps but also to do so with style.

Icelandic. Ancient breed of horse originating in Iceland.

impaction colic. Colic resulting in blockage of the intestine.

impulsion. Strong but controlled forward movement in the horse. Impulsion should come from the hind end.

indirect rein. The rein opposite to the direction in which the horse is moving.

in front of the bit. Term describing the activity of a horse when pulling or hanging onto the rider's hand. A horse that sticks its nose out is considered "in front of the bit."

inside leg. The legs of a rider and a horse on the inside of a circle in a competition.

irons. English word for stirrups.

jog. A horse's slow trot, used mostly by western riders.

jumper. A horse suited to jumping; one that competes in jumping classes. Jumpers are judged solely on their ability to negotiate obstacles.

laminitis. Condition in which the laminae inside the hoof becomes inflamed and painful. Severe laminitis can lead to founder (see definition above).

lead. The horse's leading leg in a canter.

leg up. A method of mounting a horse. Riders can get a "leg up" by standing on the ground and having someone hold their foot or leg and lift them as they mount.

Lippizan. Magnificent breed of horse from Europe famous for performances in the Spanish Riding School.

lope. A three-beat gait, mostly used by western riders.

lunging. Training or exercising a horse while the horse is attached to a lunge line (long lead line).

lunge lessons. Lessons in which a student sits on a schooled horse that is being held on a lunge line by the instructor.

Lusitano. Portuguese name for an Andalusian horse.

mare. A female horse over four years of age.

Morab. Breed of horse that is a cross between an Arabian and a Morgan.

mucking or mucking out. The removal of wet and soiled shavings from a horse's stall or paddock.

mule. Offspring of a male donkey and a female horse.

mustang. Wild horse of the American West.

navicular bone. A small bone within the hoof.

navicular disease. Degeneration of the navicular bone, a condition that causes pain and lameness.

open. Advanced competitive division in which participants are not determined by previous winnings or professional status.

on the bit. Term used to describe the activity of a horse when it carries its head in a nearly vertical position and calmly accepts the rider's contact on the reins.

overface. Putting an obstacle in front of someone (figuratively or literally) that will scare them, or asking too much of someone so that they become scared off. Often used in horseback riding circles.

packhorse. Horse used to carry goods or supplies.

packer. A well-trained and safe horse that carries its rider with a minimum of effort on the rider's part. Packers are good for beginners or nervous riders.

paddock. A large enclosed area for keeping horses. Often used for turnout and grazing.

Peruvian Paso. A breed of horse from the Paso Fino line; it is known for a comfortable, ambling gait.

Paso Fino. A breed of horse from Spain, known for its smooth gaits and endurance.

passage. Dressage movement in which a horse trots in an extremely collected and animated manner.

piaffe. Dressage movement in which a horse trots in place.

poll. The area between the ears of a horse.

polo. Game played on horseback with mallets and balls. The object is for one team to score more goals than another in a specified amount of time.

pony. A small horse, measuring 14.2 hands or less.

Potomac horse fever. A gastrointestinal disease characterized by high fever, inflammation of the large intestine, diarrhea, and dehydration.

purebred. A horse of a specific breed that has not experienced the infusion of other breeds over many generations and thus has characteristics of that breed.

quarter horse. A hearty breed of horse used mainly for ranch work, western pleasure riding, and rodeo events. It got its name from being able to run a quarter mile in excellent time.

rack. A four-beat gait in which each hoof strikes the ground separately. It is the fifth gait of the American saddlebred.

reining. A western riding class in which a horse must spin and slide in various patterns with little movement from the rider.

rising trot. Movement in which the rider rises with the rhythm of the horse's trot. Also called the posting trot.

roping. Rodeo competition in which riders catch a steer with a lasso and tie it up. The rider with the fastest time wins.

Shetland pony. One of the smallest breeds of pony; originated in the Shetland Islands near Scotland.

shying. The reaction of a horse when it has been startled. Also called spooking.

sire. The father of a horse.

snaffle. A type of bit.

sound. Word describing a horse that is not lame.

stallion. A male horse over four years of age that has not been castrated.

standardbred. Breed of horse generally used in harness racing.

star. The white marking on a horse's face. Smaller marking are called snips.

stride. The amount of ground a horse covers in one "step." Stride length will differ depending on a horse's gait.

surcingle. A strap that passes around the horse's barrel (belly). Often used in lunging.

swamp fever. Another name for equine infectious anemia (EIA).

tack. Equipment used on a saddle horse (e.g., saddle, bridle, etc.).

team-penning. An equine sport in which a team of riders separates three cattle from a herd of 30 and herds them into a pen at the opposite end of an arena. The team with the fastest time wins.

thoroughbred. Breed of speedy horse that originated in England. Used for racing, show jumping, eventing, dressage, and numerous other disciplines.

thrush. Fungal or bacterial infection of one part of a horse's foot, characterized by foul-smelling discharge. Thrush is most common when horses stand on wet ground or bedding for long periods of time.

topline. The line from the back of the withers to the end of the croup.

top-heavy. Term for the condition of a horse when its body is too large for its legs.

transition. The shift from one gait to another. Transitions can be upward (walk to trot) or downward (trot to walk).

trot. A two-beat gait.

unsound. Word used to describe a horse that is lame.

vaulting. Equestrian sport involving riders who do gymnastic exercises on the back of a moving horse back.

walking the course. Examining a course before an event to determine problem areas and strategies for the actual ride.

weanling. A horse that has been weaned from its mother.

western pleasure. Trail or show riding that shows off the manners and temperament of the horse.

western riding. Riding with a western saddle.

withers. The highest area of a horse's back. Horses are measured from the ground to the tops of their withers.

yearling. A horse that is or is turning one year old.

young rider. A competitor between the ages of 16 and 21.

Index

MORE GREAT TITLES FROM
TRAILS BOOKS & PRAIRIE OAK PRESS

TRAVEL GUIDES

Classic Wisconsin Weekends, *Michael Bie*
County Parks of Wisconsin, Revised Edition, *Jeannette and Chet Bell*
Great Little Museums of the Midwest, *Christine des Garennes*
Great Minnesota Taverns, *David K. Wright & Monica G. Wright*
Great Minnesota Weekend Adventures, *Beth Gauper*
Great Weekend Adventures, *the Editors of Wisconsin Trails*
Great Wisconsin Taverns: 101 Distinctive Badger Bars, *Dennis Boyer*
Sacred Sites of Minnesota, *John-Brian Paprock & Teresa Peneguy Paprock*
Sacred Sites of Wisconsin, *John-Brian Paprock & Teresa Peneguy Paprock*
Tastes of Minnesota: A Food Lover's Tour, *Donna Tabbert Long*
The Great Iowa Touring Book: 27 Spectacular Auto Trips, *Mike Whye*
The Great Minnesota Touring Book: 30 Spectacular Auto Trips, *Thomas Huhti*
The Great Wisconsin Touring Book: 30 Spectacular Auto Tours, *Gary Knowles*
Wisconsin Family Weekends: 20 Fun Trips for You and the Kids,
Susan Lampert Smith
Wisconsin Golf Getaways, *Jeff Mayers and Jerry Poling*
Wisconsin Lighthouses: A Photographic and Historical Guide,
Ken and Barb Wardius
Wisconsin's Hometown Flavors, *Terese Allen*
Wisconsin Waterfalls, *Patrick Lisi*
Up North Wisconsin: A Region for All Seasons, *Sharyn Alden*

ACTIVITY GUIDES

Biking Wisconsin: 50 Great Road and Trail Rides, *Steve Johnson*
Great Cross-Country Ski Trails: Wisconsin, Minnesota, Michigan & Ontario, *Wm. Chad McGrath*
Great Minnesota Walks: 49 Strolls, Rambles, Hikes, and Treks, *Wm. Chad McGrath*
Great Wisconsin Walks: 45 Strolls, Rambles, Hikes, and Treks, *Wm. Chad McGrath*
Minnesota Underground & the Best of the Black Hills, *Doris Green*
Paddling Illinois: 64 Great Trips by Canoe and Kayak, *Mike Svob*
Paddling Iowa: 96 Great Trips by Canoe and Kayak, *Nate Hoogeveen*
Paddling Northern Wisconsin: 82 Great Trips by Canoe and Kayak, *Mike Svob*
Paddling Southern Wisconsin: 82 Great Trips by Canoe and Kayak, *Mike Svob*
Walking Tours of Wisconsin's Historic Towns, *Lucy Rhodes,*
Elizabeth McBride, Anita Matcha
Wisconsin's Outdoor Treasures: A Guide to 150 Natural Destinations, *Tim Bewer*
Wisconsin Underground, *Doris Green*

For a free catalog, phone, write, or e-mail us.

Trails Books

P.O. Box 317, Black Earth, WI 53515
(800) 236-8088 • e-mail: books@wistrails.com